T0294636

TAKING LEAVE, TAKING LIBERTIES

TAKING LEAVE, TAKING LIBERTIES

AMERICAN TROOPS
ON THE WORLD WAR II
HOME FRONT

AARON HILTNER

THE UNIVERSITY OF CHICAGO PRESS | CHICAGO AND LONDON

The University of Chicago Press, Chicago 60637
The University of Chicago Press, Ltd., London
© 2020 by The University of Chicago
Published 2020
Printed in the United States of America

29 28 27 26 25 24 23 22 21 20   1 2 3 4 5

ISBN-13: 978-0-226-68704-9 (cloth)
ISBN-13: 978-0-226-68718-6 (e-book)
DOI: https://doi.org/10.7208/chicago/9780226687186.001.0001

Library of Congress Cataloging-in-Publication Data

Names: Hiltner, Aaron, author.
Title: Taking leave, taking liberties : American troops on the World War II home front / Aaron Hiltner.
Description: Chicago : The University of Chicago Press, 2020. |
    Includes bibliographical references and index.
Identifiers: LCCN 2019038422 | ISBN 9780226687049 (cloth) |
    ISBN 9780226687186 (ebook)
Subjects: LCSH: World War, 1939–1945—Social aspects—United States. |
    World War, 1939–1945—Women. | Civil-military relations—United States.
Classification: LCC D744.7.U6 H55 2020 | DDC 940.53/73—dc23
LC record available at https://lccn.loc.gov/2019038422

♾ This paper meets the requirements of ANSI/NISO Z39.48-1992 (Permanence of Paper).

For Tessa and Evangeline

CONTENTS

WHAT HAPPENED ON THE HOME FRONT

ON AUGUST 14, 1945, American troops stationed across the Pacific Rim—in Manila, Chungking, Okinawa, and elsewhere—huddled around shortwave radios as President Harry Truman announced the surrender of Japan and the end of a brutal and merciless island-hopping campaign. Soldiers and sailors celebrated by firing bullets, flak, and bright, orange tracers in the air. Some careened through the streets in jeeps, wild with euphoria that they no longer faced the deadly prospect of invading the Japanese mainland. Others formed conga lines and jubilantly sang "Don't Fence Me In."

The impromptu fireworks, joyriding, and celebrations, however, quickly turned violent. In one Pacific "liberty port," where troops took furloughs and leave, some ten thousand uniformed men poured into the downtown streets. The city crackled with a near-constant barrage of firecrackers like "a battery of machine guns." Local civilians and police watched from their now-stranded cars and sidewalk corners. Already out of booze, troops hurled bottles and bricks through store display windows, stealing alcohol, jewelry, and more. Seeing the "looting, smashing crowd" of sailors, one reporter wrote: "You couldn't stop it if you tried, not short of tear gas and fire hoses." Drunken rioters overturned cars, set them ablaze, or transformed them into battering rams to crash through more shop fronts. Some climbed atop their vehicles and reenacted the flag raising on Iwo Jima. Soon, the men were fighting each other: one marine savagely beat an army private with his bare fists, leaving him to die on the sidewalk. GIs also brawled with civilians in streets strewn with paper and shattered glass as long-standing tensions between the occupiers and the occupied boiled over. Soldiers and sailors also cornered women, tearing their dresses, kissing them forcibly, and sometimes beating the men who were escorting them. GIs, one woman recalled, "were pulling girls' pants off and sailing them down the street." Men were "kissing, and practically raping, everybody." At least six rapes did occur. "You put young girls with them and add liquor, and that's what happens," a police officer later asserted. Rather than ordering Shore Patrol to break up the riots and assaults, the rear admiral in command merely "requested" that the sailors go back to their ships.

The chaos lasted through two more nights. Hospital workers struggled to cope with the enormous number of injuries and cases of alcohol poisoning. When the police failed to investigate the numerous instances of rape, one incredulous health director asked: "What do they think we examined at the hospital last night—ghosts?" Finally, after the authorities decided that the many brawls and assaults "appeared to be getting out of hand," a combination of MPs and local police formed a phalanx and slowly cleared the streets.

Three days of "peace riots" had brought at least eleven deaths, over a thousand injuries, and tens of thousands of dollars in property damage. In the following months, city and military officials launched an investigation, but no one was charged or court-martialed. The grand jury supposedly scrutinizing the riots held that "when large numbers of young men realize that they are freed from war they are prone to celebrate overzealously." The army's intelligence summary admitted that the conduct of personnel "was generally riotous" and that "women were assaulted" but dismissed the situation as a "temporary emergency." When asked about the riot and the unremitting criminality, the mayor "gazed off into space" and responded merely that the police and navy "did a good job when they took over."

This was San Francisco at the outbreak of peace. New York, Boston, Los Angeles, and Washington, DC, also endured drunkenness, sexual assault, and riots during V-J Day celebrations. Yet this moment was not an aberration. Troop crime plagued American cities throughout the war, and civilians—especially women—lived with many of the same dangers and fears felt by the residents of occupied cities overseas. Women's groups, businesses, politicians, and police struggled to come to terms with servicemen's impact on their cities, protesting and fighting the military to regain local control of policing, regulation of businesses, curfews, and other municipal issues. While white troops proved stubbornly immune to effective oversight by civilian authorities and sometimes even military ones, African American and other nonwhite troops were harassed by police, subjected to hate crimes, and tormented by military authorities, who were often white supremacists.

This book recovers the history of American liberty ports—cities in the continental United States that were profoundly affected by military mobilization because they were destinations for millions of sailors and soldiers. The most important hubs for troops—cities like New York, Boston, Norfolk, Chicago, San Francisco, and Los Angeles—saw the relationships and conflicts that developed between servicemen, civilians, and the authorities charged with policing them. Recovering this history overturns the idea that the home front was a protected place, unscathed by the violence embroiling the rest of the globe. Indeed, soldiers effectively occupied many US cities. Sixteen million Americans served in the military, passing through towns near training camps, cities along transit lines, and ports of embarkation. During the war, over three million servicemen moved through New York City alone. Moreover, many of these troops never went abroad. Before the spring of 1944, when preparations for D-Day accelerated, 65–75 percent of all soldiers were stationed domestically. Twenty-five percent of the army never left the country at all. Liberty ports became international zones of trade and entertainment where GIs sought alcohol, sex, and other excitements. And these were not simply American spaces. The presence of Commonwealth, French, Dutch, and Chinese servicemen made it that much harder for municipal and military officials to police nightlife and crime. Taking this unexamined history into account gives us a new, unsettling picture of the home front and of World War II itself.

GI stories focus on the drama of combat, culminating in places like Pearl Harbor, Bataan, Anzio, Normandy, and Iwo Jima. Popular histories, memoirs, and films follow a common arc: young, naive, slightly scared teenagers, farmers, and factory workers join the army and leave home for exotic and dangerous locales where they soon endure their first harrowing experiences of combat, quickly form bonds across ethnic and geographic lines, and eventually become a cohesive unit of hardened, resourceful veterans. That arc mirrors that of the one often told about the nation as a whole: a young, emerging America stumbles at first but soon rises to overcome its prewar isolation and offer liberation, leadership, and democracy around the globe. This "good war" story necessarily focuses on troops outside the United States who liberate and rebuild a world broken by the horrors of fascism and imperialism—our boys in uniform become a new light for an old world in need of an American Century.

These combat stories are popular and for good reason. Anyone who has read a memoir like Eugene Sledge's *With the Old Breed* understands that the suffering servicemen faced was real. Those who fought and those who died deserve to be remembered. But the combat soldier's story can reveal only so much. Estimates vary as to how many troops actually saw combat—perhaps as few as 10 percent—but less than half were ever in a combat zone. In the European Theater of Operations, for example, combat troops made up only 19 percent of the total forces deployed in April 1945. This small tooth-to-tail ratio meant that far more soldiers spent the war working on logistics and transportation or in a vast bureaucracy that managed huge swaths of new property, paychecks, and the health care of millions.

But all soldiers dealt with the daily privations and annoyances of a regimented life. While only a few stormed a beach or flanked along a hedgerow, many exercised the privilege of the uniform while taking leave. Carousing in bars, cornering and chasing women, and beating up the guy not in uniform quickly emerged as a compelling marker of what it meant to be a soldier. Indeed, servicemen derided civilian life as a way to accept and lionize their status as military men.

GI carousing from Australia, China, and Okinawa to Britain, France, and Germany was enormously disruptive. Rape, assault, petty crime, and casual violence became all too common hallmarks of American liberations and occupations. In Commonwealth nations, the phrase *overpaid, oversexed, and over here* served as a shorthand description of GIs. By 1942, for example, the growing contingent of American personnel in Brisbane erupted into conflicts with Australian troops over women and increasingly scarce goods like cigarettes. "The Australians had grievances and they had very solid reasons to be aggrieved," recalled one officer. "The Yanks had everything—the girls, the canteens and all the rest of it—and our blokes were completely ostracized in their own city." Tensions eventually blew up in November with the two-day Battle of Brisbane, in which the city's blackout restrictions had to be lifted just to restore order. In Sydney, women stepped out into the darkened streets wielding "hatpins, bag needles, spike files, penknives, cayenne peppers, scissors, or weighted torches" as they watched for "any brown-out Casanova who makes a nuisance of himself." In Britain, Americans caused similar disturbances from London's Piccadilly Circus—where Yanks raced to find the women called "Piccadilly Commandos" for some "vicious debauchery"—to smaller coastal towns like Weymouth and Portland used as staging grounds for the D-Day invasion. Across the Channel in France, troops arrived as liberators and armed tourists but also as persistent threats to local women and civilians. And, in China, the Philippines, Okinawa, and Japan, servicemen thirsting for sex and drink repeatedly threatened both local and international relations well into the postwar era.

The American home front has long been portrayed as separate and shielded from these overseas stories. Of course, historians have recognized the conflicts that brewed back home: Japanese internment, race riots, and a wide variety of labor disputes were the most visible signs of a turbulent age. Women took jobs in the defense plants in unprecedented numbers, finding new levels of independence and fulfillment but also harassment and hazardous conditions. Popular images again and again depict wartime women as Rosie the Riveter, worried wives and daughters, or doting lovers waiting for a sailor's kiss or a letter from abroad. But, in almost all these, the home front is separate from the war front. Soldiers and sailors are absent from this landscape or make only brief cameos in events like the Zoot Suit Riots.

As a result, many people believe that Americans on the home front uniquely avoided the effects of war and of conflicts between civilians and the military. "The continental United States had escaped the plague of war, and so it was easy enough for the heirs to believe that they had been anointed by God," mused Lewis H. Lapham in 1979. David M. Kennedy's *Freedom from Fear* similarly concluded: "Beyond the war's dead and wounded and their families, few Americans had been touched by the staggering sacrifices and unspeakable anguish that the war had visited upon millions of other people around the globe." Even leading military historians like Aaron O'Connell believe that, "in World War II, civil-military friction was relatively low." But the stories of the liberty ports show that civil-military conflict was a defining feature of the home front experience.

Even when the often-poor behavior of American troops abroad has been recognized, it has been contrasted with an idealized secure home front. Mary Louise Roberts's gripping *What Soldiers Do* endorses the idea that it took exposure to a foreign country's supposedly exotic traditions and loose morals—specifically France's "primitive and oversexed" culture—to make soldiers decide that pursuing and even forcing themselves on women was justified. In this conception: "The US military protected the 'virtuous' American woman back home at the expense of the French prostitute." The home front is made safe as the people of Normandy face the unleashed urges of servicemen. The US military protected "American families," Roberts explains, "from the spectacle of GI promiscuity while leaving French families unable to escape it." But the truth is that the folks back home were not safe from the revelry and violence that accompanied invasions and occupations. An American woman in Boston likely had little more legal recourse than the French woman in Le Havre.

Compared to firebombing, the Blitz, and the horrors visited on the Eastern Front and China, what Americans experienced was mild. But civilians in stateside ports, stopover cities, and boomtowns nevertheless shared much with those living in war-touched cities abroad. Certainly, it would be safer for a civilian to be in New York than in Normandy during the invasion. Yet V-J Day in liberty ports saw uncontrolled violence and sexual assaults like those accompanying the breakout in the Norman bocage. And, while US cities were often safer than overseas combat zones, American civilians lived with some of the same dangers and risks experienced by civilians in London, Paris, and other occupied cities. They may not have seen bombings or the worst violence, but they did face uncontrolled and aggressive troops in their streets.

While some people are aware of the government's and the military's obsessive campaign against venereal disease—and the women who were treated inhumanely because of it—most stories of women and troops on the home front center on teary-eyed goodbyes and love separated by an ocean. For many people, especially in coastal cities, the military presence exerted a huge influence on everyday life. Servicemen were neither absent nor peripheral but rather central figures who dictated the often-discordant rhythms of the wartime city. From women taking a route home that circumvented areas well trafficked by troops, business owners struggling to keep brawls from destroying their establishments, to men avoiding amusement zones for fear of being heckled or assailed, civilians of all kinds were forced to adjust their daily lives. Local political officials and municipal figures likewise had to fight to retain control of their increasingly militarized cities. Civil-military conflict grew, both in the halls of political power and in the train cars, bars, and streets of port cities.

World War II cemented the rapid amalgamation of federal power that had first taken hold during World War I. Bursting with new agencies, raking in more taxes, and making greater demands on citizens, the federal government became a leviathan that demanded that civilian life turn toward serving the needs of the state. With soothing intonations and the comforting setting of fireside chats, President Franklin Delano Roosevelt consistently promoted the idea that civilians ought to serve and support a widespread militarization of American life. With this idea came an expansion of executive authority, government bureaucracy, and military power.

Yet Americans did not experience this expansion solely through taxes, propaganda, war bonds, and labor restrictions. Many also encountered it in the form of sailors and soldiers commandeering the everyday places where they lived their lives. Their streets, bars, parks, and trains regularly filled with such "friendly invasions," as one writer put it in 1944. This visceral, embodied military presence prompted bitter conflicts over who should control public space, who held jurisdiction over servicemen, and what sacrifices could be tolerated in service of the war. As municipal authorities increasingly buckled to army and navy leaders, women had to navigate the increasingly perilous streets, alleyways, and train cars, attempting to sort the decent men from the wolves. But the story of liberty ports also reveals the limits of that ballooning military authority. The American GI often remained a recalcitrant individual unwilling to abide the demands of civilian norms, military discipline, or, indeed, even the law.

Nationwide, the papers filled with lurid stories of criminal activity perpetrated by soldiers and sailors. The FBI reported crime spikes in 1941, 1942, 1945, and 1946. J. Edgar Hoover also noted that rape and aggravated assault, which increased, "have definitely emerged as wartime crimes." In major cities, a 46 percent rise in aggravated assault and a 35 percent spike in rape compared to prewar rates signaled a crisis for all levels of government. One of the key points of this story, however, is that so many men were never arrested or even stopped from committing assaults and harassing civilians. As is still the case today, numerous rapes, fights, and drunken crimes were never reported or pursued by the police. Some African American, Hispanic, and other nonwhite men were tried for and convicted of crimes, but they were not the perpetrators. Nevertheless, the FBI still counted these cases as wins in their ledger books. The data we have ultimately fail to capture what occurred in wartime.

The sexual violence that occurred in liberty ports and boomtowns throughout the war cannot be explained away as typical of the era. Millions of men coursing through ports arrived not merely with the usual levels of privilege but with a sense that the lives of civilians and women were fundamentally less important than theirs. Their uniforms and the legal privileges that came with them placed them above by-standers and municipal cops, encouraging more hostile and riskier behavior. Putting young men into barracks and camps that played up and rewarded belligerent, virile masculinity led to both sexual obsession and misogyny. The specter of death and the political pressures placed on women to provide romance and sex worsened a dangerous situation.

Worst of all, the sexual violence and rampant crime were not secret. Everyone knew that troops coerced, assaulted, and raped women with shocking regularity. Army leaders like General George C. Marshall, rear admirals, MPs, servicemen, municipal officials, writers, journalists, political organizations, civilians, and, most importantly, women in ports all knew the prevalence of harassment, assault, rape, and other violent crimes committed by troops. Again and again, these crimes went brazenly unpunished as military leaders made the welfare of civilians one more casualty of the war. Neither perpetrators nor officials even made much of an effort to cover anything up because they knew they did not need to.

CHAPTER ONE

MAKING THE MILITARY MAN

BY THE END OF WORLD WAR II, over sixteen million Americans would serve in the armed forces across a massive global network of ports, cities, towns, bases, and encampments. In early 1939, however, approximately 330,000 troops mostly waited in docked ships and decaying World War I cantonments as Nazi Germany threatened to move on Poland. The United States was not the isolationist slumbering giant depicted by many histories, but its military—particularly the ground forces—had suffered a serious decline in numbers since the Great War, and its infrastructure and traditions were crumbling. The drafting and training of millions of troops were to be an unprecedented administrative and political trial.

Military mobilization planted the seeds of conflict between servicemen, civilians, and women on the home front. From the beginning, the army and the Roosevelt administration faced severe challenges from Congress as they attempted to create a real fighting force. The draft, disorganized military buildup, and haphazard training system together fostered chronically poor morale, policing, and discipline that stretched across the services. Years of underfunding and makeshift repairs meant the military had to scramble to construct adequate camps and then muster an army. The training experiences of the first draftees presaged the coming morale and discipline issues that would undercut attempts to build an orderly and technologically adept army. The attack on Pearl Harbor initially gave dispirited men a sense of purpose and legitimized the privations they bore in half-constructed, stifling camps. Yet draftees continued to reject the old esprit de corps training style, never really embracing the idea of serving for country and freedom. Fighting for girls and brotherhood seemed much more appealing than any ideological motivation.

Lacking an efficient training infrastructure, and, at times, dealing with mutinous troops, military authorities channeled the draftees' anger and aggression toward civilians. They embraced and institutionalized a barracks culture that brought men together by celebrating swaggering masculinity and the obscene. This sexually aggressive culture devalued the lives and welfare of civilians but increased camaraderie. Demonstrating this particular kind of masculinity became the easiest way for a GI to validate his superiority and privilege even while he was trapped in a system that was stifling and that he mostly despised. Soldiers also learned that being a wolfish, tough military man outside camp could endear them to their comrades, who were otherwise strangers from different corners of the country. Their early off-site adventures taught servicemen how to act when they later reached liberty ports. San Francisco's Peace Day Riots were germinating as military men caroused in barracks and made their initial excursions into adjoining towns.

FIGHTING FOR CONSCRIPTION

Among the world's great powers, the United States was perhaps the least prepared to fight. Despite the conflagration engulfing Asia, Africa, and Europe, proponents of a peacetime draft faced political infighting and protests. Conventional wisdom held that the American public would never support a program that stole young men away from their families and workplaces, especially after years of economic hardship. Fan mail to Charles Lindbergh and crank letters to antifascists opposing American involvement in any war were shot through with anti-Semitic conspiracies. The letters captured a broad antipathy to intervention and an irrational sense that cabals were forcing the United States to confront a manufactured threat. Some Americans still felt some affinity for Germany in the wake of Versailles, and many more expressed the virulent anti-Semitism captured by Arthur Miller's *Focus*.

But President Roosevelt sensed that mobilization was near to hand—particularly since Nazi Germany had recently invaded France. Aware of the lukewarm, if not hostile, attitudes of Americans toward mass conscription, he announced his support for "universal government service for every young person" on June 18, 1940, as Paris fell. Rather than explicitly calling for a draft, the president compared this service to the Civilian Conservation Corps, a New Deal public works program that employed young, unemployed men, while praising the value of "discipline" and of fostering "a toughness of moral and physical fiber" in the young people of America. Opponents of conscription and FDR attacked the move as both a poor disguise for the draft and another New Deal program, with Alf Landon—Roosevelt's opponent in 1936—noting the president's "weasel words" that obscured the call for "compulsory military training."

Roosevelt's proposal soon took shape as the Burke-Wadsworth Act, also known as the Selective Training and Service Act of 1940. The bill called for the registration of over fifty million men between the ages of eighteen and sixty-four. From them, the army would be allowed to select—selective service officials despised the term *draft* and the connotation that the state was simply gobbling up manpower—up to 900,000 men aged twenty-one to thirty-five who would serve no more than one year during peacetime. It was a small step toward building a viable armed forces.

Military leaders and the Roosevelt administration privately confided that years of poor funding, a weak munitions industry, and mismanagement had left the US Army less prepared than its counterparts in countries like Spain, Belgium, and Switzerland. The marines spent much of their resources in the interwar years fending off attempts by the army to destroy or annex the corps. The army sought to eliminate what it saw as an annoying runt that might grow into a rival service. In addition, it had been failing to recruit men to either the National Guard or the regular army, and its leaders all but begged the Senate Military Affairs Committee to push Burke-Wadsworth through.

Prior to the introduction of Burke-Wadsworth, in May 1940, Chief of Staff George Marshall had organized a humiliating public demonstration of the army's woeful state—likely with an eye toward building support for conscription and improved funding. He had mobilized seventy thousand troops for war games along a mock front in Louisiana, Georgia, and Texas. The army's supposedly hardened regular troops performed maneuvers through mud, swamps, brush, and challenging hills, moving nearly 150 miles a day as they pretended to assault machine-gun nests, break opponent lines, and take down enemy aircraft. Families and the press gathered to see the spectacle, but anyone who watched was left with little doubt as to how poorly the military might perform in a real war. Over the course of a week, twelve soldiers died in accidents, almost four hundred suffered injuries and illness, and huge amounts of equipment and machinery failed. Later on, two flight crews totaling eleven men died when their bombers crashed. Civilians on porches and rooftops also witnessed the folly of officers unwilling to abandon cavalry. In one instance, two hundred mounted horses charged an armored brigade, ineffectually attacking the unfazed tanks. *Time* noted: "Against Europe's total war, the US Army looked like a few nice boys with BB guns."

Marshall had, nevertheless, won the day. He proved that the army needed dedicated funding and manpower, particularly for armored divisions. "It was a successful experiment," he said. "It showed us our shortcomings." Later that year, Senator Henry Cabot Lodge Jr. (R-MA) echoed Marshall: "The fact remains that our Army today is not what it ought to be."

Influential military figures like General John J. Pershing—the leader of the World War I expeditionary forces—joined the public offensive to sell Burke-Wadsworth. He argued disingenuously, however, that the measure was important less for military strength than because it would "promote democracy by bringing together young men from all walks of life." Indeed, he even suggested that the draft "might well be the determining factor in keeping us out of war." Army officials noted that voluntary recruitment efforts had failed and again asked the Senate Military Affairs Committee to pass Burke-Wadsworth.

Pershing's comments—militarist language clad in an appeal to democratic virtue—attempted to stymie the two major criticisms of compulsory military service: first, that it would bring the United States closer to war and, second, that it would foster antidemocratic or fascistic ideas among young Americans. The administration's push for a peacetime draft was quickly met with protest, with both those criticisms driving the demonstrators. In May 1940, anticipating the push toward a draft, three hundred City College of New York students picketed an ROTC drill, holding signs proclaiming, "To Hell with War." Following the introduction of the Burke-Wadsworth bill, religious organizations mobilized to denounce the draft not only for its failure to exempt priests and members of religious orders but also because they believed it threatened the nation's fundamental values. Methodist leaders protested directly to senators on the Military Affairs Committee while also releasing fiery statements to the major papers. Boston's Methodist bishop G. Bromley Oxnam and other church leaders declared that the conscription bill was "un-American and an undemocratic proposal, springing like a mushroom from swamps of unjustifiably hysterical fear": "It constitutes a weak, unintelligent proposal to take up slack in unemployment, and by its folly is doomed to defeat real democracy and tends to prepare the way for war." The draft was seen as "an insidious infection of the free life of a democratic people [that] apes totalitarian conscription." Oxnam concluded by insisting that, if Congress passed the draft, it would end the American tradition of individual liberty by resorting "to the Nazi and Fascist forms which brought totalitarian Europe to its present tragedy." Others wrote to papers to register their disdain for both the draft and Roosevelt's support for Britain. "We are not at war with anybody," wrote one critic. "England, on the other hand, declared war against Germany and is being attacked. This Nation has gone stark-mad through fear engendered by President Roosevelt." The United States ought to stay out of "Europe's power wars," and advocates of the draft "must have a guilty conscience to be shrieking about the Hun goblins."

Students, mothers, and other concerned citizens soon took to the streets to stop the passage of Burke-Wadsworth. These protests were highly theatrical, creating public spectacles worthy of press coverage. In late July, three people dressed as mummies marched through downtown Boston with messages like "Don't Be a Mummy, Speak for Peace" scrawled on their bedsheet costumes. In Los Angeles, the American Peace Crusade paraded with placards denouncing conscription, while two students posed as a newly married couple flanked by two grieving mothers. Some twelve hundred protesters crowded into Turner's, a boxing and wrestling arena in Washington, DC, to hear "speakers throw verbal lefts and rights at the Burke-Wadsworth conscription measure" and call for Capitol Hill marches and vigils. The next day, DC police dispersed several hundred protesters, fighting and arresting leaders like the Methodist minister Owen Knox. The Democratic and Republican offices in New York were surrounded by picket lines of young people carrying signs proclaiming sentiments like "Conscription Is a Blitzkrieg against Democracy." Three thousand members of the National Maritime Union violently protested in New York City, but not before publishing a resolution that framed compulsory conscription as a fascistic measure backed by a big business clique.

The protests soon reached Congress, where a thousand protesters chanted "Ain't Gonna Study War No More." One member of the Peace Mobilization Society screamed "American conscription is American fascism" from the House gallery before being removed. Agreeing that peacetime conscription embodied totalitarianism, the Socialist presidential candidate Norman Thomas told the House Military Committee that the draft was "Hitlerism without Hitler." Perhaps the most notable protest featured two hundred angry mothers, a wastepaper dummy, and a maple tree. On August 22, in sweltering heat, "a fleet of taxicabs drew up near the Capitol steps and began disgorging loads of grim faced women." Startled police watched as the women dragged "what appeared to be a man on the end of a rope," an effigy of Senator Claude Pepper (D-FL), one of the key proponents of the draft. The day before, Pepper had, according to the *Chicago Daily Tribune*, told mothers assembled to protest the draft legislation to "go home and mind their own business." The protesters found a maple tree, swung the rope over a branch, and began hauling the wastepaper man up into the air, chanting, "We're hanging Claude Pepper to a sour apple tree, so our sons and husbands can live on and be free." As a crowd of nearly five hundred applauded heartily, police arrived and declared, "You women can't do this here." A chorus of women replied, "Who's going to stop us?" Police and passersby who attempted to stop the spectacle faced insults and defiance from the assembled women, who had been organized by the Congress of American Mothers—a group that claimed ten thousand members nationwide. As debate continued in the House and the Senate, six women in widow's veils watched from the gallery as a silent warning about the potential consequences of passing Burke-Wadsworth.

The stiff opposition to the draft further delayed mobilization and guaranteed that the army would struggle to train any men it did draft effectively. In Washington, little progress was made as legislative sessions devolved into petty recriminations, insults, and fistfights. At an August 6 session in the Democratic-controlled Senate, the prodraft Sherman Minton (D-IN) accused the antidraft Rush D. Holt Sr. (D-WV) of coming from a "slacker family" that lacked patriotism and courage. Holt replied by charging that "Senator Minton is not in shape to be on the floor" before going on to defend his opposition "to this alien doctrine of conscription," which he and other opponents claimed was a foreign plot that had been "incubated in the banks and law firms of New York City on Wall Street." Outbursts from spectators led to threats of clearing the galleries, while Senator Holt was reprimanded for his language. Holt's claim appeared rooted in his economic populism, but it also echoed anti-Semitic conspiracies. His later support for the fascist America First Committee suggests that his suggestions of a foreign plot were at least partly driven by anti-Semitism. Tensions also grew in the Democratic-controlled House, where FDR's allies limited debate on Burke-Wadsworth to two days in spite of vigorous protests from Republicans. On September 4, two congressmen began brawling on the House floor. In this era, parties were not so ideologically unified, and different wings of the Democratic Party often fought each other over what US foreign policy ought to be. After Martin Sweeney (D-OH) blamed FDR and Woodrow Wilson for getting the United States entangled in the First World War, Beverly Vincent (D-KY) called Sweeney a traitor. Sweeney swung and landed a blow on Vincent's nose, and both began throwing haymakers. Fellow representatives soon pulled them apart. Sweeney apologized while not so subtly blaming Vincent for the fracas. Vincent countered: "I said I don't want to sit by a traitor, and then I moved. He attacked me and I have no apologies to make. And the speech the gentleman made is proof to me the gentleman is a traitor." The competing cheers and hisses that followed captured the divide in Washington.

To rebut the protests, the draft's proponents made their case in the press, stressing the dire situation in Europe. Roosevelt called in powerful Republicans like New York City mayor Fiorello La Guardia as well as politically connected industrialists like General Electric's Owen D. Young to speak in favor of Burke-Wadsworth. Members of the National Education Association issued statements in favor of integrating compulsory military training into schools and colleges, although they disapproved of a full year of military service. Prominent journalists like Walter Lippmann published in support of conscription. In the *Los Angeles Times*, Lippmann assailed Senator Robert Taft (R-OH) for criticizing the value of training and conscription: "These Senators are in flight from the realities and are taking refuge in sheer wishfulness. . . . If the emergency demands this much military power which we do not possess, the overshadowing concern of responsible statesmen ought to be to think up ways of hastening the process of developing this force." Chief of Staff General George C. Marshall like-wise understood that, without a peacetime draft, the army would be unable to counter German or Japanese forces. Back in June, a week before France capitulated to the Axis, he had spoken on both the complacency that existed in the United States and the challenges ahead, making a subtle call for the draft: "We have been accustomed to liberty, but after the next few days nobody knows or can say what kind of world we shall be living in." Leaders like Pershing and Marshall were joined by other veterans like Colonel W. A. Graham, who called universal training "not only wise but very necessary," especially given how long it would take to train a whole army. Graham dismissed the opposition "from religious and political objectors, from pacifists, cowards and Communists, from Liberty Leagues, and others of that ilk, and, alas, from frightened mothers, wives and sweethearts" while portraying conscription as a fundamental American tradition with its roots in the 1792 Militia Act. FDR's allies smartly passed military spending bills before tackling conscription, giving themselves the argument that men would be needed to use the already-purchased equipment and vehicles.

More than any rhetoric, probably, the deteriorating fortunes of France and Britain moved officials toward passing Burke-Wadsworth. Five days before FDR officially called for conscription, Paris had fallen to the Wehrmacht. One week after the president's announcement, France surrendered, stunning Americans. As various congressional committees met to discuss the peacetime draft, the Battle of Britain intensified. Secretary of War Henry Stimson seized on the dangerous setbacks in Europe in his recommendations to the House Military Affairs Committee on August 1. He warned: "In another 30 days Great Britain may be conquered and her fleet come under enemy control. Across the Pacific there is a powerful Japan in sympathy with Italy and Germany. We've got to very radically revise our prejudices about our first line of defense." The appeal quieted some of the objections to an unprecedented peacetime mobilization. By September, the Luftwaffe began bombing London. One supporter of conscription noted that each day of the Blitz bought Burke-Wadsworth "a vote or two in the House or Senate."

On September 14, 1940, the House and Senate approved Burke-Wadsworth by a two-to-one margin. Protests, nevertheless, continued. Peace Mobilization League members picketed the White House, futilely urging the president to veto the measure. The "anticonscriptionist" wing of the Senate held a public postmortem led by Burton Wheeler (D-MT), who warned that military training would poison American boys. "You mothers of America," he proclaimed, "they say to you they will take your sons and train them to be young brutes. They will teach them that the Ten Commandments are wrong. You will have a country of Al Capones. You will have a country where robbery will run riot." For the most part, however, Americans accepted registration and the draft as measures justified by the looming Axis threats.

The morning of October 16 marked the beginning of registration day, a massive undertaking that eventually saw many millions of men processed by a million volunteer workers across the country. Reports that day indicated a mostly smooth process even with the long lines and late hours for workers. The overwhelming majority of men reported to their registration centers, though many struggled to fill out their registration cards. Often, it was the first federal form they had ever seen. Protests at New York's Union Theological Seminary and in the Southwest among Native Americans did little to disrupt the day. By this point, Americans who might be drafted no longer rejected the idea of compulsory military service, a Gallup poll finding that 76 percent of boys and young men did not object. One father of a selectee remembered his uncertainty as he accompanied his son into the local schoolhouse for registration: "What will happen to freedom and democracy when my son and a million like him are militarized?" But he soon came to see American conscription the way the Swiss saw their compulsory service, as a guarantor of freedom, democracy, and masculine honor. "My son is going to be a soldier," he explained. "And I felt a surge of pride." Lieutenant Colonel Lewis Hershey, the executive officer at draft headquarters, took to the radio to declare: "Anyone who watched these Americans at the places of registration must have sensed a great surging pride, for America's manhood was parading through those places of registration today, America's youth upon whom the Nation depends for preservation."

"OVER THE HILL IN OCTOBER"

Despite the administration's victory with Burke-Wadsworth, the relatively smooth "R-Day," and Hershey's proclamations, military leaders understood just how unready they were to process and train the initial 900,000 men. Chief of Staff Marshall faced a wide array of problems as he attempted to build an army essentially from scratch. Before registration, the US Army totaled fewer than 170,000 regulars. The minuscule National Guard reserves lacked training and a sense that what they were doing actually mattered as the war seemed to threaten only China and Europe. Marshall was likely even more concerned by the dearth of skilled troops who could handle mortars, antiaircraft gunnery, logistics, and, most notably, tanks. The problem of integrating green recruits into the insular "Old Army" of professional soldiers loomed as well. These problems would eventually produce an army united more by a sexually aggressive and anticivilian culture than by discipline and commitment to service.

Marshall began by directly tackling supply and training problems as well as challenging the crippling traditionalism of other generals who disdained the use of tanks. Colleagues warned that he was "courting disaster," but he proceeded to assemble disparate units into divisions and pushed manufacturers to deliver needed equipment. He began, as well, the process of modernizing and centralizing the dilapidated army camp system. During the violent and brutal westward expansion of the United States, the army relied on small but numerous posts dotted throughout the country to project power and support cadres. This military and legal infrastructure had been crucial to the making of the continent-spanning American empire. Yet this meant, as Marshall said, that the army was made up of "mere hodgepodges of unrelated small units." Camps and units lacked the basic necessities of modern armies like artillery, firearms, logistics support, and basic transport. Small-unit tactics training proved impossible without these support elements.

Many members of Congress, however, still staunchly opposed any attempts to modernize this outmoded system, fearing that centralization would threaten all the small posts, camps, and forts that had provided consistent jobs, purchase orders, and income to districts throughout the Depression. Congressional resistance meant that training remained inefficient and commanding officers lacked experience directing troop movements. Initial mobilization plans called for troops to drill and assemble in public buildings, parks, and fields within major cities. But, with conscription proceeding quickly, Marshall and the War Department pushed a crash program expanding existing camps and building new centers and forts, while surveying huge swaths of land.

Marshall, the Army Corps of Engineers and the Army Construction Service also confronted a legacy of poor funding and mismanagement since World War I. At their height, the World War I army cantonments could house around 650,000 soldiers, but many of these training areas had only temporary housing, and that had fallen into disrepair. From 1920 to 1938, the Construction Service had suffered what it called "the lean years" or "the famine years." Funding for maintenance and construction plummeted during these years, and it suffered poor leadership while it was headed by Brigadier General A. Owen Seaman, who had been selected on the basis of seniority, lacked an engineering background, and ignored the suggestions of his more knowledgeable subordinates. The army had focused some funds on a few new camps but mostly had lost an increasingly futile battle against rot and dilapidation. Some of the corps' talented engineers resigned in disgust and left for more lucrative private sector work. The army saw a brief reprieve in 1924 after troops on Governors Island were forced to forage driftwood from New York Harbor in order to repair buildings. The

New York Times put the story on the front page, and other articles emphasized the poor living conditions that soldiers endured. Congress appropriated more money for construction and repairs, but funding collapsed once again with the Great Depression. From 1934 to 1936, the Construction Service received 14 percent of the appropriations it estimated it would need for adequate repairs and maintenance. With international tensions rising, FDR authorized a massive spike in construction spending of $65 million. But even the backing of the president was not enough to overcome the army's internal dysfunctions and turf wars. General Seaman—described in the army's history of the Construction Service as "peppery and unpredictable"—refused to take the new funds because Roosevelt required the work contracts be let and work. He called in a number of political favors accumulated from his nearly four-decade military career to scuttle appropriations. The exasperated General Staff broke protocol and chose to humiliate him by promoting a colonel over him. The colonel accepted the funding, and the Construction Service started to play catch-up.

Several members of Congress made aggressive bids to attract the military dollars to their states. Marshall and the Construction Service considered several factors in deciding where to purchase land and where to build training centers. The forts and training areas needed cheap, undeveloped land, space for various maneuvers and exercises, and access to water, roads, and rail. Significantly, Marshall also aimed for each base to be located near a city that could provide recreation— though some strongly opposed the army's presence near them.

Most of the new camps and major expansions came in the South or the Southwest, where units could avoid freezing conditions, train in mixed terrain, and perform maneuvers that might stretch over several states. The most important forts and camps clustered in the states of the former Confederacy. Fort Benning, in western Georgia, became the biggest army base, housing ninety-five thousand people while spanning nearly 200,000 acres. Originally a basic training camp established a month before the end of World War I, Benning was built up into an infantry training center. Camp Shelby, another expanded World War

FIGURE 1.1 US training bases and military installations
Source: Rand McNally Map of United States Military Posts. Chicago: Rand McNally & Co., 1944.

I site, rivaled Benning in population (eighty-six thousand), and its location in southern Mississippi allowed access to the Gulf Coast and
inland marches across Alabama's coastal plain. Artillery boomed at the
long ranges of Fort Bragg, outside Fayetteville, North Carolina. To the
south, infantrymen trained at Fort Jackson outside Columbia, South
Carolina. Additional training centers like Camp Hood (Texas), Camp
Claiborne (Louisiana), Camp Blanding (Florida), and Fort Knox (Ken-
tucky) all handled tens of thousands of draftees as the military expanded
throughout the South. Major installations outside Dixie included Camp
San Luis Obispo near Morro Bay, California, Fort Dix in central New Jersey, and Fort Lewis outside Tacoma, Washington. The navy focused on
expansion of its Great Lakes training center north of Chicago.

While the land was mostly cheap, surveyors, contractors, and quar-
termasters faced several difficulties during construction. Some tracts

turned out to be flooded, lacked water, or consisted of nothing but swampland. Time was short, however, and Marshall ordered his engineers to push on. Other obstacles proved harder to overcome. In 1940, the lumber market experienced a serious shortage, threatening to make the army pay exorbitant prices while still failing to meet its needs. Given that many training areas were located in the South, local mills failed to meet demand for softwoods, leading to price jacking. The Construction Service managed to break this bottleneck by instituting a new system of purchasing lumber under which purchasers would bid on lumber throughout the country, including the Pacific Northwest, which had productive softwood mills. Despite the success of driving down prices and increasing throughput, some training areas were left without needed materials. Marshall likely faced an impossible task when it came to building training areas so quickly, but many draftees found themselves arriving in unfinished camps as late as 1942. This exacerbated the disdain many inducted men had for their officers and drove them to seek delights outside army oversight.

While Marshall's much-needed rebuilding program offered some cause for optimism about the new military, the draft's first selectees and guardsmen received poor training and suffered from a lack of esprit de corps. Part of the problem came from insufficient veteran leadership in training camps and forts as well as rivalries between the new guys and the old hands. Green troops found little help from the army regulars, who often saw the "number men" as soft civilians playing soldier and too stubborn to submit to the army way of life. One sergeant of the Old Army argued that the conscripted men did not "know what the Army meant" and that the branch provided "security and pride and something good." He explained: "Putting on that uniform not only meant that for the first time in my life I had clothes I wasn't ashamed of, but also for the first time in my life I was *somebody*." Draftees, the sergeant recalled, "came in bitching about this and that, regulations, the food, a cot instead of an innerspring mattress, barracks instead of private rooms." Regulars also tended to haze and humiliate the draftees, denying them the use of the post exchange or forcing them to dig trenches for no reason. In turn, conscripts despised many of the regulars for obsessing over rank, procedure, and the "cult of the uniform." In some ways, the Old Army mimicked the clannishness and insular tendencies of the marines, though it would never embody the spiritual and monastic qualities that came to define the corps.

On an even more fundamental level, most bases proved unable to process the new trainees or to provide the most basic equipment. Although the War Department initially set bold directives such as "There will be no compromise with quality," deficiencies in the training process quickly emerged. With a chronic shortage of equipment like ammunition and mortars, draftees spent their days doing calisthenics, close-order drills, or tedious manual labor but learning little of combat or specialized skills. One senior training officer pinned the poor instruction on inexperienced officers: "Hell, you can't expect an officer to be any good if he only has as much training as the enlisted men." Noncoms would occasionally argue with and berate officers, disrupting the intended hierarchy and command structure. Unskilled and untrained majors and lieutenants—usually the leaders of platoons or companies—sometimes embarrassed themselves, losing the trust of their men. In one instance, a lieutenant maneuvered his men into a danger area during war games, leading the umpire to declare that his company had been destroyed by "friendly artillery." When the lieutenant complained that "it's our own artillery," the umpire responded: "It is, but your own shells will kill you if they hit you." Another lieutenant repeatedly became lost while orienteering his company through the forest, leading him to claim that the ground had an unusually high iron content. One army colonel publicly criticized these training failures, noting that an Illinois division "has been in camps for months, but has not had the services of a single military instructor." He concluded by grimly warning: "Valor without military education only means suicide. . . . If our boys should be recklessly thrown into battle with only the kind of training they have been receiving, they would be destroyed." Privates largely agreed with one who snarled: "The papers are always talking about how good the morale is and how ready the Army is for battle. The hell it is!"

Marshall and the brass became alarmed at the episodes of insubordination and near-mutinous behavior that spread among the selectees. Conscripts openly resented the military's hierarchy and the insularity of life in rural military camps, publicly complaining to family, congressmen, and the press. *Life* published damaging remarks from troops that captured their frustration and refusal to submit to military discipline: "To hell with Roosevelt and Marshall and the Army and especially this Goddamn hole," said one draftee fed up with camp life. Twenty-nine of his thirty fellow troops apparently agreed with his sentiment. An army-commissioned study by Arthur Sulzberger and Hilton Railey of the *New York Times* confirmed that the enlisted man "is questioning everything from God Almighty to themselves." More disturbingly, officers reported being threatened and sworn at by their men. A major, for instance, confronted a drunk soldier at a bar, asking: "Soldier, don't you think you've had enough?" The soldier apparently recognized the major's rank but nevertheless replied: "You take a good fuck for yourself." Tellingly, the major merely told the soldier to "carry on." Railey wrote to army leaders that officers lived in "physical fear" of the soldiers they supposedly commanded. The draftees often displayed blatant disregard for rank when they refused to salute an officer—a cardinal sin in the Old Army, where failure to salute could bring hefty fines or punishments like a twenty-mile run, leading one soldier to write to *Yank* that "the principles we are fighting for are being destroyed before our very eyes."

GIs and sailors also resented their superiors because of military policies on dating. Only officers were officially allowed to date the nurses, secretaries, and other women who staffed military buildings, prompting accusations from soldiers—and some women—that the brass were keeping women for themselves. Draftees' distrust of their superiors abounded in rumors that camp meals were laced with saltpeter in order to lower the men's libidos and make them more compliant and docile.

The summer of 1941 saw the number men grow even bolder in their rejection of military discipline. They also began to resent civilians, whom they saw reaping the benefits of an accelerating war economy while they were being asked to make great sacrifices. Federal funding had brought about the end of the Great Depression, but the poor pay and living conditions in the army seemed to prolong the misery for the draftees. Draftees moved into near-open rebellion in July when FDR and Marshall announced that the promised single year of military service would be extended indefinitely and that troops might be stationed outside the Western Hemisphere. Roosevelt and Marshall argued that the United States faced a great national peril, but, with Pearl Harbor still more than four months in the future, men languishing in dusty camps bereft of equipment could see little reason for an extension of their service. Meyer Berger of the *New York Times* suggested that men did not necessarily lack the willingness to serve but, rather, lacked the incentive. One draftee wrote to Arthur Krock—also at the *Times*— asking why Roosevelt did not "tell us the details of this national peril." Another group asked why they should "have to stay beyond the year prescribed in the Act when labor gets nearly everything it wants by strikes and violence and escapes the risks of Army service." The draftees also questioned the president's previous promises that jobs would be waiting for them once they were released from service. One soldier bluntly told *Life*: "So Roosevelt will get our jobs back? The hell he will! I've already been told that I can't have my job back."

Protest mail from draftees and civilians flooded Capitol Hill, signaling both the disorganization of mobilization and the draftees' rejection of military authority and discipline. The protests from troops also gave politicians who opposed American military intervention overseas ammunition. Citing the torrent of letters, Senator Robert Reynolds (D-NC) deemed Marshall's proposal to extend the service length and area of operations no different than a declaration of war. Senators Wheeler and Taft claimed to be receiving over a thousand letters a day, many from draftees opposed to the extension of service. One infantry company from Camp Livingston in Louisiana sent a petition to the Senate maintaining: "Prolongation of our service would be an actual breach of contract and certainly a blow to our morale. We feel that we have shown our patriotism for our country and now it is no more than fair that the other young men within our great country be asked to do their part. . . . Many of our families are in dire need of help." Fearing reprisals, these draftees asked not to be identified but insisted that they represented 90 percent of the camp. Privately, Marshall warned other generals and FDR that negative press reports might further exacerbate the morale crisis.

Platoons and companies that made public protests faced reprimands and reprisals from commanding officers infuriated at what they saw as mutinous behavior. A Fort Meade quartermaster company instigated a small crisis after its officials learned of a telegram the men had sent to Wheeler and Taft. Though the draftees did not "begrudge the sacrifices we have made for our country" and promised to be willing to even make "the supreme sacrifice of our lives," they questioned Marshall and Roosevelt's claim that "we are in grave danger from aggression." Instead, they argued that "the present emergency exists in the minds of war mongers in Washington and not in the actual state of affairs," before going on explicitly to "condemn the acts of the administration leaders." For the army and Fort Meade's adjutant, the telegram was a stunning public display of disloyalty and a violation of a regulation that prohibited "efforts to procure or influence legislation affecting the army." One commander threatened protesting draftees with courts-martial, while others declared they would pursue the severest of disciplinary actions. Some men responded by threatening to desert, while others chalked "OHIO"—"Over the Hill in October," meaning deserting or leaving the army after one year's service—on walls, equipment, and vehicles. In one camp, a *Life* reporter found that 50 percent of the men claimed they would desert, 40 percent "rue[d] the day they got in the Army," and the final 10 percent wished to transfer to a different branch of the military. Of the four hundred men interviewed, only two wished to stick it out in the army. Many lamented that they struggled to manage outstanding debts or prevent their families from being evicted while they drained swamps, dug ditches, and cut grass. Hilton Railey—who described the selectees as "a football team in training but without a schedule of games"—confirmed that the vast majority of troops were familiar with this damaging *Life* report and that almost every man told him the situation was far worse than it was depicted as being.

Though weakened by the protests and infighting, Marshall and the administration managed to salvage an eighteen-month extension of service for draftees and reservists, though they were forced to concede a $10.00 monthly pay raise. Low morale continued to plague the draftees, leading now General Hershey to complain that the situation would improve "if some of the parents would just leave them alone." Hershey's patronizing suggestion that the draftees were little more than mama's boys rang hollow against the terrible economic and personal pressures the men faced, leaving them little choice between serving or deserting. "I was willing to sacrifice one year but I can't afford more," one infantryman said. "You can't even see your wife. . . . One of the fellows asked for leave to go to his wife when she was having a baby. When they turned him down he went AWOL [absent without leave]. What would you do?" Marshall eased some of the pressure in camps by sending men twenty-eight and older home early after Railey reported that they were the draftees most likely to suffer from poor morale.

EXPANDING THE DRAFT

Only the horror of Japan's attack on Pearl Harbor could alleviate the political problems plaguing the army. Draftees complained about lacking a sense of purpose while in training, but much of that evaporated, at least temporarily, as the Pacific Fleet sank and smoldered in Hawaii. Fighting spirit was suddenly high, and the old battles over the draft and service length were now over. Men seemed to accept Roosevelt's language of service and sacrifice for the imminent total war. Draftees and veterans now blended manly nationalism with an almost savage desire for revenge. "It's our duty as a nation to defend it and whip the aggressors," one man explained. Another asserted that the United States would have to "take over the Western Hemisphere": "We're going to have to police the world." For the moment, the military no longer needed to manufacture motivation. Men flocked to recruiting stations "fighting mad," and most waited for hours in the cold. "We were furious," recalled one veteran. "No one's gonna come in our country. We immediately went to the marine recruiting headquarters." The navy in Boston elected to keep its stations open 24/7 as lines of over two thousand volunteers snaked around city blocks and crowded recruiting offices. "It was the greatest wave of patriotism I have ever seen," said one official. Men "pounded the doors of selective service boards" in bids to volunteer immediately.

Other interviewees emphasized a personal desire for vengeance. The recruit Charles L. Gilley gave up his $100 weekly salary, put off his marriage, and signed up for likely combat duty in the marines. He hoped to avenge his leatherneck brother Ernest, who he feared had already perished in the Japanese capture of Wake Island. Men fantasized about murdering the Japanese diplomat Saburo Kurusu—"I'd a killed that son of a gun"—and suggested that hunting season on the Japanese had begun: "No bag limit, kill as many as you want." One veteran speaking with draftees promised: "I'm going to fight with hate in my heart. What's in me, what's in my veins, I'm going to kill, slaughter."

Five additional registrations took place. After 1942, registration became a continuous process. One in ten Americans served in the armed forces between 1941 and 1945, with 20 percent of all men entering the military. Ten million men were drafted, and another six million men and women volunteered.

The government created six thousand draft boards around the country, with World War I veterans and local eminent civilians like "judges, postmasters, and men of prominence" deciding who received exemptions. Many boys hoped to be selected, and those with medical issues or physical handicaps often attempted to hide conditions that might disqualify them. Part of this desire came from a traditional sense of masculine duty. But men also faced community pressure, a tactic honed in World War I by groups like the Order of the White Feather. Any young, apparently healthy male civilian who remained at home could be ostracized and despised as a draft dodger, an especially alienating fate in small towns. The press and members of the public expressed consternation when the baseball star Joe DiMaggio was rejected because of his poor eyesight. After receiving numerous complaints about athletes being declared unfit for service, the War Department began "taking the boxer out of the ring and the ball player off the diamond, regardless of his potential value to the service, to satisfy public opinion." The administration was pleased with the efficiency and seemingly democratic and communal qualities of draft boards.

Some women's professional groups fruitlessly protested the exclusion of women from these boards. The boards also often held discriminatory views of conscientious objectors, gay men, and African Americans. One member explained that his board had met several conscientious objectors but had "always managed to talk them out of it." Military authorities brought in psychiatric examiners to find and exclude gay men, even though many wished to serve and commanders later acknowledged that gay troops became critical and effective members of the armed forces. These psychiatrists' methods lacked tact or subtlety: they simply asked whether the potential draftee was homosexual, had ever had a same-sex sexual experience, and/or thought about men while masturbating or whether he liked girls. Though some self-identified gay men found the act trying, many simply told the draft board that they liked girls.

The black press and political advocates quickly identified the reluctance of the military to give African Americans opportunities or leadership roles. Walter White, the secretary of the National Association for the Advancement of Colored People (NAACP), argued: "From the manpower angle, the largest defense headache ahead of the United States Government is likely to be the status of that 10 percent of our population which is Negro. The Negro insists upon doing his part, and the Army and Navy want none of him." Nationwide, draft officials and military leaders regarded African Americans as unsuited for combat roles, often relegating them to service and labor positions. In the South, African Americans rarely served on any draft boards, and black registrants were rejected at a far higher rate than were their white counterparts. The state selective service director in Georgia explained that draft boards "simply [did] not want them" and used a variety of manufactured excuses to reject them, including "urethritis," "inadequate personality," and "psychoneurosis." The War Department nevertheless pushed states to induct more African Americans. Each branch eventually fielded African American troops in numbers roughly proportional to the general population of registrants, aside from the marines, who never came close to bringing in enough black inductees.

African Americans saw an opportunity in this, however, and began rallying to the flag as part of a nascent Double V campaign that saw the fight for freedom overseas and the fight for freedom from racial and economic inequality at home as intertwined. African American papers like *The Crisis* passionately argued that freedom abroad could not be won without freedom at home: "A lilywhite navy cannot fight for a free world. A jim crow army cannot fight for a free world. Jim crow strategy, no matter on how grand a scale, cannot build a free world."

Despite these inequities, the processing, assessing, and drafting of millions of men represented a much-needed success in the country's plodding mobilization. Yet the new influx of manpower only exacerbated the poor training conditions that the initial selectees criticized, and troops still lacked a coherent military identity separate from their civilian selves. Roosevelt and the chiefs of staff also faced the even greater challenge of equipping, training, and supplying a still-unprepared military lacking skilled officers and infrastructure. Pearl Harbor papered over the poor morale and discipline in training areas, but the military failed to instill a lasting nationalistic or ideological drive in the draftees. The legacy of World War I taught men to be skeptical of ideological motivations for fighting. Devising a unifying narrative of why men should fight or even a basic common cause among disparate and varied divisions would prove incredibly difficult, though more so in the army than in the marines. Even after the definitive entry of the United States into the war after Pearl Harbor, the army stubbornly held to a training system that aimed at the rapid indoctrination of the supposedly individualistic and recalcitrant American civilian into military society. Ideally, men would quickly shed their civilian loyalties, submit to military discipline, and reform themselves into effective fighting units. It didn't happen.

"THEIR OWN PARTICULAR ORDEAL"

Men were made anxious by the induction process. Following their mental and physical examinations—and the long wait for the letter—they gathered to compare draft numbers. Few attempted to flee, though one inductee threw heavy chairs, damaging a room, and then fled the building, eventually being tackled by "two husky nomcoms" as he was running down the street. Men often confessed to the dread of leaving their families and girlfriends even as they expressed excitement at leaving home for unfamiliar big cities and battle somewhere across the Pacific or the Atlantic. The last ritual of leaving was the bittersweet sending-off party where family and friends gathered for a ceremony that combined elements of the coming-of-age rite and a funeral.

Arriving at induction stations, draftees readied themselves to leave their private lives for training, war, and possibly death. Awkward young men, poorly dressed and carrying items they would never need, formed misshapen lines and waited for trains or buses to take them to austere reception centers like Fort Dix in New Jersey. Many reception and training areas simply received far too many recruits each day, leading to backlogs in processing, distributing, and training. There recruits lingered for days and sometimes weeks, waiting to be assigned to a training camp or a fort and then later a unit training center. Most would also receive specialized training in a subsequent location before moving to a port of embarkation. The average trainee made six to seven moves before reaching port.

Once in camp after days on trains or buses, draftees often felt disoriented and intimidated by the rough conditions and unwelcoming regular troops. Noncoms forced the sleep-deprived men onto muddy camp roads, demanding that they close ranks. Watching the "calf-like marching gait" of green troops, regulars would yell, "Hello, suckers!" or, as the marine E. B. Sledge recalled, "You'll be sorreee." Others jeered that the recruits ought to "look out for the hook," referring to the coming smallpox and typhoid injections. "The recruits," wrote one observer at Camp Wheeler, "look about as military as a bunch of sightseers at Radio City with a guide." Draftees soon received identification tags, shoes, uniforms, and the requisite inoculations before crawling into the barracks. Settling into rough cots, men found themselves "in an alien world."

The first thing many inductees noticed was the dirt. It was everywhere and ever present. In reception centers and camps, recruits faced an endless battle against dust, grime, soot, mud, and filth. At Fort Benning and other posts, troops claimed that mud and dust somehow managed to coexist. Superior officers demanded that tents be kept clean, but as one soldier recalled: "No matter how often we swept, the broom could always collect a large pile of dust." Coal-fired stoves—at least those that worked—created piles of ash and spread soot. A recurring lack of good firewood meant that living trees were chopped down and green wood fed to the fire, producing higher levels of eye-stinging smoke and soot. Men walked through muddy pathways pocked with discarded paper and cigarette butts. Fort Dix featured streets and fields filled with "khaki-colored mud as sticky as fly paper." Latrines required near-constant cleaning, though one recruit lamented that mud and paper quickly caked the floor again. Men on KP (kitchen patrol or kitchen police) recalled the seemingly ineradicable grease that coated every pot and surface. Hastily constructed huts filled with the "heady scent of fresh pine board and tar paper," while tents howled with gusts of wind. Long marches took place "in scorching heat, in bitter cold, in rain or snow"—and in the night, each man grasping the belt of the man in front of him "to keep from getting lost in the darkness." Sledge recalled sleeping in extra gear to combat the cold. In Texas, men told of mosquitoes so spoiled that they would inspect a GI's tags for blood type before biting. Though conditions improved over the course of the war, many draftees arrived in camps that were "little more than great stretches of waste land," places where "dried top soil blew into mouth and ears with every wind." One Indiana recruit lamented the environmental hazards and physical exhaustion of living in a military post: "I cannot picture everything clearly for you for I cannot send you a box of Texas dust to pour liberally over your whole body. I cannot send you a long, hot road and a fine set of blisters or a pair of heavy G.I. shoes to be broken in." Another recalled the "all pervading barrenness" and a sense that his camp existed "in a constant state of erosion."

Life in camp became defined by the fight against discomfort, loneliness, and boredom. The vast majority of the men suffered through what the outpost soldier Ross Parmenter called "their own particular ordeal." Troops "sweated and froze in some of the dirtiest weather, and, though they were spared danger, they did not have excitement and movement to offset loneliness, separation, hardship, and monotony." At times, men were quarantined in the barracks for days following the outbreak of a disease or the death of a trainee from sickness. Continued equipment shortages had many draftees throwing stones instead of grenades or continuing to build their own unfinished camp or fort. The training infrastructure was not truly completed until 1944, and the head of Army Ground Forces later admitted: "The machine was a little wobbly when it first got going. The men knew it. The officers knew it. Everybody knew it." Teaching improved after the army and navy produced some combat veterans who could impart practical advice. Until then, instructors took a "pay-attention-you-fuckers" lecture style. Still, recruits became quite familiar with the phrase *hurry up and wait*. Paul Fussell, a veteran and cultural critic, endorsed Leonard Woolf's image of "endlessly waiting in a dirty, grey railway station waiting-room" as the best description of the "negative emptiness and desolation of personal and cosmic boredom" found during wartime. Many discomforts, he explained, were "the inevitable inconveniences of military life: overcrowding and a lack of privacy, tedious institutional cookery, deprivation of personality, general boredom."

Petty injustices, "sadism thinly disguised as necessary discipline," and authoritarianism combined to form what Fussell identified as *chickenshit*. Troops recognized chickenshit as any behavior that made "military life worse than it need be" or as some trivial but painful demand that had contributed nothing to victory. Chickenshit was being forced to dig a trench for a latrine when the camp already had a functioning sewer system. Chickenshit was not being allowed to wear an overcoat "at reveille when it is freezing, but which you will be required to wear during the sweltering afternoon." Chickenshit crystallized the stifling low-level authoritarianism baked into military training that made men aware of how little freedom and control they exercised over their lives. The irony of entering an authoritarian organization to defend the four freedoms did not go unnoticed. Some of the more intellectual draftees found the lack of choice liberating: "I was freed from even the most elementary decisions as to what to wear or eat." Most, however, found themselves confronting "the Will of the Army," a force that gave a "strange power to all those in authority, so that an ignorant drill instructor, or an uncouth corporal, who had been made barracks chief, could order us around and we had to submit or be punished." One returning veteran argued that training created "dictators who mold the thoughts and actions of men under their leadership": "The trend of this kind of leadership is to create class distinctions by making the leader king and the followers slaves." The army's caste system incentivized chickenshit while fostering an intense desire for personal liberty and comfort outside military authority. Quoting Napoléon, an army colonel observed that "misery is the best school for a soldier." For some men, misery continued far past this early training period. In 1943, soldiers at Camp Hood telegrammed the Military Police division claiming that they were "being treated more like dogs instead of soldiers" and that the German prisoners of war on-site lived in far better conditions than they did. Officers endlessly beat trainees and ignored one soldier suffering appendicitis. "Are we still in America," asked the private, "or are we over in Japan or Germany?" The irony, of course, was that few of the men would become combat soldiers; some never even approached a combat zone. Their lack of direct experience of combat left many without "the sense that their sacrifices were justified because what they were doing was vital."

The War Department eventually decided that having troops performing a slog of menial jobs like KP, cooking, operating phones, distributing mail, stoking fires, and sweeping streets was perhaps not the most efficient use of each unit's limited training time. In March 1941, the department began increasing the number of civilians employed by the army from 215,000 to 1,400,000. These civilians would free up soldiers for more direct training in their specified duty. While this idea made sense in principle, in practice it reinforced the idea, common among draftees, that while shirking duty civilians were also managing to get rich, being paid $35.00 a week when soldiers were paid only $30.00. Even though soldiers also received free food, clothing, and housing, the disparity in raw weekly salary disgusted a number of draftees, who accused civilians working in defense plants of moneygrubbing "pseudo-patriotism": "This rubs a soldier the wrong way. They don't like to see civilians getting credit. . . . We are at war, and everybody should do his duty, whether in the Army or not. They are getting $90 or $100 (per week) for the work they are doing." This pay gap became just another slight that made men hate both civilians and camp life even more. These early conflicts presaged the breakdown of civil-military relations to come.

In addition to these common indignities, African Americans suffered additional mistreatment and violence fueled by the racism of white officers and civilians. The black press covered several notable incidents in which horrible conditions had essentially forced black soldiers to go AWOL at over twice the rate of white soldiers. In Bastrop, Louisiana, several privates fled to Chicago after enduring a spate of "sadistic brutality" at the hands of white officers. After a white officer and a white soldier had objected to five African American draftees taking leave in town, a series of beatings, humiliations, and rumored murders had followed.

Besides generally facing more violent punishments, worse living conditions, and disdain for the emerging Double V campaign, black draftees also faced the effects of whites' pervasive fear of the prospect of interracial sex. The *Afro-American* reported one Birmingham man's promise: "No white man down here goin' to let his daughter sleep with a n——, or sit at the table with a n——, or go walkin' with a n——. The war can go to hell, the world can go to hell, we can all be dead—but he ain't goin' to do it." By building up training centers across the South, drafting large numbers of African Americans from the North, and failing to provide much in the way of recreation, Marshall had created a powder keg. Southerners believed that the military influx would challenge the established white supremacist sexual order. The *Afro-American* noted that the talk of white southern men always returned to the "threatened rape and the sanctity of Southern womanhood." Yet incidents outside the South suggest that white men in northern cities like Chicago, Cleveland, Detroit, and Boston had similar fears. Throughout the training period and the war, violent shoot-outs, riots, and lynchings were sparked by interracial sex, real and imagined. Georgia's Camp Stewart saw violence between troops after rumors spread that an African American soldier had been visited by his white wife. Though it was revoked by the War Department and lambasted by the NAACP, an order from Camp Stewart's Captain A. D. Robbins went so far as to treat all interracial sex—including consensual relationships and sexual assaults—as a form of rape to be punished by death.

All of the discomforts, injustices, and recurring boredom drove both black and white draftees to commit small acts of insubordination. Resistance to the assembled forces of authoritarianism, conformity, and chickenshit could be seen in the way draftees walked and the way they dressed. Europeans consistently noted the ragged, discordant marching style of American troops, as well as their disregard for a neat uniform or polished shoes. General Dwight D. Eisenhower told Marshall that American companies looked like "armed mobs," while General George S. Patton attacked Bill Mauldin's popular cartoon grunts Willie and Joe, for their sloppy, unshaven appearance. The Office of War Information eventually put out posters comparing a slovenly dressed and whiskery solder named Benny to a model sharp and stern soldier who earned a promotion. Troops shot back, using publications like *Yank* to mock the privileges given to the upper castes of the military. One recruit declared: "I'll sweat for my country, but here is one private who is never going to mop any sergeant's floor, even if it costs me six months' confinement." Men also shared "rumor-jokes" that undercut superiors and offered fantasies of rebellion. One featured General Patton dressing down a man for failing to come to attention. After Patton's lengthy tirade, the man shoots back: "Run along asshole, I'm in the Merchant Marine." In another telling, a major screams at a man in a dirty uniform. The man replies: "Fuck you, buddy. I just came in from town to fill the Coke machine."

The most famous conflict between draftees and command became known as the Yoo-Hoo Affair, and it made it clear that aggressive and disrespectful behavior from troops toward women would be tolerated. The July 1941 incident also taught men that their best chance to rebel against the restrictions and order of military life would come while off the base. The Yoo-Hoo Affair started when GIs driving past a Memphis golf course spotted a number of girls playing in shorts. Deciding, as the *Daily Boston Globe* described it, to "manifest their high-spirited free-born American independence about the Army uniforms they wore," the soldiers proceeded to shout lewd remarks and call "yoo-hoo" after the women. But they were overheard by Lieutenant General Ben Lear, who happened to be playing on the golf course. Lear was a "regular of regulars," a tough former cavalry sergeant who valued the rugged discipline and tradition that defined the Old Army. He resented the yoo-hooing soldiers' willful disregard for the standards of conduct while in uniform and their treatment of the women. He chased the men down and approached them, though he did so in his

FIGURE 1.2 "Are you like Benny, without a rating?"
Source: Created and produced between March 9, 1943, and September 15, 1945, Office for Emergency Management, Office of War Information, Domestic Operations Branch, Bureau of Special Services, Series: World War II Posters, 1942–1945, RG 44 (Records of the Office of Government Reports, 1932–47), NACP.

golfing attire. The draftees mistook the general for an elderly golfer and hooted at him, too. After retrieving his stars, Lear punished the men with a fifteen-mile march in ninety-seven-degree heat. Privately, the brass worried that the incident epitomized the recurring discipline and morale issues facing many commanders.

After the story was publicized, Lear and the War Department received a deluge of civilian complaints. To the public, the soldiers seemed to be nothing more than rambunctious boys being punished by, as one woman put it, a "mean old general." Others asserted that it would be rude *not* to catcall the women. One editorial asked: "How would the girls have felt if our dynamic Army had passed in silence? For shorts are not designed to be ignored. . . . Young ladies have a right to expect the enthusiasm and loyalty of the boys who are defending the American way of life." One woman did maintain: "Their uniform doesn't give them a right to jeer and whistle at girls. They were not gentlemen to do so and I think they should have been punished." But many women commonly agreed that "all soldiers yell at girls," though one warned: "When there is only one or two boys calling 'yoo-hoo' that's an entirely different matter and then a girl can't be too careful."

The general was unrepentant, insisting that "loose conduct and rowdyism cannot be tolerated." Lear believed in the dignity and honor of duty and the uniform—"drugstore cowboys" and undisciplined troops yelling at women had no place in the military; discipline was central to training and fielding an effective army. Congress soon put pressure on the War Department to punish Lear, while House members called for an investigation. Representative Paul J. Kilday (D-TX) accused Lear of seeking "revenge rather than disciplinary action." Lear telegrammed an explanation of his decision to discipline the soldiers, stating: "I am responsible also that members of the Second Army treat the civilian population with respect and consideration." The War Department eventually closed the investigation, backed Lear, and pleaded with the public and Congress to avoid "further hullaballoo." Nevertheless, the Yoo-Hoo Affair continued to plague Lear's career; nearly two years later, Senator Bennett Clark (D-MO) delayed action on his rank, saying: "I think those soldiers were given shameful treatment, and I still resent it." When Lear returned to the United States after his service in the European Theater—where he played a vital role in logistics and reinforcement policy—over two thousand GIs greeted him as he exited his transport ship in Boston with "an earthshaking chorus of 'yoo-hoos.'" Lear said nothing and "looked sternly ahead." The incident also inspired at least one musical number and a film script titled *Private Yoo-Hoo*.

Though it can seem like a fairly silly curiosity, the Yoo-Hoo Affair established a precedent that dissuaded military officials from publicly punishing men for behaving poorly toward women and civilians. Pressure from Congress and civilians—driven by a sense that servicemen should be allowed a bit of fun—led military officials to ignore the growing problem of violence and disorder in cities near camps and forts. The Australian war correspondent Alan Moorehead captured the almost limitless tolerance and praise that Americans accorded soldiers: "Every stop in the propaganda organ had been pulled out wide in praise of the American soldier. There was religious fervor in the phase 'our boys,' and while you could criticize everything on earth, even the most hardboiled columnist or politician would never dare to question the skill or courage of the American soldier." Outside camp, then, troops were offered a space free from military control, where civilians initially countenanced increasingly belligerent behavior.

"WHAT RABBIT EVER SLEW A WOLF?"

Despite these early conflicts, logistic problems, and training failures, draftees soon found themselves forging a military identity distinct from civilian life, though perhaps not the disciplined military identity envisioned by the War Department. Initial attempts to emphasize fighting for democracy achieved limited success in the hierarchical and sometimes abusive training camps. A vision of the "New Army" composed of "soldier-technicians" driven by their resourcefulness and know-how rather than primitive "bloodthirstiness" and "tough stuff" likewise foundered early on. The men also rejected the patriotic, esprit de corps model of the World War I army, which emphasized the obligations of citizenship and the chance for immigrant and second-generation civilians to become fully American through service. Where many doughboys in training in 1917 had longed for "a home cooked meal" from a local family and generally avoided conflict with civilians, GIs now began to see rugged, military service as superior to effeminate civilian life. When taking leave and liberty in nearby towns and cities, soldiers discovered a space where they were, for a change, empowered and rewarded for their service and even more for a kind of swaggering, violent masculinity. These experiences outside camp created and crystallized group bonds among wildly different men, setting expectations of how they could—and, indeed, ought to—behave in liberty ports.

Camp life and basic training produced their own language, rituals, and hardships. The training camp was initially uncomfortable and strange for most recruits. One GI acknowledged the diversity he found in the service: "A large number of Americans I met in the Army amazed me by their differentness. I had not known their like before, nor have I met them since." Learning the language of the barracks offered a path into the military world and a way of categorizing and understanding life in the service. Whether bullshitting, gambling on crooked card games, or telling increasingly dirty stories, draftees discovered rituals of belonging. An army study later identified the "slack times of the day and in the barracks at night" as the space in which men formed bonds and a common worldview: "It is in gossiping, carousing, smoking, and playing that consensus emerges as to who can talk, who has sound judgment, and who is a fool, who is reliable and who is untrustworthy, who gets into trouble and who stays out."

Men identified different characters in their units like the loudmouth who answered too many officers' questions or the brownnoser who committed the disgraceful sin of trying to please the officers. The goldbrick made sure to do as little work as possible, while the sad sack—short for *sad sack of shit*—was worse because he tried but failed to do anything of use. A flatpeter was more charming in that he was "so stupid and awkward as always to be stepping on, or stumbling over, his own penis."

Draftees also developed a "sociology of the obscene" and a vernacular that reveled in taboo and seemingly every possible iteration of the word *fuck*. This "army Creole" or "army Pidgin" allowed men of different regional, educational, class, and ethnic backgrounds to speak a common language and identify with the military. Army researchers concluded: "When a soldier begins to use the Army vocabulary and slang without deliberate choice, and when a situation automatically evokes the correct attitudes, he has unwittingly acquired the rules and regulations whether he knows it or not." Contemporary psychologists identified the transgressive language as "an aggression against all those who accept the taboo—in this case the entire civilian environment" or as a "defiance against the matriarchy under which the soldier grew up." Sociologists agreed, arguing: "The soldier was a morally irresponsible fellow, given to hedonistic vices and afflicted with a strong contempt for civilians."

Draftees unable to fit into the barracks vision of masculinity or incapable of completing the training became identified with the feminized civilian world. Each company produced "weaklings," "shaky kids," and "mama's boys." These men were bullied, failed to complete training exercises, and were given a blue discharge that stripped them of veteran's benefits and sent them back to the shame of civilian life. Brawny, forceful heterosexuality came to define the service itself. The epithets *blue tickets* or *blue discharges* became increasingly synonymous with boys who were supposedly *crazy, cowardly,* or *queer.* One psychiatrist argued that "sissy" draftees would be "subject to ridicule and 'joshing' which will harm the general morale and will incapacitate the individuals for Army duty." An army study concurred, explaining: "Even the man who, without homosexuality, is so effeminate in appearance and mannerisms that he is inevitably destined to be the butt of all the jokes in company, should be excluded." Officials believed that troops uninterested in participating in the heterosexual obsession and aggression of the barracks failed to fit the mold of a true military man. Indeed, a good soldier was a sexually aggressive one ready to demonstrate his swaggering masculinity.

This emphasis was a departure from attitudes prevailing during World War I, especially when it came to gay men. During the Great War, gay men might be rejected from service for previous stints in prison or sanitariums or possibly for physiological disorders but not simply because they exhibited "homosexual personalities or tendencies." Now, however, army mobilization regulations differentiated homosexuals from "normal people" while also setting guidelines for identifying and rejecting gay men. Officials noted that "effeminacy in dress," "feminine bodily characteristics," and "sissy" boys would need to be eliminated from military service so as to maintain a high level of morale. Some gay draftees found ways to cope with this heterosexualized environment via same-sex relationships and the intimate, even erotic bonds of buddy relationships allowing for what psychiatrists classified as a "disguised and sublimated homosexuality."

In its search for some form of contagious morale and camaraderie in the midst of a disorganized and haphazard mobilization, command ended up explicitly endorsing a heterosexual vision of troop aggression and virility, seeing it as an integral element of a recruit's training. General Patton observed: "A man who won't fuck, won't fight." A 1941 navy review of "essential qualities to be instilled in the draftee" made a more academic case for the same idea: "[Men] cannot, they must not, be mollycoddled, and this very education befits nature, induces sexual aggression, and makes the stern, dynamic type we associate with the armed forces. This sexual aggressiveness cannot be stifled. Imagine, if you can, an army of impotent men. . . . The Mongol hordes, who conquered all of Asia and most of Europe, recognized this fact too: 'He who is not virile is not a soldier. He who lacks virility is timid, and what rabbit ever slew a wolf?'" The *US Infantry Journal* concurred: "A certain reversion to the primitive is not undesirable." "Soldiers," the chief of the morale branch would resolutely explain, "don't want to be mollycoddled. They want to take the hard knocks." This barracks culture combined violence and heterosexual sex, driving men to play rough with women—in short, to be a wolf. It was Teddy Roosevelt's "Strenuous Life" in full force. Troops obsessed over women's bodies and getting ass while simultaneously expressing what one researcher identified as a "revengeful, contemptuous, (and defensive) attitude towards women." Popular films and stage musicals like *The Fleet's In* (1942) and *Iceland* (1942) as well as songs like Joan Merrill's "You Can't Say No to a Soldier" and cheesecake pinups all reinforced this vision of government-approved coercive heterosexual sex.

Marshall may have harbored reservations about this emerging wolfish culture, but commanders grew to value any kind of camaraderie and morale, even if it was not highly disciplined. The army's "brass hats" and morale branch accepted Napoléon's injunction that morale was far more important in battle than physical condition. They worried that, if bad morale took hold in the barracks, it would spread like a contagion. "Mental dry rot," explained a captain, "is as astonishingly infectious in an army camp because men live so close together." Commanders were happy to tolerate roughhousing, filthy humor, pranks, and bullying of sad sacks and shaky kids if they produced group cohesion and a rowdy drive in their men. Witnessing a boisterous, energetic company marching down the streets of Fort Meade, an officer remarked: "That's it, that's morale. When soldiers are still full of beans after eight hours of drill and manoeuvres they have morale."

Men who made it through training and then returned home on furloughs often remarked that they now felt irrevocably separate from the civilian world. One soldier wrote: "I found that I could not even wear one of the civilian suits which hung in the closet of my room; the gesture would have been painfully empty, and a futile retreat; in a time when reality was decked in olive drab." War Department surveys found only 17 percent responding that they felt more at ease among civilian men than among fellow soldiers. When asked whether "the Army makes a man out of you," 53 percent of soldiers strongly agreed, and another 27 percent granted that "there may be something to it."

Troops reserved particular antipathy for "feather merchants"—civilians enjoying high wages and access to women. Soldiers regularly complained that civilians were "concentrating on their individual selves instead of on winning the war." Men with deferments for critical wartime work were dismissed as "slackers" and likewise envied for their unimpeded enjoyment of the comforts of civilian life. In public, soldiers might harass and heckle men not in uniform, calling them "4-F bastards." Soldiers satirized civilian life as soft, luxurious, and almost foreign. "A Soldier's Guide to the U.S.A." captured the extent to which military men felt separated from—but also envious of—the rhythms and comforts of civilian life: "They wear a strange kind of uniform called civilian suits. . . . They eat a strange assortment of foods such as milk (direct from cows), fresh fruit (like peaches, plums, and bananas), fresh eggs (with the shell) and fresh meat. . . . These people speak a different language from the one in vogue over here. For instance, at the dinner table, instead of shouting, 'Throw over that d——n salt,' they say, 'Would you please pass the salt?' . . . They behave like 'human beings.'"

Yet troops also feared and despised civilian men as sexual threats, with some becoming "the most feared enemy of all." Marines directed their envy and hatred toward the figure of "Jodie . . . the butt of all military wrath and yet a sort of international hero at the same time." Jodie, short for "Joe-the-Grinder," represented all the 4-F men "grinding away on top of all the women back home." Soldiers obsessed over this mythical character "who could pick over our love-starved women as though they were Brussels sprouts." Army psychologists (and enemy psychological warfare divisions) quickly noticed that the fear of "the woman left behind" haunted servicemen. "Jilted GI Clubs"—with their theme song "Somebody Else Is Taking My Place"—sprang up originally in Texas to comfort men who received Dear John letters. Several camps spread "Keep 'Em Happy Clubs" for soldiers' girlfriends, asking that they refrain from writing about their dates with other men. Army researchers became fascinated by the soldier's obsession with sex and infidelity, noting that fears of civilian men stealing women at home drove his desire to reaffirm his own masculinity and sexuality when outside camp.

Military life created an in-group/out-group mentality that pushed soldiers to devalue civilian life and property. This dynamic produced disastrous results when combined with the sexual obsession of camp life and what would prove to be inadequate policing in cities filled with servicemen. The tendency of these men—already empowered by the privilege of their uniforms to believe they were owed sex—to combine lust with a deep and sometimes violent resentment of anything feminine led to the rampant abuse of women.

Many women, too, clearly sensed that they had social and sexual obligations to men in uniform. Women sometimes argued that they ought to place men's interests above their own. Even women's rights advocates like Margaret Culkin Banning asserted that women "have a serious effect on the morale of the armed forces" and that "men's happiness depends on women, even more than does their pleasure." Women's advice authors told women to excuse the misbehavior of soldiers: "Don't forget that this whole business is a great, dull, dangerous, heartbreaking trial. The life of a soldier is one of deprivation and peril. . . . Feel sorry enough, at least, to understand him—and to forgive him completely if he fails to act with all the storybook gallantry of Bulldog Drummond."

"WALLOWING IN WHAT PASSED FOR VICE"

Early on, draftees generally lacked exciting locales and opportunities to meet nice girls. Towns near training centers had yet to boom, leaving men on leave with little to do but drink. One private lamented: "The boys here hate the Army. They have no fighting spirit except among themselves when they get stinking drunk." Morale suffered because the towns and cities near camps lacked any "recreation infrastructure." The *New York Times* reported that, because the camps had "sprung up overnight," local communities quickly became inundated with soldiers, just "as army ants swarm over a crust." The men at big training centers like Fort Knox and Fort Bragg outnumbered the local citizenry forty to one. *Life* recorded soldiers' complaints: "When they go to the nearby cities they are shunned by the citizens and find it impossible to meet nice girls. Since many of them come from good families, they resent being treated as outcasts." The men ended up simply wandering "along the highways in dejected groups eager for sport and friendly civilian contact, with none to be had." Others "clustered in bewildered and uncertain knots on street corners in towns overrun with their kind."

The women who would talk to soldiers would do so "for a dollar and up." Camps that lacked a lively nearby boomtown attracted prostitutes with their own trailers, ready to take men away in "chippie wagons" or "brothels on wheels" garishly outfitted with "lush red velvet draperies and cushions." These "machine-age camp followers" joined the cavalcade of other prostitutes, scam artists, gamblers, and bootleggers looking to cash in on the "motorized vice" boom. Red-light districts also flourished, with the American Social Hygiene Association warning that "pay-day for soldiers, sailors, and marines is looked to with anticipation by practically everyone in the racket." Reacting to reports of a venereal disease epidemic, Congress gave power to adjutants and commanding officers to inform the FBI of brothels and crooked hotels. A House resolution also sought to make it illegal for "trailer women" to bring any person into a vehicle.

After Pearl Harbor, Marshall prioritized building camps and forts close to cities and towns that might serve as recreation areas for men on liberty. The morale branch also set up seven recreation camps along the Gulf Coast from New Orleans to Panama City, Florida, with areas in Georgia and the Carolinas soon following. There, the army offered chartered fishing trips, baseball games, guided walking tours of historic districts, and chaperoned riverboat dances with women from the YWCA, partly as an effort to cut venereal disease rates. Meyer Berger—a shrewd journalist unafraid to report on the crimes committed by servicemen—argued the recreation camps had become the "perfect morale builders" and a useful counter to the growing sex trade. These seven camps, however, could host only four thousand men in total, and they operated only on the weekends. They would be able to serve at the very most 14 percent of the soldiers in the army in 1941. Thus, most weekends would still be spent in the boomtowns and juke joints.

Draftees learned how to behave in liberty ports from one another. Carousing with fellow soldiers constituted, as one GI put it, "our first step into manhood, as we termed smoking, drinking, and chasing girls." Sex, liquor, and fighting also offered escapes from both military life and the stresses of training while bringing raw boys into manhood. Before their first time on liberty, new recruits participated in "bull-sessions" where they talked about "women and other fantasies" or listened to the stories of more seasoned draftees about the delights of liberty. One marine recalled: "We envied the men who were already out of boot camp and had enjoyed their first liberty. They told stories about fine-looking girls." Another marine, who "knew all about it," declared that the women "say straight out, 'Come on up and get some, Marine. . . . Want some pussy, Marine?'" Hearing these stories, one recruit remarked: "'Man, I can just taste that pussy now.'" The soldier Walter Bernstein captured how entire towns became devoted to fulfilling the desires of draftees: "The principal industry of the small town of Phenix City, Alabama [near Fort Benning], is sex, and its customer is the Army. . . . The town is at least eighty percent devoted to the titillation and subsequent pillage of that group it affectionately calls 'Uncle Sam's Soldier Boys.'" Before shipping out, soldiers might slip off to towns like Paso Robles, California, where, as one corporal described it, they "spent the night wallowing in what passed for vice," getting drunk on "too many alleged whiskey-cokes," and harassing waitresses. Hilton Railey observed men in Alexandria, Louisiana, enjoying their time off base in a "carnival of drunkenness."

Few politicians were willing to tackle the emerging problems of drunkenness and violence in these towns, and the War Department, army, and navy all rejected calls to regulate servicemen's drinking.

Only Senator Joshua Lee (D-OK), in alliance with prohibition groups, put forth a proposal to ban liquor sales in and near army camps. The various services did often set up chaperoned dances to offer men more regulated contact with women. Yet even these dances could turn rowdy, provoking protest from civilians. One concerned pastor from Elizabeth, Pennsylvania, learning that "2000 to 4000 girls will be secured as dancing partners for men in the armed services," objected not only because officials would not be able to verify the character of the women but also because the dances might put morally upstanding women "into the arms of young men who are unfit for them to associate with." He warned that the plan was "moral dynamite" because he knew the quality of the men in the service. Civilian organizations that planned chaperoned dances also admitted that "there is a real problem connected with the operation of dances and many people have objected to them." Other civilians filed careful letters of protest, noting "the liquor, prostitution, and other harmful practices near our cantonments," and requesting federal funds for improved recreation services. The Office of Civilian Defense, however, merely held: "It is expected that adjacent communities will cooperate by providing facilities beyond the boundaries of the camps." Privately, the War Department wondered what could be done to alleviate what it euphemistically referred to as "the morale problem of small communities near Army camps."

Carousing in "good-time towns" offered more than simply "smoking, drinking, and chasing girls." A draftee could be both a wolf and a soldier when he hit "the Strip." He could be a powerful, bold man worthy of respect, fear, and amorous adulation. Even more critical was that men were able to "get away from the Goddamn Army." No matter how many recreation halls, post dances, or USO shows commanders set up, draftees simply preferred the liquor-soaked slats of a boomtown bar or a dusty main street where girls could be found. Far from the control of hard-ass officers, away from the chickenshit, and outside the mud-spattered camps that functioned as desolate locales apart from the rest of the world, away from the inquiring eyes of officers, "the soldier characteristically felt supremely 'free' and sought to release his impulses and feelings," explained an army sociologist.

The army and the navy understood and tolerated this idea of blowing off steam to different degrees. Initially, the army believed it would face greater levels of troop crime than would the navy. Americans saw the navy as more prestigious and desirable, with ample opportunity for travel and adventure. Naval recruiters quickly capitalized on this perception with the slogan "Choose While You Can." The navy did not even take drafted men until late 1943, relying instead on a wealth of volunteers. It also "predrafted" favored candidates into its cadet programs while poaching others from army recruitment lines. Thus, its manpower pool was understood to be fit, educated, young, skilled, and morally upright. A similar dynamic allowed the marines and the army air force (AAF) to select their preferred candidates. In contrast, the army lacked the prestige and romance of the naval service, the cloistered martial culture of the marines, and the adventure of the AAF. It subsequently acknowledged that the other services "had the character of hand-picked organizations." Infantry draftees suffered from comparatively poor fitness and deficient training, and they were shorter, lighter, less intelligent, and less educated. The army's own postwar study stated that the ground forces suffered from the "inferior quality of the human raw material." Overall, the military failed to identify or condemn alcohol abuse when drafting and selecting men—hungover men appearing for a draft inspection received no disapprobation from inspectors—but one psychiatrist determined that "the indulgence of the Army was particularly marked in the case of alcoholics." The army also received the bulk of draftees who already suffered from venereal disease or had committed felonies. (Lobbying by the American Prison Association had pushed the War Department to accept former prisoners.) The decision to let in drunks, criminals, and those with sexually transmitted diseases did little to dispel the popular view of the army as "a haven of misfits." Two months before Pearl Harbor, the *Chicago Daily Tribune* passed on reports of soldiers in New York who exhibited poor discipline, spent their time loitering in the streets, and "seemed

definitely inferior to the enlisted personnel of the navy." Army officials, accordingly, faced far fewer illusions about the moral sobriety
of their recruits. Yet both the army and the navy would quickly dis-
cover that these expected differences in behavior disappeared as servicemen took leave and liberty in stateside ports. They also learned
the potential pitfalls of the men's wolfish behavior.

CHAPTER TWO

TAKING LIBERTY

BY 1942, TROOPS FILLED THE STREETS, docks, buses, and train stations of liberty ports, while army bases and expanded naval yards brought a military presence into the everyday lives of civilians. This liberty port network and the emerging two-front war required a massive support structure and tremendous amounts of manpower. Few realize that the vast majority of American men in uniform were stationed in the United States—not in combat zones—throughout much of the war. Indeed, the majority of men never saw combat. Many of the sixteen million troops would make their way through liberty ports multiple times, seeking various delights. This statistical reality undercuts the idea that soldiers' bad behavior was the result of combat stress or a response to the brutality of war. Troops acted poorly long before they ever fired a bullet or a shell at the enemy—if they ever did. The presence of troops in major cities and stopover towns created civil-military conflicts that shaped the lives of people on the home front. Drunken fistfights between GIs and civilian men, catcalling sailors, and unpunished sexual assaults marked the daily presence of servicemen there. Battles over jurisdiction and the right to police troops deepened this civil-military divide. The war established and bolstered the military's grip on power not only at the high levels of politics but also in the lives of women navigating streets and subways populated by servicemen looking to get plastered and chase them—or worse.

LIBERTY PORT NETWORKS

The military housed soldiers and sailors in and around the city, creating new camps and ports of embarkation while refurbishing old ones and setting up floating cities of liberty ships and freighters in harbors. Bases like Fort Hamilton near Bay Ridge and Dyker Heights in Brooklyn, and Roosevelt Base on Terminal Island in Los Angeles gave soldiers easy access to city centers, while other camps operated bus and rail services, like Vallejo's Mare Island, near San Francisco and Oakland.

Commandants and commanders retained the power to determine liberty and leave policy for men under their command, and they used this power to both motivate and punish recalcitrant individuals. Soldiers and sailors generally received one or two days of overnight liberty per week in secure Allied areas, including mainland locations. No more than a quarter of a crew or unit were supposed to be granted furloughs at a time, but commanders frequently ignored these rules to bolster morale and avoid having their men simply going AWOL when faced with the temptation of a big city's delights. This often resulted in huge numbers of men moving through amusement zones in major cities. Even in smaller locales like Norfolk, Virginia, a reporter observed that "every night is Saturday night . . . because about twelve thousand sailors come to town *every* night." Before heading out, the men lined up for uniform and card inspection, though some managed to duck that or sneak out by crawling under the perimeter fences. While on leave, they were required to wear their uniforms, carry a liberty card, and report back to base on time. Shore Patrol and Military Police were charged with regulating troop behavior and arresting insubordinate men. If arrested, the soldier was to be returned to the navy yard, base, or ship rather than delivered to the municipal jail.

Sailors and soldiers regularly circled through liberty ports as they were moved about the country for training missions, supply operations, and eventually embarkation to the European and Pacific Theaters. This meant that they would often see several major cities multiple times or regularly on weekends. Even troops destined to be quickly

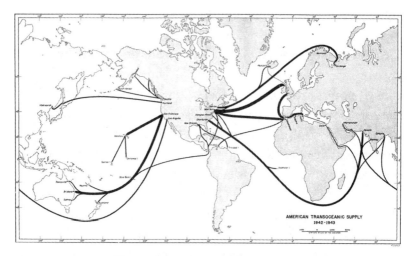

FIGURE 2.1 American transoceanic supply, 1942–43
Source: Richard M. Leighton and Robert W. Coakley, *United States Army in World War II: The War Department, Global Logistics and Strategy, 1940-1943* (Washington, DC: Center of Military History, United States Army, 1955), 349.

shipped out for D-Day in the first six months of 1944 spent anywhere from six to twelve days in New York before embarking. Nearly 22 percent of the 600,000 men handled by New York's port in these months enjoyed over two weeks boozing and carousing before leaving for Europe.

Transportation networks and destinations determined when and where sailors and soldiers took leave and liberty. Although several air and sea routes moved troops throughout the world, three primary transportation networks linked liberty ports together: The Atlantic route, the Caribbean route, and the Pacific route.

The main Atlantic route connected four key ports of embarkation: New York, Boston, Norfolk, and Charleston. Even before Pearl Harbor, New York was the world's largest and busiest port. During the war, 3.2 million troops, their supplies, and 63 million more tons of materiel passed through its maze of docks and shipyards. As the central hub for the Atlantic, New York also received from and fed subports. Troops poured out of New York's harbor en route to northern Europe and the Mediterranean or, more often, to other stateside ports and cities. They also departed from Hampton Roads at Norfolk, the second most important Atlantic port and a subport of New York until 1942. Ships at this industrial weigh station hauled nearly 13 million cubic tons of crucial supplies and over 760,000 passengers, chiefly to Africa and the Mediterranean. At the same time, another 760,000 passengers and 9.5 million cubic tons of materiel funneled through Boston—also governed by New York's commandant until 1942—on their way along the northern Atlantic line of Newfoundland, Halifax, Greenland, and Iceland. Charleston housed many of the army hospital ships while also serving multiple destinations.

New Orleans stitched the Caribbean network together, linking smaller ports like San Jacinto, Mobile, Galveston, Jacksonville, and Miami as well as the American territorial ports of Panama and San Juan, Guantanamo, leased British ports in the West Indies, and Brazilian ports like Natal and São Paulo. The smaller domestic ports were in turn fed by inland hubs like Dallas, Houston, and Memphis. Nearly 175,000 passengers and 8 million cubic tons of cargo passed through New Orleans's waters on their way south or toward the East Coast. Americans explored west Santurce and the nightlife built up next to the Isla Grande naval base in San Juan before setting off for North Africa, Cape Town, or the Mediterranean via the South Atlantic. Panama served as the key transshipment point; men destined for North Africa and Europe drank and caroused in Cristobal's red-light district in the Canal Zone before departing. Ships slated to travel the Pacific expanse crossed the canal and docked in Panama City for leave and refueling.

San Francisco and Los Angeles anchored a vast Pacific network stretching from Panama to Alaska and the Philippines. San Francisco and the greater East Bay, the major West Coast transshipment point, sent men and materiel to all areas of the Pacific, handling about half the traffic of New York—making it the second most important port in the United States. The presence nearby of Fort Mason, Treasure Island, Mare Island, and Alameda meant a near-constant stream of servicemen hitting downtown San Francisco. "There was nothing but uniforms, soldiers, sailors, just everywhere," a civilian recalled. Los Angeles was the other primary port, with B-24s and flying boats from the San Diego subport crowding the city's bustling docks. More than 217,000 people transferred through the port on their way to the western and southern Pacific, but not before slumming in barrio clubs or catching the peep shows in San Diego's Gaslamp Quarter. Seattle supplemented these two cities' output while setting up shipping lanes to Alaska and western Canada. At first a subport of San Francisco, and later fed by Portland and Prince Rupert, by 1942 Seattle brimmed with manufacturing shipments and sojourning sailors, with 12 million cubic tons of cargo and 580,000 people shipped during the war.

These port networks were connected by a sprawling cross-country rail infrastructure that handled troops, workers, and freight. While the armed forces occasionally used buses and trucks, rail was the predominant form of transport for man and materiel. Chicago notably grew as both a key zone of rail traffic and the home of the navy's main training center. Army officials selected Chicago as the central artery for all rail traffic because of its centrality and its already well-developed railway system, which featured a large amount of trackage and office space and the capacity to process constant truck deliveries readily. A section of Chicago's Junction Railway, near the quartermaster depot, allowed for quick communication and coordination between rail yard, receiving platform, and substations. As the primary consolidating station, Chicago received shipments from all over the country, broke these carloads down, and then moved the reconsolidated trains on to their ultimate destinations. Train platforms overflowed with seemingly endless tons of war supplies and lines of flatcars, while passenger terminals filled with a true menagerie of eager servicemen, migrating war workers, and wives and families following soldiers. In total, Chicago consolidated nearly half the total freight shipped throughout the war, making it a routine stopover point for soldiers, sailors, and civilians shuttling about the country for lucrative war work. Substations and smaller consolidating stations quickly developed to supplement the overwhelming traffic flooding Chicago's tracks. Midwestern and

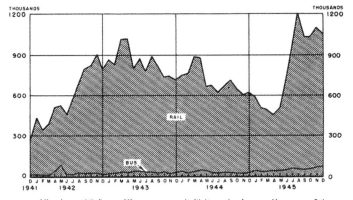

* Up to January 1943 all groups of fifty or more were routed in Washington; thereafter groups of forty or more. Rail figures are passengers actually moved; bus figures are passengers routed, some of whom did not actually move.
Source: Data originally compiled by Traffic Control Division, OCT, and reworked for a statistical volume of this series, now in preparation.

FIGURE 2.2 Army passenger traffic in the United States, December 1941–
December 1945
Source: Chester Wardlow, *United States Army in World War II: The Technical Services, the Transportation Corps; Movements, Training, and Supply* (Washington, DC: Center of Military History, US Army, 1990), 31.

heartland cities like Detroit, Cleveland, Minneapolis–St. Paul, and St. Louis emerged as the most important regional substations—pivotal points that both fed Chicago and redirected the outbound traffic. This mass expansion of rail traffic brought servicemen into contact with Americans in the heartland as troops packed into already-crowded railcars or sought diversions in stopover cities.

"A SOLDIER'S THREE DESIRES"

Most servicemen on leave gravitated toward three things on hitting port: women, alcohol, and brawling. Civilians were expected to provide them all. As their furlough periods approached, men obsessed over passing inspection, and they spent nights together reading letters from

"favorite girls" and planning where to find "some very attractive girls."
All thoughts came back to "women, women, and women and more
women and liquor" and "sally[ing] forth in search of gin and sin." Experienced soldiers reminisced about the cheap beer and women on
Coney Island's beaches, while others wrote of all "the pretty girls" in
Manhattan. Army officers noted the common view of a soldier's three
desires: "a woman, a drink, and a dollar left over." A sergeant's poem
put it more bluntly: "A soldier's the sort / For rape and slaughter / Not
fit to escort a patriot's daughter." These violent impulses extended to
fighting with 4-Fs and Jodies, activities that some men saw as both
good fun and a duty bestowed by the uniform. LeRoy Neiman, later a
famous painter but at this time an army grunt, explained: "We headed
out to the fancy midtown bars and restaurants in military uniform
just to show the slackers and café society toffs that we were real men
on a real mission, while they were just weasels." If coercing and assaulting women constituted a kind of sexual domination, then fighting with civilian men formed a corollary form of control. Men often
went after girls or fought civilians in groups, suggesting that beating
up a civilian or getting rough with a woman was partly a performance
for their fellow soldiers, a signal that they belonged to a martial, heterosexual fraternity.

Liberty ports provided spaces where men could fulfill multiple desires, often in the same spot. Troops flocked to bars, beaches, parks, cafés,
transport stations, nightclubs, dance halls, fleshpots, grind houses,
"blind pigs" (undercover cabarets), brothels, peep shows, and crooked
hotels facilitating the flesh trade. Existing red-light districts like San
Diego's Gaslamp Quarter flourished, Chicago's Gold Coast was reborn,
and Times Square was revived after hard times during the Depression. Yet servicemen did not solely head to these most famous haunts.
Newly flourishing vice quarters prompted joint civil-military crackdowns in efforts to stop an epidemic of venereal disease and under-
world crime. But these moves unintentionally drove soldier traffic
and cash to places like the Pike in Long Beach, San Francisco's Mission
District, Central Park, and Coney Island. These areas, which catered

to both working- and middle-class patrons, came to embrace the vice economy, offering seedy and dangerous delights to furloughed soldiers while defining the reputations of these neighborhoods for years afterward.

GOING AWOL

For many men, the temptation of pleasures in the city—and an escape from the military—proved too enticing. Despite the threat of being court-martialed, soldiers and sailors attempted to extend their leave by "straggling," meaning they returned to their base or the naval yard hours or even days late. These men were considered absent over leave (AOL), distinct from those who left duty without permission and were classified AWOL. Troops AWOL for thirty days or more would generally be considered deserters, a far more serious offense that worsened rampant manpower shortages and caused delays as ships and units struggled to fill positions. Absenteeism—a catchall term for straggling, AWOLism, and desertion—seemed to peak in 1942 and 1943, though the military never truly eliminated the problem.

Army and navy archives as well as contemporary newspapers feature enormous numbers of reports highlighting straggling, criminal AWOL troops, desertion, and concern among military authorities about this unshakable problem. Civilian newspapers generally attempted either to shame deserters or to expose AWOL men. Mess Sergeant Thomas Flynn was typical of the criminal AWOL soldier. After deserting his post in Pennsylvania, he stole three pistols from his regiment and hitchhiked to the Bronx. There, he attempted to assault a woman in her apartment before being arrested. Other deserters left the military to "turn Fagin," as the *Chicago Daily Tribune* described it: for example, two AWOL signal corps privates began running a gang "of juvenile purse snatchers and car thieves," "sitting in stolen cars and pointing out women victims to their youthful conspirators." One absentee serviceman was caught when his souvenir bazooka shell exploded in his hideaway apartment, and another was apprehended when his theft of over a hundred crates of cheese was discovered.

Some, like Richard Lee Bailey, attempted fantastic and foolish escapes. On August 6, 1944, Bailey stole a plane from Williams Air Field in Arizona. After nearly depleting the fuel supply, he dropped the plane to one thousand feet and then aimed it toward the sea. He leaped out of the plane, released his parachute, and landed in a small field in Mexico. Carrying his knife, gas mask, a Luger pistol, candy bars, and other supplies, he passed by a presumably bewildered Mexican family. He spent the next three weeks hiding in the mountains and tiny Mexican border villages before contracting an illness and getting arrested by the Mexican police, who returned him to a US Army envoy at Nogales. Many more absentee men, however, found quieter ways to disappear into liberty ports, avoiding the police, and alarming their commanders.

Military authorities used a number of different modes of policing to try to clamp down on absenteeism, but most concluded that little could be done. Initially, military commanders—particularly naval commandants and older army officers—attempted to enforce the rules governing liberty strictly. Men who returned to the ship late or drunk could be thrown into solitary confinement with only bread and water. Some officers revoked future liberty privileges. Sailors who went AWOL or deserted could be dishonorably discharged and given prison sentences, though commanding officers preferred to levy a thirty-day stay in the brig. Offenders might also see a decrease in rank or rating and, therefore, pay grade. In November 1942, the War Department notified all forces of Executive Order 9267, which suspended the limitations on punishments for AWOL troops. Secretary of War Henry Stimson saw the order as "a deterrent to the alarming increase in the number of such offenses" and as "mak[ing] it possible in aggravated cases to impose punishment." Stragglers and deserters were now more likely to face time in prison and expulsion from the military.

Here, however, the armed forces once again encountered the dangers of unintended incentives. By demonstrating that a serviceman would be discharged if he went AWOL or straggled enough, the military showed men a way to avoid ever facing the threat of combat. Chronic stragglers might enjoy their extended liberty time, avoiding the privations of regimented life, then eventually get booted from the military, at worst serve a short prison term, and likely pick up a more lucrative war industry job. Trials by court-martial for absenteeism also imposed an administrative burden on the army and navy bureaucracies and commanders. Drunkenness was so common among their men that officials understood that it would be impossible to punish anyone for it. Military authorities soon recognized that rampant alcoholism and the average serviceman's disdain for the military would make AWOL and straggling policies as well as guidelines governing good behavior on shore totally unenforceable.

Confronted with a strained manpower pool, brigs full of drunks, and lengthy court-martial trials, in the fall of 1942 military officials moved to revise policies on furloughs as well as guidelines for good conduct. The army and the navy set up policies that discouraged courts-martial while giving tacit approval of criminal behavior in liberty ports. Commandants on the East Coast began by establishing offices devoted to returning stragglers to their ships, while official guidelines recommended light sentences like ten days' restriction for drunkenness, the same penalty given for the "improper wearing of [a] uniform." Sailors becoming drunk and disorderly or disturbing the peace while on liberty might receive thirty days' restriction. While the navy set up some punishments for infractions like assault and indecent exposure—including the possibility of a "Deck Court or Summary Court-Martial"—San Diego's commandant, Rear Admiral Ralston S. Holmes, emphasized that these punishments were "intended *as a guide only*" and were "not to be interpreted as limiting in any way the discretionary powers vested by law in Commanding officers." The not-so-subtle message to commanding officers was that punishments by the book could well be avoided if the crime did not impede naval operations. Chief of Staff George C. Marshall echoed this in November 1942, warning commanders that "reliance on courts-martial to enforce discipline indicates lack of leadership and faulty command." He declared the high court-martial rate "unsatisfactory" and "far too high," explaining that the court-martial "should be resorted to only when adequate disciplinary action cannot be provided by other means." These official directives signaled to commanding officers that the military was not particularly interested in prosecuting men for drunken or violent furloughs. The welfare of civilians proved a secondary concern to war goals, the navy and other military branches asserting: "Discipline is not designed to reform officers or enlisted personnel nor to pass judgment on their morals. It is designed to maintain the efficiency of the Service."

Even the official punishment guidelines reflected a prioritization of military efficiency over civilian welfare. For example, while troops who stole military property might face a dishonorable discharge, those convicted of being drunk and disorderly would not. In early 1943, Stimson followed up on the previous executive order erasing limitations on punishments for AWOL men by tacitly admitting that the policy of harsher punishment had backfired. This follow-up order to all commanding generals and port-of-embarkation commanders warned that the removal of limitations on punishments for absentee troops "must not, however, be construed as encouragement for an unwarranted increase in the number of trials by general court-martial": "Trial by general courts-martial must not be resorted to unless there is no other appropriate remedy." Officers took this to mean that drunken men, stragglers, and those gone AWOL need not be punished, leading one dutiful Shore Patrol officer to complain that sailors expected "little or no punishment and feel they have committed a more or less harmless prank for which they may only be reprimanded." Despite these complaints, district officials ultimately praised the relaxing of disciplinary procedures and speedy trials, with the Los Angeles commandant noting: "This substantial improvement already has resulted in a tremendous saving of man power for the war effort." Officers were effectively incentivized to avoid prosecuting their men for their misdeeds.

Nevertheless, servicemen being AOL and deserting remained a continuing, if somewhat lessened, problem throughout the war. At the end of 1943, while docked in San Francisco, Rear Admiral Wilder D. Baker seemed resigned to the reality that no policing strategy would ever prevent men from going AWOL: "Our trouble seems to boil down to the fact that too many men are willing to be thrown out of the navy, or at least to take chances on that punishment." Baker knew that court-martialing and imprisoning stragglers and deserters would only preserve a path for men to escape the service by committing a nonviolent crime. Unfortunately, the navy's new policy, which effectively offered deserters clemency if they returned to their post, created yet another perverse incentive. When absentee sailors rejoined their ships, their shipmates noticed that they had escaped punishment. Baker noted that his own ship experienced a spike in absenteeism after the return of four bluejackets who had had their desertion convictions set aside, and he cited "inadequate punishment of flagrant offenders" as one of the key reasons for continued AOL issues. The fleet finally saw an improvement in absentee rates after it granted longer leave and liberty periods in 1945. Improvements in the absentee rate and reductions in the number of courts-martial became linked to giving servicemen more time in liberty ports with fewer restrictions on their conduct. Infantrymen even began to redesignate going AWOL as going *after women and liquor* or being *a wolf on the loose*.

POLICING AND LEGAL MANEUVERING

After Pearl Harbor, the military began claiming a wide legal purview that would make servicemen immune to civil law or policing in the vast majority of situations. Military authorities relied on a mix of legal precedent, favorable readings of existing codes, and sometimes orders that they issued without any apparent legal justification. These legal adjustments effectively granted extralegal and extraterritorial privileges to servicemen: they were no longer bound by civilian law or policing, or for that matter, outmoded codes of moral sobriety. Nor did they expect serious punishment from a military desperately scrambling to catch up in a two-front war. Absenteeism, drunkenness, "skirt-chasing," and harassment of civilians effectively constituted military sanctioned spoils of war, not just against foreign civilians, but their own.

Each branch invoked written and unwritten legal codes to assert a broad jurisdiction over both military personnel and some civilians. Some legal orders were couched in solid precedent and established military law, like the right of the service to try servicemen under a court-martial. But other orders, like when the army attempted to make civilian employees in ports of embarkation subject to military law, rested on a far less certain grounds. Some military decrees, like one preventing civilians in Miami from drinking after 1:00 a.m., were offered up without any legal justification.

The army made effective use of the Articles of War to construct a legal framework that made white soldiers mostly unaccountable to civil law enforcement and courts. The Articles of War preceded the Uniform Code of Military Justice and formed the basis for military law and justice in the United States. The War Department relied heavily on them to undercut attempts by civil officials to police GIs or try them in court, unambiguously stating: "A commanding officer is not required by Article of War 74 or by any other law to surrender a member of the military service, accused of a crime or offense, to the civil authorities for prosecution." The armed forces jealously guarded this "paramount right of custody," explaining: "The war effort should not be impeded by unnecessary arrest and detention by civil authorities of members of the military service." Article 74 established that commanding officers were required to turn over military personnel accused by civil authorities of a crime "except in time of war." It contained no other information about what should happen to troops in wartime should they be charged with a crime by civil authorities, so the War Department made clever use of this vagueness to rebuff any jurisdictional claims that civil forces might make. One official regulation stipulated that military officials would handle "civil violations perpetrated by military personnel" and that troops detained by cops would be immediately transferred to Military Police. Army leaders also relied on what one contemporary scholar called the *unwritten law* in the military code. This "common law of the army" was "derived from immemorial usage" but could be employed to justify actions that were expedient or beneficial to the army.

The navy also took advantage of the vagueness and expansive language in its key military legal code, the Articles for the Government of the United States Navy, often colloquially called "Rocks and Shoals." Legal scholars noted that the articles did not mention civil offenses like "manslaughter, rape, robbery, and assault." Instead, the navy used Article 8(1) to punish "any other scandalous conduct tending to the destruction of good morals." Article 22(a) gave the navy even more flexibility, affirming that "all offenses committed by persons belonging to the Navy which are not specified in the foregoing articles shall be punished as a court-martial may direct." The lack of specificity and simultaneously nearly infinite language likely proved a useful tool in allowing the navy to prioritize the infractions it wished to prosecute while ignoring criminal actions that threatened the efficiency of the service. Navy personnel picked up on this and criticized the articles for failing to "tell anyone in language which the ordinary person can understand what acts are punishable offenses and what are not." Who was under the jurisdiction of Rocks and Shoals also appeared to be purposefully imprecise. The articles sometimes referred to jurisdiction over "any person in the Navy," which seems clear enough. But there are also references to "persons belonging to the Navy" and, even less clear, "person connected with the Navy." In contrast to the Articles of War, the navy's legal code made no distinctions about jurisdiction in wartime. Sailors would always be under the jurisdiction of a naval court-martial should they commit an offense within the United States or outside its borders.

Though the navy almost always succeeded in enforcing this broad view of jurisdiction, it did meet some minor challenges. In 1942, a sailor, Samuel A. Rosborough, serving on detached duty as a guard on a Panamanian ship docked at Montevideo, Uruguay, became drunk.

He took hold of a mounted machine gun and began wildly firing. His shipmates tried to stop him, but in the process Rosborough killed a civilian officer. The navy took custody of him and charged him with murder, ordering a general court-martial in New York. Rosborough was eventually convicted of voluntary manslaughter and sentenced to twenty years, though he elected to appeal with a petition for a writ of habeas corpus. The resulting case—*Rosborough v. Rossell*—centered on whether the navy had the jurisdiction to try a murder charge if the offense was committed on a non-American vessel. Though the ship was registered as Panamanian, the navy argued it was commanded by a US naval officer. Rosborough eventually won his appeal in 1945. The navy later responded by amending Article 6 so that its jurisdiction extended essentially everywhere. The General Court-Martial Sentence Review Board went on to put forth a section in the postwar naval bill that declared: "The Articles for the Government of the Navy shall extend to all places."

The pervasive accommodation afforded white troops by civilians, politicians, and police allowed the military to expand its sprawling legal oversight. Beyond essentially granting American troops immunity from many crimes, the military also asserted its power to police, arrest, and try American citizens. Using a legal justification taken from the "Digest of Opinion of the Judge Advocate General of the Army, 1912–1940," commanders made civilian employees serving on transports and in ports of embarkation subject to military law and tribunals. Chief of Staff Marshall reiterated this policy in a memo declaring that all persons—including American civilians and foreign troops—"in the field" would be subject to military jurisdiction. Here, *the field* referred to any place on land or sea where "military operations are being conducted." *Military operations* was defined incredibly broadly so as effectively to mean anywhere military men were stationed or where logistics operations occurred. Much of Marshall's legal reasoning rested on Article 2(d) of the Articles of War, which held that "in time of war all such retainers and persons accompanying or serving with the armies of the United States in the field, both within and without the territorial jurisdiction of the United States," were subject to military law. Even outside US ports and bases, MPs claimed the authority to arrest civilians and confine them to army guardhouses. In one publicized case, a Shore Patrol officer arrested and then beat a civilian accused of stealing $16.00 from another officer. The municipal court judge overseeing the case censured the officer and declared that, as "far as civilians are concerned, the military should leave them alone." As Shore Patrol officers gradually took on "a complex that the whole world is out to trim sailors," the judge reasoned, "they become too partisan and lack the detached viewpoint of civil authorities." This censure, however, did nothing to change the military's expanding legal power because it failed to establish a precedent and applied only to the local, specific case.

Civilians could be blindsided by the extent of military jurisdiction. A merchant seaman who struck the civilian master of his convoy en route to Casablanca was surprised to learn that he was subject to military law because the ship was transporting soldiers and supplies. Initially sentenced to seven years of hard labor, he appealed, but a federal judge agreed with the army's claim that his presence near soldiers made him subject to military justice. The National Maritime Union angrily protested the ruling and sought an appeal "not only to determine the rights of its members but also all civilian workers who are engaged in the transportation and manufacture of supplies for the Army." To the union, the case marked a flagrant and "unwarranted imposition of Army discipline on civilians." Its protests did little to change the military's power to punish civilians who might be in the field.

Outside the continental United States, the armed forces unsurprisingly claimed and exercised an even greater level of legal power. In Shanghai, for instance, the army held three citizens without charging them for over four months, prompting a habeas corpus petition. But the greatest conflict occurred in Hawaii—not yet a state—where civilians were subject to martial law after Pearl Harbor. Hawaiian civilians described the typical provost court judge as being nothing more than "a soldier sitting on the bench with a gun on one side, a gas mask on the other, and a big cigar in his mouth." Other civilians subjected to these kangaroo courts claimed these soldier-judges forced them to purchase war bonds. Territorial officials argued that "the Army had assumed control over the personal life of everyone in the islands—including his dog." After a civilian naval employee and a stockbroker appealed their convictions, a federal judge agreed to settle the legal conflict. The civilians' attorney charged that the Hawaiian military courts produced extremely high conviction rates and disproportionate penalties: defendants could be fined $200–$500 for drinking too much. The case eventually went to the Supreme Court, and the justices retroactively struck down the territory's martial law in 1946, agreeing that the army had denied civilians their constitutional rights.

Civilian police proved unable to check this growth of the armed forces' legal and policing power. They mostly ceded control of servicemen to the army and the navy, tolerating officers' flagrant abuses and an erosion of legal authority. When local district attorneys attempted to try GIs in 1941, the army contested the effort and even ordered MPs never to testify in civilian courts unless told to by the provost marshal. The army rarely surrendered its men to civil authorities, though the few times it did the accused GIs had committed murder or rape against middle- or upper-class white civilians. These cases were more likely to garner press attention and negative publicity should commanders deny civilians their justice.

Before the war, police chiefs acknowledged that selective service would strip departments of experienced officers. At a meeting of the International Association of Chiefs of Police, one retired chief admitted: "There are very few police departments that are up to snuff insofar as numbers are concerned, and so far as trained men are concerned." He also served as a draft board member and warned that his district's best officers would be classified as the most likely to be drafted "if I don't have my way." Across the country, chiefs worried that they were facing a "very dangerous" situation that could "cripple us." The collected chiefs briefly considered agitating for exemptions for police officers but then worried that this exemption might incentivize men to "join the cops and escape the draft." Fearing a public and political back-lash for appearing to harm the war effort, they concluded that using their influence to protect officers from the draft would be "decidedly unwise": "We don't want any accusation directed toward the police."

Nationwide, police departments did suffer from a dearth of experi-enced and well-trained officers that further fueled the decline of civil-ian legal authority. The police effectively lacked the ability to hold and charge white troops except for vice violations (prostitution, homosex-uality) and the most serious of felonies (murder, vehicular homicide, arson). Civil police were also supposed to handle traffic violations com-mitted by military personnel, but the navy in San Diego acknowledged that "the jurisdiction of the civil police in their investigation of traffic accidents" had been "unintentionally infringed upon by the removal of persons from the scene without permission of the civil police."

Servicemen felt no compulsion to respect or even comply with civilian police directions. In prewar years, those who committed the unofficial crime of "contempt of cop"—essentially not behaving def-erentially to police—faced arrest or a beating (and often both). Now, by the time servicemen hit port, they knew that municipal cops held little authority over them, leading to brawls when civilian police at-tempted to challenge privileges, legal and otherwise, that came with service. In a memo to district police officers, the police chief of Long Beach, California, acknowledged the bleak situation: "There is a grow-ing resentment against police officers in general by enlisted personnel of the armed forces and . . . this resentment is rapidly being crystal-lized. This could, and may very easily develop into serious difficulties and consequences for individual officers, as well as for the depart-ment personnel in general." He then went on to warn of a complete breakdown of relations with the military and "extreme problems" that would make "work more hazardous." Finally, he implicitly called for officers to employ leniency in dealing with the military as "these are trying times." These arrangements extended to all liberty ports, giving servicemen extralegal and extraterritorial legal privileges on US soil.

The army's head of policing occasionally lamented the recurring ineffectiveness of cops. In addition to "an apparent lack of discipline in the Army as a whole," the provost marshal general cited the "failure of civil police to treat military personnel for infractions of law, as the police would treat civilians." But how could municipal cops expect to police soldiers effectively when the military had asserted that civil authorities lacked any real legal authority?

Both official wartime regulations and unwritten agreements produced a legal regime that had stripped old and undertrained cops of their power to project authority and wield command presence. Even civilians recognized the disempowerment of the country's police forces at this time and routinely mocked municipal cops, one man arguing: "American police not only do not enjoy the confidence of the public, but are loathed by it as a body of moronic bullies." He continued to guarantee that "no one above the grade of a cretin is going to take orders from a dumb cluck of a cop." This disdain for cops may have arisen when, lacking the usual projection of power, officers increasingly relied on the billy club to solve disputes.

The army generally relied on the patchwork of explicit wartime legal orders, like the Articles of War, to supersede civilian jurisdiction. Some cities felt compelled to surrender sections of their city halls for use by empowered MPs. In other areas, military and civil leaders negotiated verbal agreements to the same effect but believed that any written regulation "would be unwise." Why some commanders resisted written agreements remains unclear, but perhaps they feared that legal challenges might arise if this policing and legal regime was codified.

"BLIND ASSHOLE DRUNK"

Troops arrived in liberty ports ready to get drunk, exacerbating already growing problems of sexual assault, prostitution, and vandalism. Men often hit the bars near the dockyards before moving on to

FIGURE 2.3 The Shore Patrol in San Francisco during V-J Day
Source: © George DeCarvalho/*San Francisco Chronicle*/Polaris.

the red-light districts and honky-tonks. Before reaching port, or while on the street, sailors reported "loading up" in preparation for a weekend of liberty. Men spiked coffee and soda and tossed the empty rye and scotch bottles into the street. Whether with beer, whiskey, moonshine, bathtub gin, wood alcohol (which sometimes blinded sailors), swipe ("an ad hoc distillation of sugar, canned fruit, potato peelings, and other such ingredients"), or torpedo juice (torpedo fuel mixed with apple juice or grapefruit), soldiers found ways to get "pie-eyed" and drink "themselves into unconsciousness." The navy actually began adding croton oil—"an explosively powerful purgative" that burned the mouth, throat, and abdomen, sometimes killing men—to the torpedo fuel, though sailors found ways to distill it safely.

Other soldiers began looting whiskey and alcohol from medical supplies, stealing as many cases as possible, and then hiding the bottles in cargo holds. Some enterprising GIs even began selling the whiskey to fellow soldiers at black market rates. Others snuck booze onto trains or purchased it at stops, leading to whole cars becoming drunk and disorderly. This propensity for soldiers to get drunk at rail stations and during layovers consistently resulted in delays and missed trains. British officers remarked that American soldiers were "drunk all day," and one GI reported: "We got blind asshole drunk every chance we got." Subsequent medical studies confirm that World War II veterans died from alcoholism at significantly higher rates than did nonveterans.

In November 1942, Chief of Staff Marshall wrote to Provost Marshal General Allen Gullion—the head of army policing—regarding alcohol abuse among soldiers. After referring to the recurring issue of "soldiers drinking on trains," he acknowledged the "touchy problem in the matter of drinking elsewhere, especially in cities where enlisted men congregate during the week-ends." His main concern appeared to be the civilian enmity created by the rampant drunkenness and violence of his men, admonishing Gullion: "It is essential that the mounting wave of criticism and resentment be stopped." Months later, however, commanding officers received notice that "many reports continue to reach the War Department relative to drinking and misconduct of military personnel on public carriers and in towns and cities adjacent to posts, camps, and stations." The inspector general and General Gullion demanded that commanding officers require their men to "correct defects in conduct, dress, and military courtesy," though they offered no specific ideas as to how they might accomplish this. Reducing drunk and disorderly conduct in port was a formidable task. Military leaders had already discouraged the use of dishonorable discharges, courts-martial, and confinement as these punishments all resulted in manpower loss. Aside from reductions in rank and the levying of extra duties, commanders could revoke liberty privileges. Once again, however, naval protocol warned that "loss of liberty becomes a more onerous punishment when opportunity for liberty is very limited." Indeed, losing liberty could spur waves of absenteeism and desertion if men began to feel homesick or "cooped up." This web of contradictory policies left officers with no clear, effective method of preventing the poor conduct and performance caused by drinking. Civilian police did little better, with one civilian observing that cops failed to stop drunk troops taking swigs from hip flasks in cafeterias and cafés prohibited from serving.

Some district naval commandants' attempts to curb drinking had limited effect or even backfired entirely. In July 1942, Miami's Rear Admiral James L. Kauffman and Brigadier General Ralph Wooten unilaterally decided that all places serving beer and liquor in Dade County would close at midnight Mondays through Saturdays and at 1:00 a.m. on Sundays. Military authorities explained to *Variety*: "It is imperative that these measures be taken because of the increasing difficulty in controlling drinking among service personnel." They proceeded to admit publicly that the sheer numbers of men coursing through Miami had left only a scattered number of MPs and SPs struggling to keep the peace. Notably, Miami's command included civilians in the ban, explaining that, were civilians allowed to continue drinking, morale would collapse and troops would feel that this was "discrimination in favor of the civilians." What legal authority this decree rested on remains unclear. *Variety* explained: "Previous legal restrains [sic] have been sketchy." Bar operators grumbled, but no major protest emerged against "the most stringent liquor and nitery regulations ever instigated in this resort area." The order ultimately did little to shelter Miami from the disruptions brought on by excessive drinking. In March 1943, the *Daily Boston Globe* explained that "the Army and Navy have taken over" Miami and that the swarms of uniforms had "profoundly change[d] things." Bars and liquor stores still did a regular trade, shops more and more sold GIs "cheap and tawdry stuff," and streets swelled with singing men. Similar attempts in New York to cut off drinking before midnight only led to evenings filled with soldiers engaging in "unpaced drinking," heading to modernized "clip joints" with "shoddy women," and then more drinking and "'necking' in dark hallways." Moreover, the curfew appeared to severely affect the morale of the men.

THE "GI GAUNTLET"

Most ports of call featured well-known red-light districts, explicitly catering to the drives of servicemen. American-controlled areas like San Juan, Trinidad, Bermuda, and the Panama Canal Zone emerged as desired stops for men on transshipment routes, who specifically sought out their vice zones. In Colón and Panama City, American sailors mixed in the wild, colorful, and dangerous streets filled with vendors, prostitutes, barmen, other foreign soldiers, and taxi drivers calling out the names of brothels like "La Casa del Amor." For one naval officer, it was "the tropics, maturity, and the Fall of Man simultaneously." Sailors hurried off the docks after the canal trawl to find "the honky-tonk main street of Panama City lined with bars." Amid the cacophony of competing jukeboxes, men could buy "cameras, silk hose, liquor, handbags decorated with the stuffed heads of baby alligators, bracelets of Mexican silver, and jade supposedly from the Orient." Packs of servicemen drank their way through Ancón's open-air taverns to El Chorrillo's sweltering cabarets. Along the way, they picked up "pictures made of butterfly wings, or coconuts, . . . or red bananas, or bottles of rum" from peddlers and hawkers dotting the streets. At nightclubs, men danced with hostesses, watched striptease shows, and listened to music as women "shook [their] giant naked breasts" in their faces. As sailors with "red faces" and "unfocused eyes" stumbled through the night, prostitutes beckoned from flung-open shutters. Military Police and Shore Patrol made no effort to stop the vice trade but instead transported passed-out and inebriated men back to their ships. Privately, the army conceded that MPs remained ineffective in the Caribbean owing to poor training and the lack of Spanish-speaking officers.

Yet Panamanians and other populations in American-controlled ports did not just passively accept the US military's use of their cities as pleasure zones. Some civilians saw opportunities to exploit visiting soldiers, while others found ways to actively challenge the military's domination. Some Panamanians—including the local police—beat and robbed drunk personnel, while others profited off the vice trade. Civilian groups organized protests aimed at expelling troops. Riots and other disturbances involving servicemen and civilians made major newspapers throughout the period, reflecting active resistance against the American presence. Often, the violence could be traced back to nightlife, women, and liquor. Troops and MPs in Colón were injured when "a free-for-all in a cabaret spread to the street." Later, in Natal, Brazil, sailors sparked "a quasi riot" when a drunken crew of nearly three hundred "annoyed" and "seized" several women, provoking a "general brawl" that had to be put down by police and firemen wielding hoses. These brawls and riots and the general comportment of Americans in port fueled anti-American sentiment and possibly contributed to Panama's decision to expel the army's defense bases in 1947 after protests by civilians.

One might suspect that Caribbean ports afforded American troops a kind of anonymity, that it was their foreign location and racial hierarchies that allowed for the suspension of normal moral codes. Yet the same kind of raucous, violent hedonism could be found in US mainland ports. New York City, for example, emerged as the world's busiest and most popular liberty port during the war and the most desired place for men trying to find a girl before shipping out, whether across the ocean or, more likely, to another US city. For many men it was "Last Stop, U.S.A.," the key Atlantic hub of transshipment and transfer for soldiers, sailors, and marines of every Allied nation. Entering New York Harbor amid the fog, recurring clanging bells, and freighters, men could see "the most beautiful sight in the world . . . Manhattan floating on the water." And, in "the Crossroad of the World," servicemen gathered at the heart of what English transplant Alistair Cooke termed "Tijuana on the Hudson," crowded with servicemen surging through the dimly lit streets. Seeing the hordes of bluejackets, GIs, and merchant marines, the naval officer Robert Edson Lee wrote: "Virgil and Dante saw nothing more spectacular in Hell than those hundred thousand servicemen circling Times Square endlessly walking, continually replaced. Desperate, lonely, forlorn, but certain to find there the excitement for which they had gone to war."

Times Square functioned as both the center for liberty activity in New York and a central hub for civilian transport, once again bringing troops and civilians into tense contact. On Broadway, women filling wartime jobs and visiting civilians confronted a sea of colors, "the red pompons of French Navy caps mingling with the bright blue collars of the British seamen, the somber khaki of American, Australian, and Canadian soldiers." But this was not a peaceful, romantic meeting of allies, nor was Times Square the center of well-ordered spectacle and international consumerism that it is today. Instead, its appeal lay in its suspension of civic virtue and raucous celebration of wolfish aggression. Just like overseas staging grounds, it was a militarized zone where each week millions of soldiers could get drunk in dank taverns, carouse and fight, catch a peep show, and then chase women through the dimout streets of the wartime city. "Canteens, above-the-street dance halls, shooting galleries, bars, [and] honky-tonks" dominated "the mecca of the pleasure-seeker, the curious, the odd, and the homeless." In this aggressive mix of violent masculinity and frontier spectacle, servicemen provided Times Square with the "greatest boom in its history."

In Times Square, women, Meyer Berger of the *New York Times* noted, ran "a kind of GI gauntlet," threading their way past the American, British, and French servicemen "forming the nightly stag lines" as they ogled the "girls and women surging toward Forty-second Street subway stations." Cops warned women to "look out for them Coney Island wolves," but the police ultimately did little to discourage the "wolf whistles," stares, and physical intimidation that greeted women on their commutes. The film critic Pauline Kael remembered that soldiers picked up "techniques they saw in the movies": "If you were walking down the street and a guy in uniform tried stop you and you weren't interested . . . they tried to make you feel guilty for not wanting to go to bed with them." Indeed, consent did not usually factor into a serviceman's approach. Secretary of the Navy Frank Knox received direct complaints about drunken troops "bullying civilians and frightening women and children," while Times Square women protested that "sailors call you the vilest names if you ask them to leave you alone." Even pregnant women could not escape "being insulted and chased right up to [their] very door." Women often found little recourse for this chronic pattern of harassment, threat, assault, and rape. In the early hours of the morning, Berger observed one woman with "a damaged right eye" repeating to herself, "'He hit me, he hit me.'" "But she's alone," Berger notes. "No one stops her. No sympathy."

For servicemen, however, Times Square—and New York itself—became a place to break sexual and racial taboos while consummating the identities they had forged in training. After beginning the night by pouring "raw whiskey" down his throat, one sailor found himself "in an orgy": "I kissed, my God, I kissed a hundred women, two hundred women in an hour. . . . I kissed a gorgeous Negress. . . . I fondled breasts. Somebody screamed, and we chased the prettiest girls up and down. . . . We staggered away, our lips a raw mass of cold sores for days to come—badges, envied by all the others on the ship." Reporters ominously wrote of the "soldiers and sailors pacing the streets looking for a 'pick up'" after being tossed from the bars. From the beginning of the war, the temptations of New York proved too much for some Allied soldiers, and many British, Canadian, French, and Chinese sailors went AWOL there, leading American civil police forces and MPs to try to track these international deserters down.

At times, New York and other stateside cities struggled to house the huge numbers arriving on furloughs despite the efforts of volunteer and religious organizations to offer housing, apartments, and dormitories. Many hotels refused to give rooms to enlisted men fearing the trouble they might well bring, driving them to sleazy establishments or the street. The New York Times noted that members of the "friendly invasion of soldiers, sailors, and marines"—and the women they were with—could be found sleeping on benches and crowding the walk-ups of Fifth Avenue and Central Park West. Others, after carousing in Times Square, holed up in bus stations and subway terminals. On hot nights, troops slept in Central Park despite Mayor La Guardia's order that it close at midnight. The *Times* noted: "It would require a small army to make the order fully effective."

Gay soldiers—and men who identified as straight but enjoyed ho-moerotic experiences—also took to liberty ports for dancing, carousing, and sex even though they disproportionately attracted the attention of policing and vice squads. Like other servicemen, gay troops smartly followed the lists of bars that had been declared out-of-bounds by the MPs, vice boards, and command. By quickly changing out of their uni-form and into civvies, men hoped to find a blacklisted gay bar without attracting attention. Large public areas like Central Park also offered an ideal space for cruising, though MPs also began cracking down on well-known meeting spots. Police also focused on raiding drag shows and burlesque theaters, though wartime gay life in the military can hardly be characterized as nothing but crackdowns. Indeed, gay GIs and men interested in homoerotic encounters regularly found and adopted previously straight taverns and clubs, remaining there even when opposed by civilian and police forces. In other instances, gay servicemen found established spots like Carroll's bar in Washington, DC, where government employees cruised for military men. Carroll's maintained established traditions and codes of conduct that made it a reliable and safe spot to pick up a guy in prewar years. But, just as heterosexual troops turned on civilians and made nightlife more ag-gressive, the gay servicemen in Carroll's sometimes bucked the bar's long-standing customs, became drunk, and then turned violent to-ward the civilian clientele. Waitresses warned their regulars about troublesome troops, and many civilians ultimately departed for less dangerous establishments.

In Los Angeles, sailors found vice to be more decentralized as they made their way from the navy yard and Terminal Island to the nightlife of Long Beach, downtown, or Hollywood. Main Street and East Fifth Street in Los Angeles, San Pedro's South Beacon, and Long Beach's West Pike and Ocean boomed with servicemen looking to drink and maybe "buy a piece of 'ass.'" Bluejackets and army grunts also took advantage of LA's relative proximity to the fleshpots and amusement zones across the Mexican border. Los Angeles, San Diego, Tijuana, Tecate, Mexicali, and Ensenada effectively formed a single stretch where soldiers could tour the taverns, brothels, and bars. Locals suggested that visiting servicemen pursue the "good neighbor policy by going to Tijuana in quest of liquor."

While some soldiers viewed the border towns as spots for carousing, others identified them as the ideal spots to go AWOL. Mexico and the United States lacked an official agreement regarding the return of deserters, leading Mexican authorities to demand compensation for cooperation. Army administrators acknowledged their relative lack of leverage and advised commanding generals negotiating the extradition of absentee soldiers "to avoid any possibility of controversy with Mexican authorities who, it must be understood, are under no obligation to enter into such agreements."

The American vice traffic also sometimes strained relations between the US military and the Mexican government. After a night of drinking, an American corporal was shot by a Mexican policeman while drunkenly driving away from a Tijuana cabaret, leading to recriminations and demands for justice from both sides. In Reynosa, the first stop for south Texas–based troops hopping the border, intoxicated sailors and soldiers were regularly arrested by the Mexican police "for anything from arguing with a taxi driver about an exorbitant fare to an assault on a Mexican, and are almost invariably fined the amount of money in their possession." The army attempted to declare Reynosa's prostitution district off-limits, but, because the Mexican army enforced these regulations, soldiers "understood that for a sum . . . this restriction is waived." The army eventually formed joint American-Mexican police forces to patrol Juarez and Reynosa in an effort to control "prostitution, liquor, and high prices." Despite these attempts to police the stag trade, soldiers quickly became accustomed to having women, no matter the law or regulation in place.

Across American liberty ports, women "both young and old"—often working late into the night—were approached by men in uniform. When told "no," one woman wrote, sailors would call her "the most vulgar names." Other servicemen would "hide and wait for ladies passing on their way home," catcalling and following after them, "which makes it very unpleasant and unsafe—as these men seem to disregard a persons [sic] age and make the same advances to both young and old." At the Pike in the Long Beach Amusement Zone, criminality among naval personnel ran unchecked as "thousands of usual visitors have been driven from the beaches and pleasures" as "hordes of drunken sailors, running wild, insulting and man-handling women," claimed the area as their own. Male civilians escorting women "have been beaten insensible" while "trying to protect their families from the moronic desires of these hoodlums." "Irate husbands," one civilian remarked, "may have to kill a few of these gangsters before proper action is taken." On trains and railways, women often could not avoid the advances and attention of soldiers, some of whom spent these trips becoming drunk and disorderly to the point of assaulting conductors and porters.

Soldiers and sailors regularly engaged in a practice later labeled *prowling* by Pearl Schiff, a novelist who lived in a liberty port. Describing the mind-set of the sailors, she explained: "You prowled the Square and took your time, seeing what the evening had to offer." This generally meant groups of servicemen stood at high-traffic areas, like busy street crossings, bus stops, and subway stations, assessing the women and girls passing by. Men would give women "the eye," a mix of seductive glances and outright leering. Wolf whistles, aggressive come-ons, and chasing after a girl might follow. Servicemen, Schiff wrote, debated which girl to pursue and described hoping to avoid committing "to a profitless evening with a girl who soaked up . . . liquor like a sponge but gave nothing back when squeezed."

Some in the military hierarchy acknowledged the unchecked mistreatment of women in liberty ports, but they initially found ways to ascribe the problem to a tiny minority of scoundrels rather than admit how widespread this behavior had become. After witnessing the violent carousing in Hampton Roads that had previously disturbed General Marshall, Rear Admiral David McDougal Le Breton admitted: "Some men appear to believe that because they are in the military service they are privileged to molest women in public places and to insult and disregard the rights of civilians who are not wearing the uniform." Generals in the army offered similar warnings about the rampant lawlessness and poor behavior defining wartime life in liberty ports and military camps. Lieutenant General Brehon Somervell, for example, warned: "Adverse criticism of the discipline and soldierly bearing of the members of the Army has been received in the War Department. This criticism results from observations of Army personnel not only in cities, public conveyances and other public places, but also in our posts, camps and stations."

Le Breton was an old hand—an experienced career officer dedicated to the service who genuinely believed in the ideal of a gentleman officer. This ideology informed his declaration that "the conduct of these men brings the entire Navy into disrepute and should be a matter of serious concern to all decent, self-respecting men in the Naval service." Given the range of offenses—swearing, insulting women and civilians, destruction of civilian property, assault, highway robbery, and manslaughter—he surmised that the navy was losing the respect and confidence of the public, who increasingly saw nothing but "disorderly and rowdy conduct in public places."

While the admiral chose to step up Shore Patrol efforts, issue stronger punishments, and encourage a culture of more gentlemanly behavior during stays in stateside cities, he failed to recognize how the navy's culture of swaggering masculinity and anticivilian clannishness fueled enlistees' criminal behavior. Instead, he blamed the port's troubles on "criminals, gangsters, and other undesirable persons of bad character" who had unfortunately found their way into the service. Here, Le Breton ignored the fact that the navy generally had its pick of the best recruits and did not rely on the draft like the army did. Hampton Roads's struggles with crime and sexual assault also began in 1942, when the navy was generally filled with disproportionally educated, middle-class sailors. Criminal behavior, then, could not simply be attributed to poor education or a dearth of men raised in good homes. Instead, each service saw the effects of a training system that emphasized virile masculinity and disdain for civilian life combined with a legal framework that allowed troops to use liberty to relieve stress and have a rollicking good time.

BRAWLING

Servicemen demonstrated their superiority to nonmilitary men by fighting them. Male civilians—thought of as 4-Fs and Jodies—were often targeted, usually with no consequences for the aggressors. Fighting with civilians asserted a soldier's dominance over other men as well as over spaces like Times Square. On many nights, reporters watched as "soldiers, sailors, and civilians exchanged blows" while servicemen vandalized property, but MPs rarely arrived to make any arrests. On other nights, service personnel hammering drinks ended up in "drunken brawls." Store owners expected riots and vandalism whenever an election or New Year's Eve brought masses of servicemen to Times Square, boarding up their storefronts and windows to deter theft and vandalism. In New York and elsewhere, soldiers drinking, stealing cars, and joyriding created a sense of helplessness among civilians. Stories of sailors even murdering civilians in local hotels cropped up.

Servicemen's targeting of civilian men could cause whole cities to be declared out-of-bounds, as happened in Sacramento when "mounting trouble between sailors and civilians . . . culminated in a riotous fight." There, twenty-five sailors insulted and then attacked a smaller group of civilian men, including a Mexican American prize fighter. City officials warned that "friction between sailors and civilian young men had been increasing" with earlier brawls at a Chinese restaurant where belligerent sailors clashed with waiters who "fought with hot soup," scalding one of the men.

Men sought out establishments that became known for consistent brawling. On San Diego's Mission Beach boardwalk, soldiers, marines, and civilians could scrap in hard-edged bars like the Casino Café, where management made no effort to stop drunken fights, which lasted thirty minutes at times. Nearby civilians lodged formal complaints against the chronic "fighting and profane language," soldiers using their yards "as a toilet," and the intoxicated servicemen sleeping on their property. One resident saw these carousing men and the bars they frequented as "a menace to the welfare of my wife and family."

Brawls could quickly change from low-level street fights into massive, deadly riots. In August 1942, over twelve hundred people crowded into the ballroom of the Elks building in Cambridge, Massachusetts, for a dance. As the servicemen, women, and civilians danced and mingled, a fistfight broke out between a GI and a civilian over a woman. A cacophony of insults, fists, and screaming overtook the hall as the fighting spiraled out onto the dance floor. Men broke bottles, smashed windows, and readied knives. A police matron was punched in the eye and knocked to the ground. Witnesses saw a soldier thrown from a balcony, plummeting fifteen feet onto his head and disappearing from view as the combatants on the dance floor trampled him. Joint Shore Patrol and civilian police squads stormed the building, and the riot spread into the streets. After police arrested the instigators, the crowd turned against them, brawling with the SPs and municipal cops. Army MPs soon joined the resurgent riot, and the police quelled the melee only by firing tear gas into the crowd. Brawls that escalated into riots consistently harmed relations between soldiers, civilians, and police.

Civil challenges to military authority and privilege as well as enforcement of chickenshit regulations could also prompt brawling. Troops knew that municipal cops held little authority over them, leading to fights when civilian police encroached on the de facto and de jure privileges of the uniform. The "Battle of Astoria" in New York—a ninety-minute bar fight between scores of sailors and policemen

witnessed by four hundred spectators—started when officers demanded to see liberty passes and identification cards. The sailors ral-
lied to the cry of "so this is democracy!" and began "the free-for-all."
Glass panels were smashed, stones were thrown at policemen, civilians joined in the fray, and scores were injured. Although the sailors
were in violation of liberty regulations and publicly assaulted police
officers, the magistrate presiding over the case chastised the police:
"A bar and grill at 1 o'clock in the morning is likely to become inflamed
at the slightest provocation. I cannot understand the physical force
used by the police in arresting these defendants."

Liberty ports also often shifted the focus of brawling. Previously,
GIs and sailors fought among themselves. These interservice brawls
could be massive; one street fight just outside Seattle involved over 150
sailors and marines. But, when faced with Allied troops taking leave
in stateside cities, American troops increasingly began to fight the
interlopers. In Bermuda, "a bewildering potpourri of fighting men,"
including American sailors, British navy men, Scottish Highlanders,
Free French out of Tahiti, and other Commonwealth conscripts, congregated in the same bars after long ocean trawls. In an area where
rum was cheaper than beer, international punch-ups proved inevitable. One bar fight allegedly began after an American sailor and a
British merchant marine began exchanging insults. "To hell with your
king!" said the American. "To hell with Babe Ruth!" replied the Brit.

British and American men suffered perhaps the poorest relations.
Relations between them eventually became so poor that British command instituted a program aimed at training American and British
recruits together in order to avoid inter-Alliance conflicts. The brawls
between them were partly sparked by sexual jealousy and competition. Many British soldiers and sailors abroad had heard rumors of
all the Yanks in the United Kingdom supposedly reducing their wives
and sisters to prostitution. British soldiers also resented the higher
pay, better food, and access to beer that US servicemen enjoyed. Prominent Bostonians responded to street clashes by creating the Union
Jack Club for passing British sailors, the idea being to keep them out

of rowdy spots and stop them from sleeping on the Boston Common. American troops, for their part, despised the potential competition for women they saw in British men. British sailors seen with American women were sometimes targeted by groups of American troops. Nevertheless, British sailors did end up meeting American women and marrying them. Some British servicemen deserted in places like Brooklyn to marry, while Australian merchant marines found wives in Los Angeles and took them back to Sydney as war brides.

British and American political and military leaders also clashed over unequal legal treaties. While the British assented to the claim that American merchant marines and sailors charged with crimes in the United Kingdom and the Commonwealth territories should be tried by US courts, the Americans made no similar concessions for British sailors charged with crimes in the States. The Americans additionally demanded that none of their troops ever be tried by a UK court. The British Admiralty bristled at this clear inequality but generally cooperated with the American demands.

"TELL YOUR TROUBLES TO THE PRESIDENT"

Military officials readily understood the primary causes of trouble on leave and liberty, with one naval official listing "drank too much," "detained by civilian police," and "couldn't keep away from girls" as key factors. Following General Marshall's complaints in 1942, General Gullion—the head of army policing—likewise identified "intoxication," "disturbing civilians," and "general obnoxious disorder" as deeply troubling signs of "an apparent lack of discipline in the Army as a whole." Gullion made a number of requests and recommendations. First, the army should greatly increase the number of MPs in key liberty ports, in towns near bases, and on trains. Second, he wrote to the International Association of Chiefs of Police asking that civil police across the country "arrest and confine all military personnel for drunkenness" before turning them over to the nearest military station. Finally, he

attempted to institute better policing by threatening the commanding generals. "Misconduct of military personnel, especially outside
the confines of military reservations," he explained, "is an indica-
tion of poor leadership, training and esprit de corps and of the failure of officers to carry out their responsibilities." Those who failed to
correct this chronic misbehavior promptly would face "disciplinary
measures."

Gullion's words were sharp, but he lacked any real way to back them
up. The military's policing problem did not result simply from a lack
of effort among commanding officers and the police. Both military
and civil policing remained ineffective for a number reasons beyond
the lazy explanation of poor leadership.

First, the War Department believed that recurring manpower problems made devoting more (and better-trained) men to policing an impossible request. After Gullion demanded more MPs and patrols, it
admitted that "the number of military police in all categories is below
the number allotted" but maintained that the army would not accede
to an expansion of Military Police units: "It is obvious that as the Army
increases in size, the vital question of manpower must increasingly
influence decisions. . . . Assignment of additional personnel to duties
which are not closely associated with the support of combat units in
active theaters must be kept to a minimum." Even as the number of
combat and support troops grew—and, therefore, the number of men
taking liberty increased—the War Department refused to make pro-
portionate increases in police forces. A report in August 1942 made
an even more desperate case, noting that MPs were already short
over seventeen thousand officers and would ideally need twenty-six
additional battalions, a 41 percent increase in the total number of
MPs. With only forty-five thousand officers—some of them dedicated
to internal security efforts at defense plants and, thus, not contribut-
ing to keeping order in urban areas—attempting to police over three
million GIs, MPs were operating at under half their target strength.
By January 1945, Military Police numbers in the continental United
States stood at ninety thousand, though the army's total personnel

had also grown to over eight million, leaving the provost marshal general with a continued shortage of men.

Rather than addressing servicemen's alcohol abuse or increasing patrols to prevent street harassment and rape, joint army-navy boards used military and civilian policing to focus on preventing the spread of venereal diseases, attacking homosexuality, and investigating black and other nonwhite servicemen. Any area of the city or any business could be placed out-of-bounds if it was thought to harbor venereal disease, rendering it theoretically inaccessible to servicemen (though lists of such places often told troops exactly where to go). In centering policing efforts on venereal disease, the military redoubled its commitment to maintaining manpower while allowing soldiers to engage in a few port sins. But this also drove more and more soldiers into areas with civilian women uninvolved in the sex trade.

Both the Shore Patrol and the Military Police lacked tradition, morale, funding, and the backing of higher-level commanders. Indeed, some ship captains bitterly protested the loss of morale and manpower when their men were held for drunkenness and carousing. When the Los Angeles Shore Patrol attempted to enforce alcohol and location restrictions, a skeptical vice admiral asked senior officers to legitimize the policy. A 1942 army study of Military Police personnel problems argued that the whole force suffered from "unqualified personnel" as it was seen as a place to dump "useless individuals." One inspector remarked: "The most frightening situation is personnel—the first thing referred to at all posts." By the war's end, few improvements had been made, and War Department headquarters continued to receive complaints from generals that they could not obtain qualified and well-trained MPs. Major General James L. Collins asked that the army move to concentrate the scant Military Police resources in "cities that are centers of population having a large impact on military personnel," but this proposal was scuttled without explanation. Other commanders pleaded that they required "additional military police badly" and warned of "tremendous headaches" should the War Department ignore their requests. Consistently understaffed, and given unremarkable trainees, MPs continued to be cast as underpowered misfits. Jokes abounded claiming that color-blind draftees were made MPs and tasked with directing traffic. Another joke featured an illiterate MP telling a speeding colonel's wife: "You're damn lucky, ma'am. If I could write I'd give you a ticket." Civilian women joined in mocking officers as they passed them on the sidewalk, calling them "flatfoots," implying that they could not hack it in the infantry.

Servicemen thus held little respect for either Military Police or Shore Patrol. Each force struggled to assert effective control and authority over unruly men, many of whom outright refused to obey the commands of police from a different branch. GIs like Bill Mauldin saw MPs as matriarchal figures determined to impede any kind of fun. In one of Mauldin's *Star Spangled Banter* cartoons, three GIs analyze a scowling MP waving his baton. When one asks, "Whaddaya s'pose makes an M.P. become an M.P.?," another answers, "They want t'keep us boys innercent—it the mother instinct." Other troops hypothesized that *MP* must stand for "miserable prick." A 1943 War Department report, "What Soldiers Think about Army Branches," revealed that soldiers indeed despised the MPs. The average grunt identified them as having "the least amount of work to do" and "the least dangerous jobs" while also seeing the corps as the least-liked branch and the branch least important to winning the war. Some commanding officers chastised the casual disrespect shown the corps and feared the sometimes vicious disdain GIs displayed toward law enforcement. One brigadier general—noticing a growing number of "incidents indicative of an attitude of disrespect toward military and civilian police, and toward military and local law"—cautioned that soldiers were showing "contempt for the requests and orders of military police." This was leading to "violence committed upon the persons" of MPs. Naval files swell with reports of sailors cursing out Shore Patrol officers or assaulting them. One officer described being surrounded after attempting to make an arrest, with troops grabbing at his pistol. Army reports include grisly accounts of soldiers ganging up on isolated MPs and savagely beating them.

Some Shore Patrol commanders like Clarence Fogg seemed genuinely concerned with the levels of crime, drunkenness, and sexual harassment and assaults. A naval district patrol officer in San Diego claimed that the SPs gave "the accosting of women more attention than any other offense, operating special details in some sections for that offense alone." But how could undermanned patrols enforce the rule of law when naval protocols informed them that "arrest should not be resorted to where corrective measures will suffice?" One woman complained directly to the admiral in command of San Diego: "The Police say they don't get co-operation from the Navy. If you or some of your command would only investigate, you will find that the papers don't write up half of what's going on." She concluded by remarking: "Where I am living the women don't have a good word for the Navy."

The authority and effectiveness of military policing rapidly diminished over the course of the war, with officers coming to accept their lack of control in liberty ports. Even as civilians protested to the military that women were forced to "run the gauntlet" and civilian men had to "stand idly by to the abuse and humiliation of their women," little was done to bolster military policing. Instead, "patrols," one civilian seethed, "advise the victims they are under orders to NOT stop these boys." When women complained about these "troubles," some MPs would dismiss them, saying: "Old gal you tell your troubles to the President." Other MPs abused their power to coerce women for sexual favors. Several women told the *Chicago Defender* that MPs "bully them into affairs with them, sometimes on threat of 'taking it out' on their soldier boyfriends or husbands."

RACE IN LIBERTY PORTS—HOUSTON, CHICAGO, DETROIT, LOS ANGELES, HARLEM

Reconstructing the wartime lives of African American servicemen is a far more difficult task than doing so for white military men, whose experiences are well documented. Military, police, and civic records were all written and documented by whites. Aside from a few notable black newspapers, most crime beats were covered by white journalists informed by the era's prevailing racism. After the war, publishers provided far more opportunities and support for white combat soldiers' memoirs and journals. The army's weekly intelligence summaries dedicated whole sections to the "racial situation" and "negro crime," sections suffused with blatant racism. The administrative division of the Military Police kept detailed records of individual incidents involving black soldiers and assessed the degree of "racial agitation" occurring in each command area. Once again, these accounts lack the perspective of the soldier, and their claims of crime cannot be independently corroborated. African American servicemen also likely felt pressure not to publicize their activities in liberty ports. While white soldiers could safely recall fond memories of carousing in Times Square or getting rowdy on Mission Street, individual black veterans were held to the impossible standard of representing the moral character of all African Americans. Moreover, rape accusations and convictions against black troops—and subsequent lynchings— were commonly used as tools to enforce white supremacy. Reminiscing about bawdy adventures in port thus had to be excluded in favor of the rhetorical power of the Double V Campaign.

Nevertheless, some indications of how black servicemen experienced liberty ports and other stopover cities exist. Like white troops, black men desired women, alcohol, and an escape from the regimentation and authoritarianism of military life. Black marines lusted after "fine-looking girls" and "hot-coeds" offering "pussy." Old hands taunted new recruits by asking, "Didja bring your sister?" Conversely, one marine being "razzed" by older troops for wearing a zoot suit responded by boasting about his access to nightlife: "Y'all jealous 'cause I seen the city an' y'all h'aint." Bill Downey, a black marine, remembers his first night in DC as a "search for easy women." Black troops took particular delight in waving to women "who had not been indoctrinated with racism." These women waved back, and "when they saw our black faces and Marine uniforms they yelled like cheerleaders."

Overall, black servicemen echoed white troops' obsession with liberty, describing it as a chance "to get back to civilization." As it was among whites, time on long train rides was spent playing poker, enjoying bullshit sessions, and talking about women. Unlike their white counterparts, however, black troops' train journeys into liberty ports often required an uncomfortable ride in "the standing room only aisles of the Jim Crow Special."

In further stark contrast to the experiences of white troops, African American servicemen regularly faced harsh and violent treatment from both military and civilian police forces. The uniform often protected white troops from police action even when they acted in the most profane and repugnant ways. But black men in uniform were even greater targets for cops eager to enforce the white supremacist order (and perhaps to exercise their own power and masculinity in a time when police were despised and disempowered). Yet it was more than just the combination of the light olive uniform and black skin that so incensed whites. Black troops taking leave in cities became the ultimate threat because they were—for that brief period—outside the control of their white commanders. Knowing that these men would possibly be looking for both liquor and women only exacerbated the fears of white police, civilians, and military authorities. Liberty ports quickly emerged as significant conflict zones between black servicemen and whites, and attempts to prevent black troops from enjoying the urban nightlife fueled a number of riots and violent incidents throughout the war.

African American servicemen on leave committed three sins in the eyes of whites. First, their exhibition of military identity in public could be seen as unpatriotic. Using the war and military service to gain greater freedom and access to major urban areas than they could have as civilians struck whites as disloyal and exploitative behavior. In the strange reasoning of white observers, black troops were politicizing war. Second, black troops were seen not only as sexual threats to white women but also as sexual competitors for the black women desired by white men. Third, groups of black servicemen moving through liberty ports threatened both the de facto and the de jure seg-regation of many urban spaces. Police, military, and urban officials responded by issuing a new set of wartime segregation policies while also terrorizing black troops on leave. The conflict and brutal hatred that black servicemen faced, however, made African Americans more cognizant that amusement and access to public space could become key political battlegrounds.

From the beginning of the war, civilian police forces and military police forces seemed to find rare common cause in threatening and harassing black troops on leave. In early 1942, Houston city cops and MPs entered bars and taverns in the "the heart of the Negro section of [the] city" to taunt and insult black soldiers. The combined police forces told them that "they were 'niggers' and that as long as they re-mained in the South they would be 'niggers' and would be treated as such." Soldiers replied that they were not "'nigger soldiers' but . . . American soldiers." One of the cops responded, "You are a nigger sol-dier if I say so," before threatening to kill them. The police began ar-resting the men and charging them with "inciting to riot," a common catchall charge used to intimidate and harass black troops. On releas-ing them the next morning, the cops warned one of the soldiers that "he would be arrested everytime he came into Houston." And, indeed, that soldier was arrested later that night for remaining in the city. Other GIs reported being forced to leave restaurants, being told to re-move their hats when speaking to whites, and suffering beatings with billy clubs. One claimed to have been almost blinded after being struck by an officer. Major Smith, the head of military policing in Houston, defended the conduct of the Houston cops, maintaining that the po-lice could treat black soldiers "in any way they wished." He went on to claim—with no legal basis—that, when black soldiers entered the city, they were under "the authority of city law," a marked contrast to the assertions of the supremacy of military law for white troops. The *Chicago Defender* and the NAACP concluded that "a campaign of terror and intimidation is being waged against Negro soldiers by civilian and white military police in this area," and they protested to the War

Department's "Negro advisor," Judge William Hastie. Such an early action to harass and arrest black soldiers suggests a deliberate strategy among the police to prevent any black troops from even attempting to go to Houston during their leave and liberty. Local commanders likely collaborated in this scheme when they took ammunition and firearms away from black companies, fearing armed troops preparing to confront Houston's racist police forces. Nevertheless, the *Defender* reported: "Negro soldiers have brought arms and ammunition to defend themselves if things get too hot for them in Houston."

The War Department investigated the situation and the claims of John H. Thompson, the author of the *Defender* piece. Thompson warned the army about the lack of black MPs, who might be able to police black servicemen more effectively, while also noting the consistent police brutality that defined GI-police interactions and the numbers of northern blacks apparently unaccustomed to such virulent segregation. The specter of riots loomed in the mind of Thompson, who recalled the Red Summer riots of 1919 and advised that "the present day soldier which we see here, is not taking the abuse the white people are placing on them." If Houston did not learn to "respect the United States uniform even though it is worn by a Negro," then the danger of riots would continue to grow. "These soldiers have told me and other newsmen," he advised, "that they are not going to stand for a lot 'foolishness' by whites as long as they are in uniform." Though the War Department acknowledged some of the abuses of Houston's police force and advocated for improved recreation for black soldiers, its report mostly justified the prevailing principle of simply segregating the black divisions. The report concluded: "Negro training camps should be widely distributed throughout the country. . . . In other words, suppose that negro camps are placed in Arizona or New Mexico and are not located adjacent to cities or towns having a substantial negro population." A different solution presented itself in Ohio, where black infantrymen argued that they were kept from enjoying liberty because of burdensome workloads: "The mistreated colored serviceman," wrote one GI, "is discriminated, segregated, ridiculed, misjudged and frowned upon. He is given, in most cases the hardest dirtiest work in the service and during his spare time, if he has the energy left to go to town, he is confronted with the same treatment."

While police commanders in Houston attempted to prevent any and all black troops—even black transport drivers delivering important supplies—from entering the city, Chicago's authorities sought to redouble the hypersegregation that defined the city's North-South divide. However, they reinforced the city's racial order in an unexpected way. In July 1942, a navy lieutenant commander declared that much of Chicago's South Side would be off-limits for white sailors. Black business owners received notice that they were to bar white sailors from their establishments. Shore Patrol officers soon moved in to enforce what the *Defender* considered an extension of Jim Crow, forcibly ejecting white sailors from well-known South Side nightspots like the DeLisa. White sailors carousing at the Rhumboogie responded by nearly rioting when "Shore police attempted to invade the night club." Whites were allowed to frequent only White City, an amusement park that had long been segregated, and they were required to reach this fun zone only by public transportation. A local NAACP branch attorney explained that the order effectively blocked all white sailors from the South Side's streets, shops, and nightlife. The NAACP and the *Defender*—both fervent supporters of the black businesses that stood to lose significant revenue from this action—argued that the order was a form of "discrimination based on race or color" against whites. They also rejected the unstated but intended effect of the order to reinforce the de facto ban on black sailors visiting the North Side. This policy of keeping black troops contained within the city's "negro section" became standard policy in other northern cities as well. For example, in New York, black servicemen were expected to remain in Harlem.

Naval authorities in Chicago framed the ban as an effort "to protect Negro women from being approached by white sailors." Lieutenant Commander Lowe even said this explicitly. But this explanation seems dubious. The navy, however, might have recognized that competition between white and black men over women would likely create fierce

episodes of racial violence. In the army's weekly intelligence summaries, officers consistently posted reports that "attempts by white
soldiers to date Negro women is [sic] creating resentment among
Negroes." These reports acknowledge instances of white MPs and
enlisted men accosting and making advances toward black women,
prompting their black servicemen escorts to defend them physically.

Even the rumor of an interracial transgression could be enough
to provoke citywide violence. Detroit witnessed the power of race
and rumor in June 1943. While the Detroit Riot had many long-term
causes—particularly the deterioration of public services and housing
as well as overcrowding—the conflict between blacks and whites was
sparked by rumors of military men committing acts of racial violence.
In the summer's heat, white Detroiters spread wild rumors of black
men who "slit a white soldier's throat and raped his girlfriend," while
African American residents passed on stories of white sailors throwing a black woman and child off a bridge into the Detroit River. (Investigators later dragged the river but discovered no bodies.) When
the riot began, however, stories of interracial conflict involving servicemen formed key parts of the narrative. Brawling, looting, and
firefights soon spread outward from Belle Isle Park as black Detroiters, white sailors, and police—and later soldiers—battled for three
days, leaving thirty-four dead, hundreds wounded, and the US Army
occupying the shattered streets. Only a day before the riot erupted,
black and white troops had exchanged gunfire at Camp Stewart in
Georgia—leaving four dead and many wounded—after a white man
was accused of assaulting a black soldier's wife.

Questions of who could control access to both women and public
spaces—and demonstrations of the way rumor could inflame existing
tensions—would arise again in Los Angeles with the Zoot Suit Riots as
well as in Harlem with the riot over a black MP shot by a white policeman. For five days in June 1943, white marines and sailors went to war
against Mexican American zoot-suiters and pachucos in the streets of
Los Angeles. The Chicago Daily Tribune claimed that it all began after
some zoot-suiters tried "to 'push around' lone men in uniform and

to molest their girls." Servicemen reacted to this unsubstantiated claim, the zoot suit uniform—with its gleeful disdain for wartime regulations and implicit challenge to the servicemen's uniform—and the perceived threat of young, nonwhite men competing for women. The military men stationed in Los Angeles stormed the city to repeatedly and ritualistically beat the zoot-suiters, strip them, and then tear their suits apart. Hordes of servicemen and civilian spectators watched as they marched through Main Street with liquor and clubs in hand. Troops cried: "We'll destroy every zoot suit in Los Angeles County before this is over." Eventually, the navy temporarily banned sailors from entering Los Angeles for liberty. Newspapers and city officials mostly blamed the zoot-suiters, with the *Los Angeles Times* concluding: "Those gamin dandies, the zoot suiters, having learned a great moral lesson from servicemen, mostly sailors, who took over their instruction three days ago, are staying home."

Weeks later in Harlem, a white policeman's possibly unlawful attempt to arrest a black woman blew up when a black MP attempted to intervene by striking the cop. The policeman then fired on the MP. As news of the MP's death reached Harlem, reality quickly fused with rumor. Locals heard that a cop killed a black soldier in front of his own mother—a false narrative that nevertheless captured just how little value white officials placed on the lives of black men who served their country. Crowds formed, windows were shattered, fires blazed, and riot squads rushed in. By the end of the night, six citizens lay dead, and hundreds were wounded. Riots, fights, and protests would continue throughout the war as black military men fought for access to the privileges of liberty ports and black communities strove to obtain the freedoms the United States claimed it was fighting for overseas.

V-J DAY

The mythic view of wartime romance and a safe home front was ironically founded on perhaps the most dangerous moment of troop crime in liberty ports: V-J Day. San Francisco's Peace Day Riots—almost completely unknown today—proved the most destructive and deadly, but other liberty ports experienced similar outbreaks of coerced kissing, assault, and looting. The War Department anticipated that victory over Germany and Japan would likely bring dangerous revelry to American cities. It requested that the army and navy augment their police forces in advance of the celebrations and asked military authorities to lobby governors and other officials to implement a twenty-four-hour ban on the sale of alcohol. While the report spent considerable time worrying about the possible reactions of Japanese Americans and "the colored races," it also recognized the "large numbers of military and naval personnel [who] will be on leave, pass, or furlough, particularly in the metropolitan areas." "It is possible," it noted, "that the actions of such personnel during an impromptu celebration might react to the detriment of the service as a whole." The army also prepared some troops for riot duty and readied the auxiliary Military Police. The War Department's report accepted that disorders and riots were likely but vowed that the burden of policing would fall on local cops and state guard forces. In this sense, the memo was both a plan for preparation and a way of preemptively shifting blame.

In Boston, army officials wisely moved to confine all soldiers to their bases for two days after learning of Japan's surrender, though some GIs managed to sneak out. Store owners, now well aware of the dangers of carousing sailors, hurriedly boarded up their shop windows again. Boston's police chief mobilized all two thousand municipal cops while calling in auxiliaries and MPs. Nearby Cambridge, Medford, and Falmouth banned all sales of alcohol for twenty-four hours. The navy was less cooperative, giving liberty to sailors. Bars and liquor stores in Boston shipped in huge quantities of liquor to profit off the coming celebrations, though perhaps these proprietors also realized that servicemen would loot their existing stocks of alcohol if it was not willingly provided. By night, Boston's downtown turned "into a joyous madhouse" as "pent-up tension . . . exploded like a giant firecracker." An estimated 750,000 people coursed into downtown Boston with "soldiers and sailors dominat[ing] the throngs" to celebrate "a dozen New Year's Eves rolled into one." Car horns, church bells, Chinatown torpedoes, and fire sirens blared out across Tremont, Washington, and Boylston. In South Boston, mobs of people marched into the streets banging dishpans. Huge bonfires blazed on Boston Common, in the Public Garden, and in the North End, while hundreds of sailors climbed fire engine ladders and joyrode the trucks. The bars and taverns became overpacked with crowds, while each man spilling onto the street had, as the *Globe* described it, "a bottle containing his favorite beverage." Bostonians rolled beer kegs and barrels of wine onto street corners as the city enjoyed the delirious "bedlam" that came with peace.

"When the excitement really got under way," one *Globe* reporter noted, "servicemen—and again sailors seemed to dominate the picture—began the interesting game of trying to kiss every pretty girl they saw." Compelled mass kissing of women became the hallmark of V-J Day across the nation, with every sailor being "entitled to at least one kiss." Well into the second day of "tumult," the *Globe* reported, "sailors still kissing girls as holiday roars on." Servicemen sometimes demanded more than a kiss. At "the orgy of kissing" around Tremont and Boylston, sailors were reported picking up girls, tearing off their skirts, and then waving their prizes like flags. "Uncooperative" women who refused to be kissed were grabbed by "exuberant sailors" and then "flung" into the Common's frog pond as the men chanted, "No kiss, then kerplunk!" Women familiar with the behavior of furloughed soldiers who "sort of got out of hand" knew to avoid certain areas. Alison Arnold, the *Boston Herald* society editor, recalled that "young ladies were more or less advised to keep away from Scollay Square." Civilian men and servicemen also fought throughout the region. In New Bedford, civilians and soldiers exchanged blows in the city center, sparking a riot involving one hundred people. State guardsmen, police, and SPs armed with bayonets and tear gas managed to restore order after two hours of fighting in the streets. Throughout the Boston area, several died and hundreds were injured during the course of the raucous "victory whoopee."

In Los Angeles, thousands of "gobs, G.I.'s, gyrenes, [and] Coast Guardsmen" took to the downtown streets for "street kisses" as the "growing roar of sirens and whistles" marked the Allied victory. "Masses of humanity" overflowed into Pershing Square and Main Street, intermixing in the confetti snow and "the carnival spirit." Autos were smashed by the surging crowds of servicemen, while liquor stores were busted open before police could arrive. Other men began "jerking trolleys from the wires," sparking fires. Throughout the night, fights broke out between men, and "servicemen kissed every pretty girl they met." Marines, GIs, and bluejackets stayed up through the night feeding blazing street fires with the "paper strewing the streets." Altogether, eight people died—mainly in traffic accidents—and hundreds were treated for injuries ranging from gunshot wounds to firecracker burns. The police, who marshaled their entire force after learning of Japan's surrender, took a "good-natured" approach to the celebrations, allowing drinking and coerced kissing while trying to prevent "robberies and drunk-rollings." Having seen the disorder and violence committed by servicemen during the war, police forces in Los Angeles "contented themselves with the philosophy: 'It could have been worse.'"

Despite the violence, rioting, and sexual coercion that marked V-J Day and all the wartime chaos in liberty ports that had preceded it, only one scene has managed to gain a foothold in most Americans' memory of the home front: Alfred Eisenstaedt's *Kissing Sailor*. For the public, it became a romantic token of postwar America's relief and promise as it moved from the good war to the Cold War. Yet the photo actually captures a drunken sailor, George Mendonsa, forcibly accosting and kissing a dental nurse running the gauntlet that women had faced on a nightly basis in wartime ports. Eisenstaedt's series of photos reveals her attempts to struggle free of Mendonsa's control and prevent him from yanking up her dress. An alternate angle likewise focuses on Mendonsa's arm pinning her head and neck against his body. The woman, Greta Friedman, recalled: "I couldn't speak. I mean somebody much bigger than you and much stronger, where you've

FIGURE 2.4 An alternate view of the famous V-J Day kiss
Source: Victor Jorgensen, "New York Celebrating the Surrender of Japan: They Threw Anything and Kissed Anybody in Times Square," August 1945, General Photographic File of the Department of the Navy, 1943–1958, RG 80, NACP.

lost control of yourself, I'm not sure that makes you happy." In another interview she maintained: "It wasn't my choice to be kissed. The guy just came over and grabbed!"

Over two million crowded into Times Square and another 500,000 marched to Coney Island, with police making no effort to stop the groups of sailors and soldiers. Men strung up effigies of Hirohito and Hitler and crashed the "champagne parties" in Broadway's bars and dance halls. *PM's* man called it "the wildest, loudest, gayest, drunkest,

kissingest hell-for-leather celebration the big town has ever seen."
Police stood by as "showers of confetti and streamers fell in abun-
dance," watching the "service men exact[ing] kisses from strolling
girls as tribute for their part in the victory." Indeed, "kissing became
a popular and public pastime" with sailors taking firm hold of nearby
women. One woman, seized by a kissing soldier, yelled, "I'm Married!
I'm Married!" The "gob" replied, "Well tell your husband this is with
the compliments of the Third Division." One nurse who "wanted to
be part of the celebration" soon found herself "retreat[ing] into the
next opening of the subway" because of "amorous sailor[s]." Reporters later witnessed GIs and sailors tearing the clothes off a woman and
fighting off a police officer trying to stop the attack. Alexander Feinberg of the *Times* reported: "One girl, her lipstick smeared, marched
down the street indignant. 'They don't ask a girl's permission—can I
kiss you?—they just grab,' she said."

Over the next two days, fire brigades struggled to put out the 275
fires started throughout the city. The hospitals overflowed as at least
four people died and nearly a thousand suffered injuries. Servicemen
looted liquor stores, brawled, and reveled in the streets. All the while,
women and other civilians hoped, as they had throughout the war, to
make it past the servicemen dominating their cities.

CHAPTER THREE

WOMEN FACE THE UNIFORM

IN A CHAOTIC WARTIME ENVIRONMENT where newcomers with extraordinary legal privileges swarmed cities, women were often left to protect themselves. Constant risk and even mortal danger lurked when military men came to town. Every trip out, every step on the street threatened to become a humiliating ordeal or a frightening trial. But, in the wake of the disorder troops often created, women also took advantage of the changes visited on cities. Wives, workers in the flourishing defense industries, enlisted members of the WAC (Women's Auxiliary Corps) and the WAVES (Women Accepted for Voluntary Emergency Service), and con women and others profiting off the vice trade—all experienced life in liberty ports as a contradictory time defined by the immense danger but sometimes also by the new possibilities posed by servicemen.

Military mobilization created new economic, sexual, and social opportunities for the women who flocked to defense plants for work and downtowns for fun. Even housewives uncovered ingenious ways to enjoy the town and take greater control over their lives. The army's WACs and the navy's WAVES discovered that, like their male counterparts, they could leverage their military privileges to carouse and avoid consequences. B-girls—short for *bad girls* or *bar girls*—and con women developed innovative ways of exploiting the ubiquitous drunk serviceman, and they contributed to a liberty port economy that fed off the government wages of the military and armament industries.

This expansion of opportunities for women does not negate the fear, harassment, and violence that so many experienced. But women's lives at the time were defined as much by their own negotiations, responses, and tactics as by the oppressions they endured. The history of American women during World War II is filled with narratives about liberation in the defense factory, bittersweet goodbyes, and USO dances. Other stories depict how women became targets of the government's obsession with venereal disease. Those histories are not wrong. They miss, however, what the war worker did with her money, how women worked to find romance in a period of unchecked rape, and how wives managed marriages strained more by time and jealousy than distance. For many women, the war was not just a story of working and waiting. It was also a story of taking part in a mixture of rebellion, accommodation, experimentation, and repression that brought them into direct contact and conflict with American and Allied servicemen.

"UNIFORM-CRAZY"

Despite a growing reputation for aggressive conduct, sailors—and, to a lesser degree, GIs—were seen as exciting and desirable. Fiction serves as a useful portal through which to understand how women might have fantasized about servicemen, but it also allowed writers to criticize the aggressive behavior and rapes in liberty ports. Novels like Pearl Schiff's best-selling and scandalous portrait of wartime Boston, *Scollay Square*, became clever ways for women to circumvent the taboo of criticizing servicemen. Schiff lived in Boston during the war, and her book gives voice to women who lived through rape and assault while also offering a compelling and detailed look into how women saw men in uniform as rugged, sexy, and powerful.

The novel focuses on Beth, a respectable woman from upper-class Beacon Hill, and Jerry, a rough, hard-drinking sailor taking furlough in Boston's cheap amusements quarter of Scollay Square. When Beth first meets Jerry, she immediately takes in his "impressive shoulders,

wide and muscular under that taut fabric of the blouse," and his towering, six-foot stature. She also notices another sailor looking marvelous in "his trim naval lieutenant's uniform": "His body was lean and
well-proportioned, his skin a healthy tan."

Other genres reinforced similar themes and images. Musical com-
edies like *Two Girls and a Sailor* (1944) depicted navy men as attractive
and charming but also as "racy, sly, and wistful." Popular films—many
adopted from stage musicals—like Victor Shertzinger's *The Fleet's In*
(1942), H. Bruce Humberstone's *Iceland* (1942), Gene Kelly's *On the
Town* (the 1944 musical was followed by the 1949 film), George Sidney's
Anchors Aweigh (1945), and Hal Walker's *Sailor Beware* (1952) featured
sailors as handsome, hopeless romantics but also as coy and possibly
lonely, longing for a girl. Other women hoped for the kind of liberty-
born romance captured by Judy Garland and Robert Walker in *The Clock*
(1945). Some likely found such romance in real life.

More often, however, troops were depicted as tough paragons of
masculinity—physically intimidating but also warm and comforting
because of this macho presence. In Schiff's *Scollay Square*, Jerry's impos-
ing stature is both threatening and reassuring. Small actions like Jerry
placing his sturdy arms around Beth's small waist to steady her against
a harsh gust of wind slowly build the sense of strength and security
Beth associates with the uniform. Schiff repeatedly describes Jerry's
tough, weathered hands wrapping around Beth's tiny hips and roughly
pulling her toward him for an embrace or a kiss. For Beth, that tight,
even forceful grip becomes "strangely comforting." Jerry's forearm
tattoo—Josephine, a nude dancing girl that he makes move with each
clench of his fist—forms a physical symbol of his virility and association with the taboo. Beth enjoys "the easy way the blasphemies rolled
off his tongue": "After all, he was a sailor." But a sailor's appeal could
also come from the rare instances of vulnerability and loneliness that
women perceived in moments of intimacy. Women could lust after the
deep, colorful eyes of servicemen that might betray their softer sides.
When Jerry softly brushes her hair, Beth stares into his brown pupils
and watches as "the flames in his eyes bobbed and curtsied at her."

After she tells him of her paraplegic soldier brother, his voice becomes "kind, gentle, full of understanding." Unlike the civilians in her life, he can understand the perils of combat and how it can destroy a man and his family. The military man, then, was not just a brawny, sexy hunk but also a reassuring and empathetic figure.

Perhaps the most unsettling recurring theme of wartime romance is the desire of women to have their military escorts take charge on these dates. For the first two months of their relationship, Beth refuses to go all the way even as Jerry increases the amount of pressure and physical force. As the sexual tension builds between them, she thinks: "Oh God. I want him. I wish he'd force me so I wouldn't have to decide." At other times Jerry kisses her "fiercely, angrily." When they have sex for the first time, Beth dreamily remembers "upon her body his hands had been strong and uncompromising, breaking down resistance." After this first instance of rough, forceful sex, she throbs "with desire for the feel of his skin and the taut muscles under it and the outline of bone under that." Another character, Emily, enjoys a similar dynamic with the sailors she picks up, playing a game of consent and power. After a night of drinking and flirting, Emily revels in the sense of control she had "to carry things just as far as she wanted and to stop them where she wanted." She could happily let "a sailor rub up against her in a doorway" with the safety of knowing that she could still say no and escape. This game was "exciting, intoxicating, dangerous fun." This longing for a strange kind of consensual force or aggressive seduction did not indicate an actual desire to be raped; instead, it may have been a strategy that women employed to overcome social and religious pressure to avoid premarital sex or casual encounters. If the man simply took charge, then she would be blameless for the subsequent moral transgression. Popular works from the era like Margaret Mitchell's *Gone with the Wind* featured these fantasies, while novels like Zelda Popkin's *The Journey Home* focused on hard-drinking troops fondling women's legs on trains or bluntly telling them: "Enough of this bourgeois romancing. Take off your clothes." These desires fall into the rape fantasy genre or, perhaps more accurately, the forced seduction fantasy that first appeared in the romance novels of the Victorian era, continued with the bodice ripper category of pulp fiction, and became even more popular in the 1970s after the publication of Nancy Friday's *My Secret Garden*.

The uniform drew women in precisely because it could mean so many different and contradictory things at the same time. For some, the man in uniform promised grand passion. He was an exotic lothario ready to sweep a woman off her feet. One of Schiff's female characters spends time fantasizing about "that intense, dark sailor lounging near the subway entrance." Another longs for a chance romance with a wholesome boy next door or "the shy blond kid" who made a clumsy but charming advance.

Many women echoed the themes of novels and films when they confessed to being "uniform-crazy" and to lusting after "the handsomest thing you ever saw in his uniform." Married women worried that they might be unfaithful if they spent too much time with a man in uniform. Print columnists readily dispensed advice to girls who had "simply been dazzled by a uniform." Civilian groups such as the War Camp Community Service (WCCS), a secular aid organization, worried about "the problem of the young girl" in the vicinity of soldiers and sailors and hoped to persuade women to be more careful around servicemen, all the while tacitly admitting that little could be done about the behavior of the draftees. With the surge of thousands of men into sleepy communities near bases, WCCS members argued, women and girls would succumb to "the lure of the khaki." Seeing uniformed men, a young woman would become "thrilled to pieces" and so excited that she could not be trusted to her own "chaperonage." The WCCS explained that the attractive, friendly woman believed "everything in uniform is a hero to her" but then cautioned that in reality "everything in uniform is not a hero" and men would be "quick to offer advances."

Despite these admonitions and potential threats, young women and girls eagerly sought out dates with troops. Appearing before a Senate subcommittee, Dr. William Healey, a children's mental health expert, emphasized that "the adolescent girl quite normally tells herself that a serviceman, for instance, is entitled to all the pleasures she can give him before he goes off to war." One seventeen-year-old girl from New York admitted that "you read and hear much about young girls walking arm in arm with sailors and soldiers" and that the public blamed the girls for "promiscuous sex relations, venereal disease and pregnancy." Another girl argued: "Many girls go out with a soldier or sailor just because of the excitement of it. But most of the girls run away if the guys try to get fresh." But several other girls disagreed that they had much control while on dates with servicemen. One teenage girl explained: "Many of the girls don't realize what they are doing because they are taken into bars and given drinks, and most of them never had any liquor before. Then they get drunk and before they know it they are doing something they would not be likely to do otherwise." A Baltimore boy suggested that the police start actually cracking down on bars that served these girls and asked: "Why don't the Army and Navy instruct sailors and soldiers to stop leading girls astray, to stop taking advantage of the silly, stupid ones who fall for their line and think it's glamorous to be a Victory girl?"

The army khaki or the navy blue sometimes reminded girls and women of husbands, brothers, or fathers, drawing them to potentially risky dates. Spending time with a uniformed man offered an opportunity to comfort one's "husband by proxy." But uniforms were also standard issue—something mass-produced and given to men mobilized by the millions, which encouraged women to see the GI as a classless, regionless totem of security and state-sanctioned romance. The serviceman's anonymity also provided women a soft escape or semideparture from the moral and religious norms of their communities. Precisely because military men were often on the move, they held the promise of short and sweet relationships or even casual sex. After such a fling, the soldier or sailor could simply disappear back into the crowds of khaki and blue.

Women sometimes banded together to "adopt" a "lonesome" sailor—an image popularized by musical and films—by sending him pictures and letters. The navy even went so far as to warn "well-meaning but misinformed . . . Juliets of unknown vintage" that most sailors were not suffering from "lonely hearts." These proclamations could not tamp down some women's fascination with uniformed men. In 1944, twenty-five hundred "Miss Manhattans" flocked to "dance and jitterbug" with "GI Joes" and "shy" sailors "on a moonlight patch" in Central Park. Papers featured front-page stories like "'Cinderella' Finds Her Bill the Sailor," in which a down-on-her-luck girl, lost in the city, found a kind, handsome sailor to marry her. By the end of the column, "she was the happiest girl in the world." Some young women, taken in by the lure of the uniform, would end up assisting their beau's misbehavior. At Fort Jackson's hospital in South Carolina, young women snuck alcohol into wards filled with recovering soldiers. Even after being warned about her troubled and irresponsible soldier boyfriend, one young nurse's aide thought: "He was a soldier. He could not be anything but a marvelous, magnificent human being."

Some women simply enjoyed the opportunity to sample men with a chance for fun and romance. Dellie Hahne, a substitute teacher, stated: "A young woman had a chance to meet hundreds of men in the course of one or two weeks, more than she would in her entire lifetime, because of the war. Life became a series of weekend dates." Going out during wartime meant heading "into bars and drinking," and romancing troops, nearly a civic duty, made this activity more acceptable for women. Some women remembered going to a nightclub to see a "striptease" or getting "mixed up . . . drinking and running around." Workers said that they "wanted to live . . . wanted to dance . . . wanted to go out." Some spent too much time "drinkin'," leading them to take NoDoz tablets or nap in the bathroom for fifteen minutes during their shift at work. At Lockheed, young female workers almost revolted when the nearby social clubs closed because of electricity shortages. The GI or sailor about to depart also proved a recurring temptation for married women, and some fantasized about getting "toujours gai" with a comforting but roguish officer.

Many war workers seized opportunities to transgress sexual boundaries and enjoy the chance to date multiple men. While this willingness may have driven troops to be more aggressive and possessive, women found ways to take advantage of the situation. One riveter remembered all the "boots" she could meet in Portland, Oregon, remarking: "Gee, there was no lack of knowing men, for goodness sakes. I was right at the source of supply—and whoopie! You'd wade in barefoot and have a great time." Another young woman, Margarita Salazar McSweyn, remembered that she had "boyfriends in the service" and wrote to "three or four different fellows" using the same letter. Because troops were often present only for short periods of leave, workers like McSweyn would "concentrate mostly on what could be done" and resist getting tied down to one man. Servicemen often attempted to marry girlfriends or get them to promise to marry when they returned. Yet McSweyn and other women could ignore these demands, rebuffing constant pleadings from her service boyfriend: "We would see each other and he would pressure me to get married. Then I wouldn't see him and I'd see other fellows, and he'd see other girls and he'd go his merry way. . . . He knew that I was going out, but he also was doing it, so why not?"

The quick turnover of troops meant that encounters could be brief. One worker said: "Most of the fellows that I knew, by 1943 were gone in three days or in a week. I mean they were just gone!" Other women, like Marilyn Renner of Iowa, worried that too many men were marrying abroad, dooming her and others to "spinsterhood and lives of loneliness." Writing to the *Sydney Daily Telegraph*, she asked that the military do all it could "to prevent marriages between United States soldiers and Australian girls." Women in coastal centers of production, however, did not suffer similar absences of available men. Jean Bartlett—who started seeing sailors and soldiers in the Bay Area at age fourteen—described how she went "through fifty or hundred" servicemen, eventually failing to "keep track of what they looked like": "They were just coming through this revolving door of my life." She claimed to be "engaged fourteen times" and later reflected: "The war absolutely ruined me. The more men I had, the more my ego was fed. I had no attachments at all."

The war also meant that women would get a chance to meet men from outside their neighborhoods and social circles and even indulge in the exotic. Allied soldiers could be particularly tempting. Women quickly found sport in trying to distinguish one uniform from another. "In the metropolitan war centers like New York, San Francisco, New Orleans, Toronto, Montreal, the gamut of uniforms is bewildering," explained one married woman. "On their streets of a fine Saturday afternoon one can see the uniforms of Britain, the United States, Canada, Australia, New Zealand, South Africa, the Free French Navy, airmen of the Royal Norwegian Air Force and the Royal Netherlands Air Force, Dutch Marines from Java, six-foot Polish officers with orange tabs and their curious square-cut caps." Women shared sodas with, dated, and married Australian merchant marines, with the *Los Angeles Times* declaring: "Australian lads who lost their lovely lasses to Yankee doughboys find at least a measure of consolation—one of their number has claimed a pretty American girl as his bride." Some women expressed a particular preference for Scottish troops: "When you get into the tartans and kilts of the Scottish regiments the thing becomes a whirl, although you'd give your eyeteeth to have your beau show up in kilts and a balmoral, so outrageously handsome would it make him look." Observers in marriage license bureaus recalled the "occasional flash of red" that "indicates a French seaman, his pompommed, cap-topped presence proof that a strange country and a strange language are no bars to romance."

Other women used the USO to pursue their own desires. Most USO hostesses were in their late teens and early twenties, unmarried, and quite often looking to meet men. The military fingerprinted each hostess and demanded personal references. Romance was officially discouraged, but women routinely went out with soldiers and married them. One hostess explained: "I'm supposed to be doing this for patriotism, but frankly I've never had so much fun in my life." "Center girls"—essentially the servicemen's center's equivalent of USO hostesses—flocked to the clubs so that they could chat, dance, and flirt with men from all the Allied forces. One center girl, Lois Brown, scoffed at "the idea that girls go to the center for purely patriotic reasons." Instead, the center girl did it to have "a good time": "She loves to dance and it's fun following the lead of a boy from Brooklyn who does the Lindy Hop, a coast guardsman from Michigan who waltzes, or a sailor in the Queen's navy who does some strange gyration akin to the Lambeth Walk."

Women sometimes mimicked the tactic of "treating" that turn-of-the-century working girls used to buy a good time. Here, a girl or young woman hoping to see a film, head to an amusement park, go dancing, or get a drink implied the promise of romance or sexual favors in exchange for the man footing the bill. Rather than rotting away at home, the women in Schiff's *Scollay Square* reason that they ought to enjoy the pleasures of the city. One character figures: "If she wanted to see a movie she got a feller to take her. So if he slipped a hand under her sweater to make it worth while, what the hell? At least she was out of the house. At least she was having fun."

Servicemen's wives also found fun and temptation, defying both established social norms and encroaching boredom. They remembered being "blighted [by] evenings with bores" and "crazy to get out and around with a man." War wives argued that they now existed in a social netherworld. "We women are neither wives nor widows and are therefore a kind of social nothings," wrote an army wife. "We are the abandoned wives and the world expects us to stop living and lie quietly on the shelf until our men come home and dust us off." She went on to explain that "the neighbors sit behind their curtains with field glasses to see who goes in and out of the home." Many women agreed that remaining cooped up would be impossible. Though married women would likely face the whispered rumors and disapproving glances of neighbors, many still went out. "Don't decide against going out with other men because of neighborly gossip. Gossip will come no matter what you do," a guide advised. Middle-class wives in big cities also found value in a world without husbands. Full control of the pocketbook and a need to be self-reliant could be fulfilling. "Majordomos without portfolio, they pay the bills, pay the insurance, pay the taxes," wrote Nancy MacLennan. "They mix the cocktails for a party, draw the Extra Man at dinner. Alone, they name the baby." These women found work, new circles of friends, and education at lectures, exhibits, and plays. MacLennan concluded: "The lonely wife admits she is becoming more 'capable,' more 'resourceful.'"

Providing entertainment for troops constituted a state-sanctioned way for young women and wives to interact with men who were not their husbands. Guides advised wives to volunteer at the local USO, though unmarried women were still imagined to be more suited for the role. Married women also joined hobby clubs and recreation committees organizing troop entertainment. These committees charged wives with "trying to get the unattached girls attached to the timid boys" while also giving them opportunities to dance themselves. To mitigate the idea that dancing with other men constituted a dangerous temptation, guides preached confidence and a feeling of security in one's marriage. Dancing with troops was additionally thought of as a useful preventive measure. If wives could dance and entertain men in a well-ordered and supervised USO event, they would avoid more enticing situations and proposals. Boston's hostesses found that conga lines and jitterbugging with scores of marines and sailors were regarded as perfectly acceptable provided they were overseen by well-established neighborhood organizations.

When military men hit port, they brought fun, dancing, dating, even romance and sex. But, as many women quickly discovered, they would also bring challenges, anxieties, and dangers.

"SO YOUR HUSBAND'S GONE TO WAR!"

Wives' attempts to maintain their marriages offer an instructive view of how liberty ports both constrained and expanded women's social lives. Although only 8 percent of women were actually married to servicemen, these war wives exercised an outsized influence on the politics of infidelity and debates about women's roles on the home front in general.

Ethel Gorham—the author of *So Your Husband's Gone to War!* (1942), one
of the most influential guides for war wives—told their story. She became a kind of Emily Post for the middle-class war wife, dispensing advice on appearance, letter writing, and travel while also issuing cheer-
fully worded warnings about the dangers posed by wartime city streets.
Her guidebook—full of interviews and field observations—offers a rare
look into the predicaments of military wives.

Wives tried to use liberty and furlough visits—the "Week-End
Marriage"—to maintain the health of their partnerships and the loyalty of their husbands. Because women never knew how many of
these visits they might get, they placed immense importance on making them perfect occasions. Gorham counseled her readers that the
short furlough presented "a kind of microcosm of your marriage,"
an opportunity "to gather up all the loose ends of your life and try
to knit them together without dangerous stitches that may one day
run." Though wives saw this as much more than a simple opportunity
to have sex, friends and acquaintances often reduced these visits to
nothing more. Gorham asked whether other wives had been "embarrassed by people who drool and leer when they hear you're to see your
husband?" Too often, wives were "made to feel like the forthcoming
participant in a Polish wedding ceremony where all the family and
friends remain close by to cheer the bride right into her marriage
bed." The constant gossip and planning, however, were reminders that
troops never fully left.

For leave and furloughs, war wives sought to emphasize their
beauty. Many seemed to understand that their husbands would roman-
ticize their appearance while in the barracks, and this heightened the
pressure to wow them on furlough. As men endured the petty annoyances and dangers of military life, many coped by describing what
they called the beautiful girls they left behind. After weeks obsessing
over a wife's beauty, the husband's mental image "suffered no chapped
skin or excess weight or frowsy hair." Soldiers failed to account for the
hardships of the home front and would not "excuse a sloppy figure or
broken nails or a scalp in search of stimulation." "What a glamorous

creature you would be," Gorham concluded, "if you only looked half as pretty as the man at the front remembers you."

Guides advised that a poor appearance or a decline in one's beauty regimen could drastically increase the potential of infidelity. Wives were warned that they would need to look enchanting if they hoped to pass the "once-over." Staying fit required vigilance as his wife's figure would be the first thing a husband noticed. "Fat is the most obvious disfigurement," noted Gorham. The women's columnist Antoinette Donnelly offered similar advice. She warned that, since their husbands had left, wives had begun to gain weight, failed to maintain their nails, and grown lazy. She counseled war wives: "If you neglect your appearance, there will come a time you may regret it. . . . A good motto to keep before you is: 'When he comes home, he's going to find a more attractive woman. So help me!'" Pressure mounted when a wife saw that her husband was now slimmer, fit, and dashing in his uniform. Gorham advised that, if a woman did not "want to be taken for the dowdy elder sister, or even—heaven forbid—for [her husband's] young-looking mother," she would need "a regime to compensate for his." Women ought to wear something familiar rather than chic—something their husbands could easily remember from before the war. A lasting, beautiful image was the main bulwark against a husband falling prey to temptations in port. The burden of keeping husbands happy and faithful fell on the wives, but they also needed to avoid coming across as jealous.

Even with a successful weekend marriage, wives (and girlfriends) sometimes experienced recurring fears, loneliness, and anxiety. From the moment the draft notice arrived, women reported a simultaneous dread and desire to ignore the coming strains on their marriages. Thinking about the inevitable departure of their husbands was like "the contemplation of death," according to Gorham.

Beyond the threat of losing their husbands to grievous wounds, capture, or death, wives reported an encroaching loneliness and sense of abandonment. The *New York Times* called them "the loneliest women in America." They feared a daunting "lonely and endless" daily routine.

The *Chicago Daily Tribune* reported: "Wives argue they're lonely, and no doubt many of them are, lonelier than they ever were." Yet women's writers warned them to avoid boredom and even blamed them for their feelings of loneliness. "What is loneliness, continued loneliness?" asked the pseudonymous Doris Blake. "It's a self-centeredness, inertia, the will to victimize oneself." Wives ought to pursue "work, study, and personal advancement." "They may not cure loneliness, but they remove the sharp edges of it." Besides, some wives argued, husbands moving into the service had to take on "the strain of a new environment," a lack of privacy, and "the tastelessness of official food, official clothing, official lock step." "If you're going to feel sorry for anyone," Gorham concluded, "you ought to feel more sorry for your husband than you do for yourself."

Loneliness created temptations, as did time away. Both husbands and wives confronting the intransigent reality of war often came to see it as a time of hiatus. For sweethearts, infidelity, and fears of infidelity, flourished. Troops feared the Dear John letters and the male civilians who might be trying to take their place at home, and sometimes they violently deterred or punished unfaithful conduct. At the same time, they obsessed over the other women they imagined would be waiting for them when they hit town.

Indeed, even as military husbands fantasized about carousing in port they issued warnings to their spouses. An army chaplain declared: "Any service man's wife who is playing around here with another man is about the lowest thing I know. And about the next lowest thing I know is that man who plays around with her." In Brooklyn, a sailor with the merchant marine—"prompted by jealousy"—fatally stabbed his wife, sister-in-law, and others after the wife failed to answer his questions about her faithfulness. Civilian men likewise forcefully and sometimes violently opposed affairs. One husband viciously stabbed his wife after she confessed her love for a soldier, whom he then knifed. Women also condemned unfaithful wives. The opera singer Grace Moore recommended that each adulterous woman "should have her head shaved forthwith as a mark of shame and disgrace." She went on to blame such women for "driving their men into the arms of women of Europe."

Government officials also raised the specter of wives who, in their infidelity, proved themselves disloyal to both their husbands and the war effort. Agents of the state used social pressure but also judicial and legislative power to punish women suspected of adultery. Presiding over a petty officer's divorce case, the circuit court judge Julius H. Miner declared that unfaithful wives sinned against both their husbands and the military, damaging both morality and morale: "In time of war it is wicked and ignoble that the wife of a man in military service should invite illicit association of another in our fighting forces. She thereby undermines the morale of her husband and corrupts the morals of her paramour." Referring to them as "nonessential wives," the judge railed against those women who "demoralize the home front and impede the prosecution of the war": "National welfare demands their divorcement." Beyond granting more divorces, other officials tried to use shame and even prosecution to prevent "the disillusionment of the returning soldier" who found "his wife living with another man." One state's attorney—denouncing the "dark side of the civilian picture" and "the cheater wives" who had yielded to "moral weakness and cupidity"—promised that he would criminally prosecute adulterous wives to deter "these unsavory situations." "Flagrantly fraudulent wives" would also face "public disapproval and punishment . . . through the initiative of the State." Representative Dewey Short (R-MO) went on to declare that immoral women were "marrying soldiers" and that "harlots [are] free to run around while drawing [dependency benefits] from a boy they hardly know." Rumors swirled that these wives might be taking advantage of the tax exemptions granted to military spouses. A congressional committee demanded that the army investigate suspected "wayward wives" and determine their faithfulness. The army opposed the demand as the measure might exacerbate an epidemic of soldiers questioning their wives' fidelity.

Wives experienced a mix of dread, pressure, and resignation when contemplating their husbands' potential infidelities. Here, World War I was a cautionary example, the divorce rate having ticked up then. During World War II, the divorce rate nearly doubled. Women—especially brides who met their grooms when they were on furlough—expressed anxiety over what their husbands might be up to outside camp or the city dockyard. They were told: "You'd be a foolish wife to ask your husband what he does with those leaves of his when he can't get home." One wife recalled that, even when her husband went on leave, he was liable to "run around with other soldiers who are free." A twenty-one-year-old bride affirmed: "If a marriage weathers this, it's fool-proof." Another young furlough bride mused: "If my husband comes back even remembering me . . . I suppose our marriage has a chance. But when I think of those Southern lulubelles down in Georgia where he's stationed my blood runs cold." Gorham noted: "The young wife down in Georgia is probably shivering over what the Yankee girl is going to do to her darling." Despite this obvious double standard, guides asserted that women ought to excuse the misbehavior of soldiers. Wives also despaired when civilian husbands, now raking in generous wages in defense plants, spent "their time in beer joints drinking and carousing with the women they have met on their jobs." These women contemplated tolerating husbands who went "out with a cutie" and spent "$25 or $30 on showing her a good time."

Beyond the difficulties of maintaining a marriage and dealing with real and imagined infidelity, women also confronted new men in their lives. Here, wartime expectations about female propriety and duties became more byzantine and even contradictory. While troops and the broader public—especially newspapers—condemned wayward wives, wives were also expected to entertain servicemen and even go out with male acquaintances. This mandate provided wives opportunities to explore the city nightlife but also created new dangers when men attempted to take advantage of them.

Married women prepared themselves to fend off threats from both troops and civilian men, who saw the "lonely wife" as a vulnerable target. "Don't think there won't be any men," warned Gorham. "You can be cross-eyed or bowlegged or hide your light under a bushel at night—but you'll find a cross-eyed man to follow you, a bowlegged one to phone you, a blind one who will petition you in Braille. Especially if you're 'alone.'" Civilian men seemed to target married women more than soldiers and sailors did as they were less likely to frequent the entertainment zones favored by enlisted men. Civilian men also had more access to married women as their neighbors, social acquaintances, and, increasingly, coworkers. The lonely wife became a temptation for these men. She was simultaneously available and unavailable, in need and forbidden: She gave the vain wandering male a chance to act like a gallant gentleman, comforting a supposedly melancholy woman in need of masculine support.

Married women attempted to identify men who might be wolfish, but they could easily fail to guess which former friends, new acquaintances, or servicemen would ultimately become aggressive or lascivious. There were men seeking to use women, one woman lamented: "And the most unexpected ones they turn out to be too. Why is it that all the towers of virtue, the monuments of sobriety, the ideal husbands and fathers turn out to be the garter-snappers, the stray pinchers, the wolves?" Husbands' friends could be the most flagrant offenders. Wives sometimes despised the burden placed on them to placate coercive men, but most agreed that little could be done to change this double standard. They were usually left with little more than intuition.

Despite instances of fun and independence, women understood that they needed to be vigilant about the potential dangers posed by both civilian men and servicemen. Yet many still blamed themselves if their date became amorous or forceful. Gorham cautioned fellow wives that "it takes two to make a bargain" and that they should not "blame everything on the man if a nice casual date goes moaning low" and "then whine and weep because men are beasts." Both experienced couples and furlough brides were counseled not to "try it with temptations" or let their loneliness lead them to a lapse in faithfulness. Guides like *So Your Husband's Gone to War!* and social pressure demanded that a wife place fidelity and loyalty above these temptations, even if her husband could not be asked to do the same. If wives were not faithful, it would be "the woman who takes it on the chin," meaning that they would face social condemnation and economic consequences. Other wives ruefully noted that the press and society seemed eager to criticize "army wives abandoning children, running around nights, and in general conducting themselves as the fuddy-duddies say they shouldn't." Married women needed to be diligent, careful, and shrewd when maintaining their marriages and dealing with new men. Gorham offered these wives a final, key aphorism: "But now it's other times, other customs, and the wolf only takes the hindmost."

Women's columnists also advised unmarried young women to learn their "escort's marital status." Readers were warned that married men would pose as single and that their easiest prey was "the inexperienced young girl who may innocently enough meet this shatterer of her dreams." Married men on the move would be strongly tempted "to deny their marital ties, or ignore the subject entirely, when meeting young women." Fears of infidelity also populated women's fiction. Books like *Sailor's Star* (1944) centered on navy wives rushing to New York, only to find their sailor husband entranced by a new woman. Ultimately, women expected poor behavior from their husbands, despite the double standard. "Let your blood run cold," wrote Gorham. "But don't imagine he remains pure as the driven snow to match your own temperature. Men aren't made that way, but they certainly expect women to be."

"ASSAULT WITH INTENT TO PLEASE"

Aside from the threats of new men in their lives, women confronted new challenges in booming wartime metropolises. Finding adequate living quarters, managing lascivious male coworkers, and safely traveling through the city constituted the daily privations of life in liberty ports.

Taking a defense job, despite its wages and promise of greater independence, often required women to relocate closer to troop bases, transports, and fun zones. Yet the sheer number of troops in the city during weekends and furlough periods drastically reduced the number of available short-term rooms, while the surging defense worker population claimed most long-term rentals. Housing thus became scarce and expensive in many metropolitan areas, pushing women into crumbling, dingy, or unfinished apartments in rowdy, unsafe neighborhoods. Workers sometimes resorted to moving from hotel to hotel: "You could only stay in a hotel for X amount of days and you had to move. This was a wartime thing." Even if workers could find housing through their company, its quality was not guaranteed. Marie Baker, a worker who assembled tail sections for North American Aviation, discovered that her brand new $46.50 a month apartment in Redondo Beach lacked both lights and a stove, leaving her to heat soup on an electric percolator or buy hamburgers at the pier.

Yet, compared to other housing arrangements, no lighting and a missing stove were little to complain about. Early in 1942, the Women's Bureau of the Department of Labor called on local organizations and state governments to "improve living conditions for women workers snared in the maelstrom of migrating peoples surging into defense industries." In boomtowns and West Coast industrial centers, women faced "housing and general living conditions" that were "appallingly below desirable standards," with five to six women sharing one room or two to three sharing a bed. By 1944, little had changed. According to the *Women's Bureau Special Bulletin*, "the lack of adequate housing, recreation, transportation and child care facilities" was endemic to industrial areas, causing "discontent, absenteeism, turn-over, and other production saboteurs." Even though women were earning "good money," landlords stated that they disliked female tenants, in part because they "entertain more, especially men friends."

Even military wives struggled with housing since, as one recalled, "property owners do not like to rent to military personnel." Upscale hotels, too, began refusing to serve enlisted men, leaving one husband to apologize for taking his wife to a boardinghouse "where all the sailors are staying." "If only I had known what I was going to be up against," his wife said, "it would have made things easier. You plan so for such a week end; you buy a new hat, new perfume, new dress. And when you see the kind of place you're dumped in you feel that much worse than if you had known." Women were also advised to look out for potential threats beyond just enlisted men: "There's the lecherous clerk who would pinch your behind if he could reach over the counter. There's the seedy house detective who almost does." Little could be done to avoid these ramshackle hotels and rundown boardinghouses. Gorham suggested to "come prepared for the worst accommodations and do what you can to forget them." Many decent and even shabby hotels were claimed early because of the huge numbers of servicemen passing through ports. Trains, too, were "predominately stag." In New York, hotel associations put out pleas for couples to avoid the rush for rooms on Saturday or plan in advance. Travelers Aid even suggested that couples who owned homes and apartments in New York might take in servicemen and their wives on the weekends.

Work could also be difficult and demanding, leaving some women with little time or energy for anything other than the job. Part of the daily drudgery included male coworkers harassing or propositioning them. Female war workers dealt with men asking whether they were married, with one male coworker replying: "All the good looking girls around here are." Even when told that they were married and, no, their husbands were not in the army, men responded: "Well, let me know if he goes. . . . I'll see you don't get lonesome." Other women struggled against stereotypes that defense workers were "frivolous" or "gum popping, silly, flowers in our hair" or the type who went "roaming the streets looking for soldiers." "It's not true," said one factory laborer. "By the time you got out of work, you were so damned tired you didn't want to do anything. In my case, the first thing I wanted was a bath." Beauty columns pressuring exhausted war workers to "superimpose on her day's labor hours of work trying to make herself into a glamour girl" likely only added to the weariness they felt after a long shift.

Adding to the burdens of housing and work, simply traveling through or between liberty ports could become a dangerous proposition. The immense numbers of troops moving through cities made transportation a taxing and sometimes hazardous challenge. Gorham described trains as "crowded, noisy, often held up," and as spaces where "the war is brought home" by "so many men in uniform, going, coming, on the move." Sailors and soldiers took up whole sections, crowded into sleeper cars, and filled the smoky aisles making passes as women tried to squeeze by. Given the difficulties of travel, the marriage advice columnist Mary Day Winn recommended that women should not even attempt to follow their husbands as they moved about the country.

By 1942, the War Department recognized that poor discipline on both civilian trains and troop transports required a bolstered Military Police presence. One report acknowledged that more MPs "have been placed on public carriers to solve the many problems created by hundreds of thousands of men in the armed services traveling under orders or on furlough." Nevertheless, women still faced misbehavior and disorder while traveling—scenes that Bill Mauldin's servicemen cartoons captured. Chief of Staff George C. Marshall acknowledged "soldier drinking on trains" as a recurring issue, complaining in November 1942 to the army's head of policing that he was "still receiving reports of drunken soldiers on trains." Marshall even read and cited complaints from a woman and her daughter who had been traveling on a train "filled with drunken soldiers who molested her to the extent that she and another lady were forced to ask civilians to sit with them as protection from the soldiers." He went on to note tersely: "Military Police were on the train but apparently did nothing." The Office of War Information went on to produce posters warning troops not to misbehave in front of civilians.

Women's safety, too, was imperiled on city streets. War workers reported being attacked and assaulted, especially late at night. Chicago's Phyllis Blair, for example, a "slight and attractive war worker," died after being hit over the head with a brick and assaulted by an

FIGURE 3.1 "Only a Benny would say . . . I always relax when I travel"
Source: Created and produced between March 9, 1943, and September 15, 1945, Office for Emergency Management, Office of War Information, Domestic Operations Branch, Bureau of Special Services, Series: World War II Posters, 1942–1945, RG 44 (Records of the Office of Government Reports, 1932–1947), NACP.

unknown man. Her attacker, like many others, had followed her when she left her factory job after midnight. Her fellow workers told police that Blair had complained about being trailed on other nights. Other young workers reported similar instances of men striking them and then attempting "to molest" them. Soldiers often managed to commit multiple attacks without repercussions. Private Edward Green was arrested five or six times in Atlanta before being transferred to New York for guard duty. There, he mugged and raped multiple women in Gramercy Park and Brooklyn late at night before slashing a woman's sailor escort with his bayonet and assaulting her in Madison Square Park at 3:00 a.m. Many women experienced the kind of startling, seemingly random episodes of violence visited on Alberta Burgett of Boston. As she was leaving the Old Howard Theatre in the servicemen-dominated Scollay Square, an army sergeant "grabbed her, pushed her into an alley, and choked and beat her when she resisted him." In Los Angeles, women described similar instances of men stalking them while they walked Hollywood Boulevard or having to exit streetcars before men attempted to rape them. Some women, like Fanny Christina Hill, avoided "gallivanting" because of the dangers that came with it: "I knew how to get around, and I knew how to stay out of danger and not take too many chances." Another woman testified that her newfound experience as a welder had given her the strength to fend off an attempted rape.

Brazen assaults like these took place at an alarming rate throughout the war and attracted the attention of the First Lady. After the rape and strangling of Jessie Strieff—a young Washington, DC, worker—Eleanor Roosevelt urged other young women in cities to "go home early, or with a reliable escort," and to "accept no favors from strangers or casual acquaintances." She also cautioned against going out with men "until assured of their good character" and suggested that, "if a girl drinks at all, it should be done with well-known friends." The House District Committee subsequently asked the military to assist in policing the capital under the authority of *posse comitatus*. The committee's chairman argued: "It seems logical that the military should have some part in relieving [the] situation." Similarly, by 1945, Chicago's crime commission declared a "war on rapists" in response to an explosion in the number of rape cases caused by the "lowering of moral standards because of war." Attacks like these and a general fear of nighttime assaults may have prompted labor leaders like Elizabeth Gurley Flynn to demand "special transportation for night shifts." Early on, the National Council for Women demanded "women patrol officers" who would "protect girls in defense centers." Yet many continued to live with the omnipresent fear of being attacked without warning while going about the most mundane activities or walking home. Even worse was the sense that a rapist's uniform would save him from prosecution or punishment.

Women who were attacked often never found justice or recompense. The papers became especially infatuated with cases involving young, white, middle-class victims, which stood a somewhat better chance of receiving a full investigation. Women of color, however, saw that a white assailant's uniform and race granted extraordinary cover for his actions. In Detroit, the furloughed coast guardsman Mike Stephanchenko attacked and raped a twenty-three-year-old black mother. He grabbed her from behind and dragged her into a field obscured by tall weeds. "See these hands," he told her. "I'm the maniac of the neighborhood and I'll kill you." After he raped her twice, she managed to escape to a friend's home. Despite the fact that he lived near the scene and confessed to having drunk over eighteen beers that night, not to mention extensive physical evidence, he was found not guilty by an all-white jury. The judge subsequently admonished the jury: "You've made a serious mistake." The wife and her husband wept in the courtroom.

Even in Pearl Schiff's wartime romance *Scollay Square*, the female characters initially enchanted by handsome, virile sailors eventually learned the dangers that came with them. Jerry—Beth's sailor love interest—cannot break out of the endless cycle of drinking, fighting, and sex. When Beth attempts to end the relationship, the tight grip she once associated with a reassuring strength becomes a threat. Jerry refuses to break off the relationship, picks her up, and flings her onto a bed. Beth protests, "This is rape," but Jerry merely agrees, "Sure. Assault with intent to please." Schiff concludes the scene: "When he let himself out of the apartment, she was lying face down on the bed crying silently into the pillow." The other female protagonist, Emily, is likewise assaulted by a bluejacket: "He hit me. . . . He got me up to a room and he took off his clothes and he hit me. He kept hitting me with his fists. He *enjoyed* hitting me." Schiff, a Bostonian in her twenties during the war, captured what many women were never able or allowed to express.

"LISTEN LITTLE LADY"

Some of this violence occurred because of the revulsion against feminine and civilian life tacitly condoned, even encouraged, during military training. Because command routinely failed to check crimes that ranged from drunkenness to harassment to rape, men understood that violent carousing was essentially sanctioned. Given the manpower crisis, flagrantly inadequate police numbers and training, and the legal privileges granted to men in uniform, women were mostly left to fend for themselves. Of course, understanding the endemic harassment, assault, and rape that occurred on the home front requires more specific explanations.

Troop aggression may have partly been a response to newly independent and financially self-sufficient women, particularly war workers. Women working relatively lucrative jobs in defense plants could take home more income than the average GI or bluejacket, upending traditional power relationships. One riveter, Helen Studer, stated: "People didn't know what to do with their money when they were making so much." Another claimed: "[I have] six or eight checks laying in my dresser drawer" uncashed. Betty Jeanne Boggs, also a defense plant worker, agreed. She said: "I would buy everything: my shoes, lingerie. The more I worked, the more clothes I bought. I could go out and blow my whole pay in one day if I wanted to." Another remembered: "Everybody was talking about the overtime and how much more money it was. And it was exciting." Because wartime rationing put limits on consumer goods, women, like servicemen, often directed their disposable income toward plentifully available entertainment and nightlife. Gorham told working wives: "The whole city is yours, depending on how much money you both saved for the excursion, and you can do pretty much as you always have when you've gone big-city gallivanting. You'll find you get somewhat more for your money in amusement than you did before." The *Chicago Defender*, however, warned black workers "not to indulge in reckless spending." Seeing women reaping greater rewards because they chose to upset social norms may have disturbed servicemen, who were supposed to be symbols of strength and power. Confronted with the question of how a military man could be the epitome of strength when he did not earn as much as the women next to him at the bar, some may have lashed out at these female threats to their machismo. Psychologists, doctors, and military officials argued that the new economic and social opportunities afforded to women drove a postwar epidemic of "wife-beating." These officials "placed a good share of the blame on the wives" and called on them to be "very tolerant and understanding" of this domestic abuse.

Women were also compelled by patriotism to tolerate the abuses of servicemen. Over and over, single women were reminded of their key role in boosting and maintaining servicemen's morale. "Suddenly, single women were of tremendous importance," said one young worker. "It was hammered at us through the newspapers and magazines and on the radio. We were needed at USO, to dance with the soldiers." Propaganda especially drove women to see dancing with, dating, and romancing soldiers and sailors as a wartime duty, one that young women later acknowledged had exercised "a tremendous influence" on their lives. "Listen little lady, it's the order of the day / Issued by the highest of authority / Fellows in the service simply can't be turned away / You know that defense must get priority," instructed one characteristic song popularized by Joan Merrill. "Patriotically inclined" women were advised to get out their "lipstick and powder" before dancing with a sailor or soldier. "You can't say no if he wants to dance," Merrill explained. "If he's gonna fight he's got a right to romance." On the radio, in magazine shorts, and in films, women recalled a recurring narrative: "The central theme was the girl meets the soldier, and after a weekend of acquaintanceship they get married and overcome all difficulties." Women who did not fulfill this kind of prescribed political obligation were seen by peers as failing to live up to the duties of a citizen in wartime.

Even as military commanders privately exchanged escalating worries about the lack of discipline among their men while on leave and fielded protest from female citizens, they also moved to scapegoat women as a threat to their men and the entire war effort. For government officials, women's sexuality was a disturbing force that posed a danger to the health of the armed forces. It could be contained only by a vigorous legal and policing regimen aimed at destroying vice and venereal disease. By the end of the war, accusations of prostitution and promiscuity began to lose real meaning. A US Public Health Service physician even developed the portmanteau *patriotute* to describe a woman who was both patriot and prostitute. But in deeming most women a health threat—in a time when men in uniform were a far more obvious and recurring danger—and hopelessly licentious, authorities ended up targeting the victims of sexual violence and blaming them for it when it occurred. Officials also found it far too easy to dismiss a woman's concerns and protests as sob stories or the excuses of promiscuous girls. One official equated prostitution and venereal disease with treason, pushing the army-navy vice boards to attack female bodies as a source of infection. At the same time, the military's campaign for men to engage in safe sex became a tacit incitement for men to prove themselves sexually as it essentially made condoms standard issue.

"WOLVES IN FRIEND'S CLOTHING"

Across the country, women prepared for the wide range of threats that came with mass mobilization. The majority of soldiers and sailors did not perpetrate outright assaults, but many engaged in other kinds of coercive, wolfish behavior. They catcalled, leered, followed women down the street, or became aggressive when a date did not become something more. A typical instance of harassment took place in Norfolk, where a soldier repeatedly made advances toward a woman watching a film at the cinema. The woman was not physically harmed, but neither was the soldier arrested for his behavior. Gorham warned women to guard themselves from these "wolves in friend's clothing." She also recognized that men in uniform would become more aggressive on streets, "where women are appraised and approached via the once-over and yoo-hoo techniques." "When American men get into a masculine groove they sharpen their eyes and give the girls the once-over as they go by," she wrote. *Good Housekeeping* published guides for women meant to help them navigate a city populated by "stag parties": "Don't overdress. . . . [W]ear simple clothes. . . . If you want to avoid whistles and caustic comments on your excursion . . . thread your way along quietly." "Stags are jovial as a rule," the author warned. "Cast a couple of warm glances in their direction and, presto, they're ready to move in on the party—ribald jokes, liquor, and all." Above all else, women should "be inconspicuous and dignified" in order to avoid unwanted attention.

Given the lack of policing and the freedom accorded to men in the service when off base, some women sought out a decent military man to protect her. This need to find a reliable escort may also have pushed women to see multiple men in case one was unavailable, sometimes resulting in jealous men becoming violent. The First Lady, as previously mentioned, suggested the necessity of a reliable escort but offered few guidelines as to how to obtain one. A Doris Blake column early in 1941 acknowledged that women would soon lack a "steady escort" and that the problem of choosing new escorts "really boils down to one of intuition." Women often lacked a totally reliable soldier to choose, forcing many to pick between going it alone or taking their chances with a somewhat rough GI who could ward off less savory interlopers.

The Catholic priest and writer Daniel A. Lord explained the escort's role in starkly military terms: "That word is used to designate the cruisers that protect a line of merchantmen during a war. The job of an escort is to protect that which is being escorted." "What," he asked, "would you think of an escort cruiser that suddenly started to try to sink the ship it was sent to protect?" Wartime made sorting out the protector from the wolf even more difficult. According to Lord, "modern young men" increasingly argued: "If she lets me get away with murder, then it's her responsibility." Men sought to "find out as soon as possible how much a girl" might let them "get away with." Other young men suggested: "If a girl says, 'No,' pretend that she has said 'Yes.'" They maintained that, if an escort "paid for the girl's evening," she ought to pay him back with "familiarities." Moving unaccompanied through the city was likely more dangerous than taking a chance on a military man as an escort. Still, intuition went only so far when assessing a man's character. And, with the movement of millions of troops throughout major cities, women found more men who believed that "chivalry is a fine thing in poetry, but has no place in a taxicab."

Women in liberty ports, however, did not passively accept aggressive conduct or attempted assaults. Imogene Stevens, an army major's wife, gained a minor celebrity after shooting and killing a sailor "in an 'aura of sex recrimination, beer, and window smashing reprisals.'" Late in the night, the "beautiful and socially prominent" Mrs. Stevens heard some noise and noticed the absence of her neighbors. She made her way next door and confronted two sailor brothers enjoying their liberty. After demanding to know why the two intoxicated servicemen were there, an argument ensued, and the brothers attacked Stevens, ripping her clothing, and leaving her with bruises and scratches on her throat. Stevens pulled out her pistol and fired on one of the sailors three times as the other fled. Although Stevens was initially put on trial for manslaughter, the prosecutor eventually agreed that the evidence supported her claim of self-defense.

As the war went on, many women decided that their best chance at self-defense was arming themselves. At Terminal Island in Los Angeles, "prompt, unpleasant surprise overtook a 21-year-old Navy coxswain who tried to bite the hand that fed him a Christmas dinner—and found it held a gun." Edna Olson, a fifty-four-year-old mother of a sailor, described as "diminutive" with "graying hair," invited a young bluejacket to her home. On arriving, the sailor produced a .45 service automatic and demanded the family's car and cash. Olson "marched to a closet and seized the family .38-caliber revolver" and then "won a brief battle of nerves," after which the sailor fled the showdown. After posing with the pistol for the papers, Olson declared: "Do you think I'd let that young whipper-snapper take our car when we worked so hard to get it?" Those who fought off attackers, however, risked prosecution. In San Diego, a navy wife shot and killed a sailor—not her husband—who accompanied her home after midnight. After an initial fight and struggle, she seized a rifle from the sailor and fired two bullets, mortally wounding him. At her arrest, she attempted to demonstrate her patriotism and avoid prosecution by remarking: "I have a friendly feeling for all servicemen because my husband is in the Navy." She nevertheless faced a murder charge.

Women also confronted attempts to push them into prostitution, another flourishing industry in wartime. Sarah Killingsworth, a black worker in Long Beach, recalled that during wartime she faced "so many opportunities to go wrong." While she was waiting for the bus, prostitutes would approach and tell her: "We got good jobs. You could make as much money in one day as you do in a month." Killingsworth explained: "They'd go out and date these white fellas and spend the night with 'em." Other prostitutes worked "a red-light district in San

Bernardino, where the soldiers would go." Many of them "were married, very attractive women" whose husbands acted as their "pimps." One young woman accused a couple of pressing her to join "the largest and best call house in Los Angeles" where she "would entertain no one but film executives and celebrities, earning as high as $400 a week." The recruiters promised "easy money and jewels" when luring women to work "as a call girl." The FBI became so concerned about prostitution among war workers that it directed women's counselors to investigate prostitution recruitment occurring in factories. Susan Laughlin, a counselor at Lockheed, began spying on women in the restroom after "the FBI had word of a certain woman who was recruiting for the camps, for the girls to go up and sleep with the men." "I had to catch her at it," Laughlin remembered. "And I did." Most workers, however, found ways to avoid what Killingsworth called "selling my body for a few dollars."

"SPAWNING GROUND OF EVIL"

Though the fears of military and federal officials over promiscuity and patriotutes were unrestrained and ultimately harmful to many women, the vice trade boomed on the home front. When men hit port, they left their ships and rail cars full of desire and loaded with back pay and booze. For GIs and sailors from podunk towns, the liberty port could be an extravaganza of towering buildings, boisterous clubs, and nearly endless drinking. These men and boys, however, desired sex above all else, and this desire drove the economy and geography of vice.

Men flocked to the bars and saloons. Most of these establishments at least took on the facade of a café or bar to avoid the scrutiny of the military or civilian vice squad. Other establishments became "water joints," or bars that had their liquor licenses revoked after being identified as trouble spots. Enterprising operators developed "breakfast clubs," which opened as the regular bars closed, beckoning in troops for liquor served surreptitiously. In saloons and soda shops like the Stag Café, the Victory Canteen, Ye Olde Winery Club, and Shanghai Red's, attractive B-girls waited to part servicemen from their spending cash. Men would buy the girls liquor or, more likely, soft drinks, which the girls then spiked with rotgut. In exchange, the B-girl offered a kiss, a wandering touch, and perhaps more. The drinking establishment profited, while the B-girl received a cut and a drink. Other young women—single girls, defense workers, and lonely wives—sometimes populated these cafés and clubs, hoping to meet a dashing navy man or a bold GI. Cafés and bars with B-girls also brought the desires of servicemen into direct conflict with civilian patrons. This mix of alcohol and swaggering masculinity meant competition for women could be fierce—and men did not take rejection from their female acquaintances lightly.

Military and civilian authorities quickly recognized the potential for crime and exploitation in the rough taverns and heady fleshpots of Main Street in Los Angeles, Times Square, and San Francisco's Mission Street. If these threats were not contained, they imagined, both the war effort and the safety of the home front might be jeopardized. Yet they did not focus on preventing drunken brawls, vandalism, or troops assaulting women. Instead, commanders and municipal officials identified women as the great recurring threat to the furloughed serviceman. These fears and suspicions contributed to the crackdown on prostitution and a demonization of some women as nothing more than a conduit through which to spread venereal disease.

But many women were a threat, though not in the way officials obsessed with venereal disease imagined. Even in an environment that encouraged soldiers and sailors to commit crimes and prey on vulnerable women, B-girls, con women, scam artists, and female gangs were ready to take advantage of inebriated men and their flush pocketbooks. Rather than passively submit to the coercive and violent impulses of military men, many civilian women actively exploited them as they caroused the burgeoning entertainment zones. Los Angeles became a port plagued by "murder, robbery, shootings, bunko games, drunk 'rollings,' the spread of venereal diseases among combatant servicemen granted leave . . . and general hoodlumism." Military authorities publicly decried the "feminine bar flies, thieves, degenerates, and habitual criminals" who made service personnel loaded with back pay their "natural prey."

The army's head of policing sought to ban B-girls almost immediately. "When is a bottle of pop dangerous to the Army and Navy?" asked the *Los Angeles Times*. When it was served by one of the "harpies of Main St.," apparently. Employing crackdowns, raids, and the revocation of liquor licenses, municipal and military authorities attempted to drive the B-girls from their usual haunts.

But these techniques were often ineffective. How could you tell a B-girl from any other young woman? And what should an officer do if a soldier drunkenly objected to a woman's arrest? Usually the girls just moved to a new café or water joint, directing the flow of vice traffic into areas of Los Angeles beyond South Main Street, including downtown and Hollywood. They also developed new methods. As the men poured out of their ships, B-girls beckoned to passing uniforms from "photographic studios." Luring the men into ramshackle storefronts, the girls promised to pose with them for a twenty-five-cent photo. After a few shots and perhaps a kiss, the men soon discovered that the photograph cost much more.

Other women participated in robbery schemes that directly targeted GIs and sailors. Many worked in pairs, running routines that exploited men's desire for drink and sex. One pair of young women picked up pairs of sailors as they arrived at the docks, barhopped with them, and then suggested a ride in their car. They would then knock the drunken men out and make off with hundreds of dollars of back pay. Young women also worked with older women and wives as part of a "mother-daughter" combination. The pair would invite a soldier "to a private home for chicken dinner." Once in the car, the mark received "a bump on the head and a missing wallet." Girls in the West End of Boston committed similar robberies. One British sailor reported losing $1,500 after being lured into a darkened apartment hallway by a blond and brunette he met in a café. As he stepped into the hallway, a male accomplice—a common third member of these teams—grabbed his throat while the women searched his pockets. Sailors could be stabbed to death after following a female pickup home. Teenage girls, including a thirteen-year-old who called herself "Queen Dorothy," even ran "crime clubs" that broke into department stores to steal watches and jewelry that they would then sell to sailors in Boston's Scollay Square. In Staten Island, the New York Times profiled "two blond 'glamour girl' burglars, who apparently have invaded another field of male activities in wartime." In Washington, DC, women sometimes posed as women's police bureau agents, accusing sailors of some fabricated infraction, and demanding to inspect their identification cards and wallets. Then, claiming to be taking the confiscated items back to the receiving station, they would make off with the cash. Back in Los Angeles, two blond sisters who worked in defense factories doubled as holdup girls. After making dates with sailors whom they met in cocktail parlors, they invited the men outside, where they received a beating and a liberation of their earnings. Los Angeles authorities estimated that army and navy men visiting the city lost nearly $100,000 to robberies in just one year. "It's just the same old story," remarked Shore Patrol commander Fogg. "Money is plentiful and there are enough crooked men and women after their share of it to make our job tough." Yet officers also admitted that "it is the serviceman, in many instances, who is to blame for his predicament, and victimization," having chosen to frequent the crooked establishments.

Nationwide, officials worried that the war was becoming a "spawning ground of evil" for girls and women. FBI director J. Edgar Hoover consistently used the press to warn the public of "the alarming upswing in crime among women and girls" and to publish regular annual jumps in both arrests and offenses. In just one year, the FBI recorded a greater than 50 percent surge in the number of women under twenty-one years of age arrested. Subsequent years saw similar increases in the number of arrests of young women and girls. Women's police bureau officials declared the girl gangs of Washington, DC, to be "the true counterparts of the Werewolves and the Forty Thieves." Armed with knives and razors, these girls were not the "'gun molls' of the cheap movies and magazines" but rather "truly criminal, well on the road to professional standing." They "hover at night waiting and watching for a soldier or sailor," cautioned a women's police captain. "Rolling drunks is one of their elementary accomplishments." Academics made similar claims. The sociologist Elizabeth K. Norton suggested that, though the war prompted "a new stimulus to emancipation—even including economic equality," this transformation would be "dearly bought." She advised that, in wartime, "feminine behavior that would once have been described as vicious became respectable or was at least condoned."

WACS AND WAVES

In contrast to war wives, workers, and even con women, female members of the military might experience a fundamentally different dynamic with servicemen. While military men generally viewed civilian women as prizes or objects of pursuit, WACs and WAVES could be seen as belonging to the military and, thus, not targets. Military sources are limited, but what exists suggests that male soldiers treated their female counterparts as fellow carousers. They shared a sense of belonging to their branch, one that was forged through the common experience of training as well as the uniforms that set them apart from the civilian world. Female troops even got military tattoos in hard-edged martial zones to cement their bond to the armed forces. Military authorities realized that, like their male comrades, women were drawn to military service because it brought them to exciting locales like liberty ports. When WACs and WAVES took leave in the big coastal cities and inland waypoints, they might well act like male troops: drinking, swearing, cruising through juke joints and taverns, and mocking the authority of the police.

Like male soldiers, female troops became drunk and belligerent on trains. In one example, a female first lieutenant on the train from

FIGURE 3.2 "Don't miss your great opportunity"
Source: Created and produced between March 9, 1943, and September 15, 1945, Office for Emergency Management, Office of War Information, Domestic Operations Branch, Bureau of Special Services, Series: World War II Posters, 1942–1945, RG 44 (Records of the Office of Government Reports, 1932–1947), NACP.

Nashville to New Orleans was reported for "using loud and profane language; drinking to excess; creating a disturbance." The male MP attempting to deal with the situation proceeded to treat her with the same deferential, even obsequious manner used when approaching male offenders. After repeated requests that she desist and produce identification, the lieutenant pulled rank and stated that she "did not have to obey the orders of enlisted men." Similar incidents occurred when female and male troops went out partying together. On Union Street in Memphis, several MPs confronted three WACs, a marine, a sailor, and an army captain who were drunk and disorderly. The MP's report specifically identifies the women as the most belligerent. Swearing, drunk, and with their uniforms disheveled, the assembled personnel were creating a scene that "did attract the attention of people passing by." According to the MPs, the WACs repeatedly ignored their requests and asked what right the police had to tell them to do anything. The women's male counterparts apparently attempted to get them to go back to base, but the women refused. One WAC struck out at one of the officers, while another accused the ranking MP of being a "damn shavetail"—meaning an inexperienced officer—and of having nothing but "brass" to back him up. The women continued to mock the MPs, calling them "chicken," "bitches," and "yellow." Increasingly agitated, one of the WACs swung at a Military Police sergeant and then kicked him in the groin.

These examples do not erase the well-chronicled hostility that soldiers directed toward female enlistees and the hateful rumors they spread about them. In some instances, however, the behavior of female troops mirrored that of servicemen. Getting drunk and disorderly and disrespecting MPs and fighting were not solely male domains. Indeed, servicewomen occasionally managed to invoke the privilege of the uniform either to escape punishment or to beat an unfair charge. A contingent of African American WACs at Fort Knox used the respect garnered by their military position to force a white civilian police officer to resign after he struck one of them. Even civilian observers drew more similarities than differences between male and female sailors. For example, profiles of Coney Island depicted sailors and WAVES as equals, making no distinction when describing their domination of the park. In other instances, however, servicemen, especially officers, used their power to abuse female troops. A San Francisco naval lieutenant was reprimanded for repeatedly breaking into the WAVES barracks in an attempt to solicit sex. In Tampa, a corrupt army captain coerced a WAC to have sex with him in exchange for a promotion to the rank of sergeant. Female troops ultimately did not escape the sexual violence visited on civilian women.

Though the wartime lives of WACs and WAVES differed substantially from the lives of other American women, they nonetheless capture the contradictory dynamic of the military's effect on liberty ports. Men and women could be both allies and adversaries, though the real relationship often lay somewhere in between. In the war within the war, many women could not avoid the suffering caused by the military's sanctioning of rampant assault and harassment. Yet others leveraged these disruptions to obtain a new range of movement and opportunity within liberty ports.

CHAPTER FOUR

THE MILITARIZED CITY

WRITING IN 1990, Mike Davis envisioned Los Angeles as a dysto-pian metropolis not unlike the brutal fortress cities of Ridley Scott's *Blade Runner* or John Carpenter's *Escape from New York*. Beginning in the 1960s, the rise of "megastructures and supermalls" brought about the destruction of public space with the help of a police and private security apparatus dedicated to middle-class demands for "increased spatial and social insulation." This "militarization of urban space," Davis explained, ended the democratic ideal of classes mixing in the lost "paradise of free beaches, luxurious parks, and 'cruising strips.'" He specifically identified Mayor Fiorello La Guardia's New York City and downtown Los Angeles in the 1940s as exemplars of the Olmstedian tradition of heterogeneity and democratic space. Wartime Los Ange-les, New York, and other liberty ports certainly featured more mixed public spaces and less corporate urban planning. But just because a space was more democratic does not mean it was not also militarized.

Cities had previously been militarized by the pursuit of military dollars and the growth of the modern defense industries. Since World War I, city boosters in areas like Norfolk, Virginia, fought other offi-cials angling for new bases and shipyards and the federal dollars that came with them. These efforts signaled a political and economic shift that presaged the arrival of a powerful alliance between the military, the defense industries, and Congress. The militarization of liberty ports, however, went far beyond the buildup of defense plants, army bases, and dockyards. It also meant military control of urban policing, neighborhoods, businesses, and municipal politics.

World War II brought about a wave of urban militarization that was far more direct and disruptive than previous instances of defense dollars hitting areas like Norfolk. Cities were transformed not just by the presence of millions of servicemen but also by the military's annexation of property, policing, and regulation of businesses. Civilian and military leaders sometimes cooperated but often argued over who should have control. Some municipal leaders like Mayor La Guardia chose to build their own auxiliary police forces to retake some power. Religious leaders, antivice organizations (often with roots stretching back to the Victorian era), and business groups joined the fray, seeking to shape local policies on issues like curfews, out-of-bounds zones, and urban order making.

The streets of wartime cities where millions of conscripts took leave and liberty certainly featured the dynamic and vibrant life that Davis romanticizes. However, they also fostered bitter civil-military conflicts and drove the growth of military power in urban America. Civilian life itself experienced its own militarization too. Civilians responded to the friendly occupation by America's men in uniform with a mix of cooperation, accommodation, profiteering, and protest, though many found themselves powerless to stop the military's control of liberty ports.

"THE CROSSROADS OF HELL"

In booming ports like Boston, servicemen revitalized and expanded red-light districts, creating whole new sexual networks that brought martial masculinity into everyday life. Each city frequented by troops on furlough or en route to training grounds or combat zones had at least one quarter where men could hit the taverns, cafés, bars, cabarets, and brothels for booze and B-girls, dope, and "well stacked" prostitutes. Hotels with "special offers" and bellboys connected to the flesh trade proliferated. The reinvigoration of red-light districts produced both cooperation and conflict between troops, businesses, anti-vice crusaders, slumming civilians, politicians, and military authorities, all of whom sought to determine the order and character of these spaces. Major port hubs contained neighborhoods where civilian life and the civilian economy were defined by the presence and behaviors of the soldiers flooding the streets. One such neighborhood was Scollay Square, an area whose reputation was changed for decades to come by militarized vice. It serves as a case study for understanding conflict between municipal and military authorities over city spaces.

Boston's history of catering to the sailor on shore leave began long before World War II. In the 1850s, ships released their crews along the original waterfront, sending them onto Anne Street, home to a host of criminals, swindlers, and prostitutes. Rushing out with their wages and "pent-up desires," the sailors crowded the bordellos, burlesque theaters, gambling houses, "rat pits," and "jilt shops" where the staff ran scams and robberies on drunken patrons. Men surging out from Dock Square lost themselves in blood sport, drinking, and whoring without much fear of the police, who dared not send lone officers into those "vicious highways." Richmond Street in the North End became known as the Black Sea, another center of sin and slumming, where both sailors and wayward students could place bets on ratting—how fast a dog could kill twenty rats released into a pit—or find a girl in one of the combination dance hall-brothels flourishing near the wharfs. Vice squads and moral reformers periodically raided these "streets of sin," but Boston's economic transformation into a center of finance generally proved more effective in driving out the purveyors of drink and flesh.

During World War II, Scollay Square emerged as a rival to Times Square for revelry and risky fun. Originally a cow pasture, then host to a quartet of grand hotels, Scollay was regarded as "a disreputable slum" by the early years of the twentieth century. During and after World War I, with the great expansion of the Charlestown Navy Yard and the battleship fleet, sailors thronged the square, searching for last-minute amusements before their ships departed. Still, the square of the 1930s remained a classic red-light district, full of any types from the Brahmins to the down-and-out. Troops taking liberty blended into, rather than dominating, the scene. World War II changed this as bluejackets swarmed in not only from the navy yard to the north but also from the new South Boston Naval Annex. The square's businesses capitalized on the cycles of paydays and benders, and the sector was soon ruled by naval legal codes, the Shore Patrol, and, most influentially, the whims of servicemen. By 1945, the rush of sailors would transform Scollay Square into a projection of the navy's power in the heart of Boston and a cause of intractable civil-military conflict.

Before troops even arrived in Boston, most knew about Scollay Square. It had developed an almost mythological appeal as it was conveyed in mostly apocryphal stories. In one tale, marines holed up on a Pacific island mark their bivouac with a sign reading "Scollay Square." In another, two ships sailing the Atlantic approach one another and begin sending a flurry of wigwag flag signals. The message is quickly translated and read back as: "How are things on Scollay Square?" Civilians recalled GIs wandering down Washington Street and asking, "Hey bud, where's Scoll—," but, before they could finish the question, they were already receiving directions.

For Boston's citizens, the square could be many things. Boston mothers employed it as a warning against immoral conduct, telling their teenage daughters that too much lipstick and waggling of hips would damn them to being streetwalkers in Scollay. But, at the start of the war, all kinds of people—not just those wearing navy blue—went there. High school boys and undergraduates treated it as a kind of coming-of-age rite, frequenting the notorious block for "burly distractions." Some underage boys recalled burying themselves in big winter jackets to hide their youthful appearance and then affecting a deep voice when trying to purchase a ticket to see a striptease. Harvard students—and some professors—ventured across the Charles River to visit the premier burlesque theater, the Old Howard Athenaeum (nicknamed the Old Howard). Before graduating as a Crimson man in 1940, JFK was rumored to have fallen in love with a stripper named "Peaches Strange." Even women from the city's elite Cabot family visited and remembered the "nice, healthy looking girls" performing stripteases. "There was no special class that went there," insisted one of the square's film projectionists. "You'd see the affluent, you'd see the poor, and you'd see all in between." An African American woman agreed, asserting: "It was everyman's place."

Officially, Scollay was only one city block among the many populating the serpentine streets of Boston. The actual square featured a small number of establishments, including theaters, "dine-and-dance spots," restaurants, a tavern, two cinemas, a pharmacy, a penny arcade, a bowling alley, tattoo parlors, shooting galleries, and a liquor store. Patrons understood, however, that Scollay also enveloped the surrounding streets, including businesses like Joe and Nemo's on Cambridge Street, known for its hotdogs. But even describing Scollay as a red-light district fails to capture how novelists, visitors, and reporters thought about it. Boston's Pearl Schiff, the author of the scandalous and best-selling romance *Scollay Square*, saw the area as "a mood, a rhythm," "a catchy tune with dirty lyrics." A GI also identified the area as synonymous with the obscene, the dirty, and the shocking. "Scollay Square was the closest thing to a four letter word that you could've had," he put it. The district offered a place to "escape into make-believe," a place where someone might "drink and make love and let the world go to hell." Scollay offered a bit of make-believe for everyone. For the man on liberty, it was an escape into "an almost infinite choice of pleasures." Spots like the Tasty, Jack's Lighthouse, and the Red Hat Tavern offered reliable access to the three desires of men on shore leave. For the Harvard crowd and the Beacon Hill elites, it provided a titillating brush with "the earthy kind." Respectable women might enjoy a night of rowdy fun without risking their social standing.

Both sailors and civilians originally came for the many varieties of burlesque. The Old Howard was "Boston's Temple of Burlesque," and

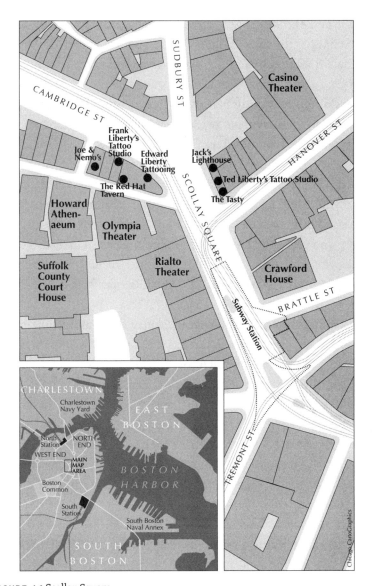

FIGURE 4.1 Scollay Square
Source: Dennis McClendon and Chicago Cartographics.

wartime audiences regularly packed its fifteen hundred seats. Originally famous as the site of William Miller's nonascension into heaven, the Howard found fame in the years between the world wars in the signature stripteases of Ann Corio, a queen of the genre. By World War II, Corio was making movies, but many other striptease artists took her place. Even without her, the war produced regular audiences for the burlesque routines offered by the Howard, with signs proclaiming "Always Something Doing." Other theaters featured fan dances with scantily clad women seductively waving huge, white feather fans, covering and uncovering skin to music. Visitors also sought out the tassel dancers at the Crawford House, where one act featured a woman who could rhythmically move her breasts so that each tassel would swing in the opposite direction. Punters would catcall and yell from the audience, "Take it off!" to which the performer gamely replied: "I can't take that off. I'll catch a cold!"

But, in time, the war transformed Scollay into a more militarized, hard-edged, dangerous place, far less welcoming to civilians. Shore Patrol officers, who increasingly replaced city cops, were soon "everywhere, their gaitered legs and belted waists with the small businesslike clubs swinging at their hips, investing them with authority," Schiff recalled. Civilian men who had not joined the service learned to avoid the square. Women and girls who were not prostitutes congregating to capture military dollars charted alternate routes through the city and carefully scanned the avenue when exiting the nearby subway station.

Wartime Scollay was defined by its sights, smells, and sensations. "Jack Ashore" understood, as one historian put it, that "Scollay Square, like the ladies who frequented it, was best seen in the evening." Furloughed sailors were greeted by the blazing electric bulbs of café signs and the penny arcade's neon tubes that "glowed with jewel-toned brilliance of ruby, emerald and sapphire." When sailors and women stumbled out of the gin joints and saloons, jukebox music filled the street momentarily before fading away as the door slammed shut behind them. The air was heavy with the mix of sauerkraut, vomit, smoke, and pungent cologne. Visitors and observers uncovered rhythms that dictated movement and actions within the square. At the beginning of the night, Schiff observed a "slow shuffling tempo" as day drunks, bookies, and horseplayers lounged in the streets. As the women and girls hit the square at dusk, sailors poured out from taxis, subways, and side streets, and the tempo began to build. Catcalls, obscenities, and raucous laughter formed a kind of sound track, while men increasingly threw fists at each other. Homeless men, derided as "stewbums" and panhandlers by troops, begged for cash as men hunted for a girl. The "grand finale" occurred when the cafés, honky-tonks, and dance halls ejected their patrons out into the wide avenue late at night. Then, sailors fought over women, and women fought over sailors. Shore Patrol frantically attempted to keep the peace and clear the zone. Some departed near dawn in taxis for crooked hotels, while others left for the Common, "where the ground is hard but free." More settled for doorways and sides of buildings, where car headlights briefly illuminated a flurry of hands, mouths, and thighs. By early morning, the quiet was interrupted only by the occasional giggle, cry, or smashed bottle.

Businesses capitalized on the near-constant military traffic. Street hawkers and shops began appealing to servicemen's various desires for trinkets and mementos associated with their time in the service. Many sold large, heavy rings that sailors wore on their middle fingers. As an alternative to the more noticeable and illegal brass knuckles, the rings worked well as both a masculine accessory and a fighting implement. Each ring featured a huge plate of metal placed on top of the band and imprinted with the faces of women or "wild west" Indian warriors. After a brawl or a scuffle, men might find these designs stamped into their faces and bodies. Photo studios, similar to ones featuring B-girls in Los Angeles, offered a place for sailors and women to capture a keepsake of a wartime romance. The Rialto Theatre explicitly catered to sailors by screening films into the early morning hours. Sailors explained that "Boston is like a morgue at one o'clock," so many would hole up in the Rialto until dawn. Night-shift workers joined them to watch vampires attack "some Hollywood cutie" and to "sober off before going home to the wife."

Scollay's tattoo parlors were dominated almost entirely by GIs, marines, sailors, and men from the coast guard—often called *coasties*. The square's main parlors were all owned by members of the appropriately named Liberty family. Edward "Dad" Liberty and his sons Ted, Frank, and "Lefty" ran a cluster of studios. Amid the myriad colors, designs, and insignias spattered across shops' walls, sailors picked from "ships and girls, in memoriam and religious motives, patriotic emblems, pirates, cupids, Mickey Mouse, and such mottoes as 'one home, one flag, one girl.'" Many went for their service's emblem, a visual commitment to their new lives as military men. Ted Liberty, the barrel-chested son, explained: "Servicemen comprise the biggest number of our customers and nowadays they go in more for military emblems and sentimental motives, in contrast to the old-timers who were apt to favor female forms." Paying cash in advance, coasties and bluejackets pointed to the tattoo's desired location, then received a quick shave with the aid of a "murderous looking straight razor" and a "sturdy forearm." After a dash of Vaseline, the tattooist placed the stencil and used lampblack to outline the design. Then the needle danced across the skin, stinging the ink fifty times a second. Besides being a boon to civilians like the Liberty family, getting tattoos together offered servicemen a shared experience of pain and camaraderie.

Sailors idolized Scollay's full embrace of vice and the power they exercised in the district. In Schiff's *Scollay Square*, a sailor extols Boston because it cherished "the tradition of its narrow streets, and set aside its widest thoroughfare for drinking and whoring." While other cities might hide their red-light districts "on mean back streets far removed from the wide pleasant avenues of respectability," Schiff wrote, Boston's hub for fun had become the home for the military man on leave: "The beer joints were his children." Other troops sentimentally remembered it as "gay, raucous, and uninhibited," a spot to escape the war and make full use of the privilege of the uniform. As the end of the war approached, officials even announced plans to

cordon off Scollay Square and designate it as the official V-E Day celebration zone.

City officials and civilians, however, saw the growth of military-
specific businesses as proof of Scollay's descent into iniquity. Many
denounced this shift as "a disgrace to Boston" while using whatever
municipal power they had to counter the spillover of crime and hedonism that had overtaken the square. In 1942, Boston police issued a
10:00 p.m. curfew order for both Scollay and the Common, with city
cops, SPs, and MPs sweeping both areas for any "girl or man in uniform." Police commissioner Joseph F. Timilty's board on wartime vices
cleverly invoked a previous Park Department ordinance to clear the
Common and surrounding areas. Timilty also assigned more police to
the Common and streets near Scollay in an attempt to crack down on
"young girls in those places." Though he couched the curfew and the
step-up in police presence as a response to the "teen-age girl situation," he also explicitly mentioned that "thousands of servicemen are
here over the weekends," suggesting that he viewed them as part of
the problem. Though the curfew did not last, city bureaucrats found
other ways to curb what they saw as Scollay's descent into depravity.
Timilty, for instance, went on to campaign for a large servicemen's
recreation center at the junction of Tremont Street and Beacon, just
a block from every sailor's favorite spot, Scollay Square. He likely
intended to capture the sailor traffic before it got to Scollay, but his
strategy was scuttled when the navy rejected the plans. Undeterred,
the Boston Licensing Board employed health checks to close down unsanitary establishments. Occasional citywide blackouts forced temporary business closures, though many establishments failed to dim
their lights until compelled to.

Despite these efforts, the area's nightlife grew increasingly difficult to control. Even one soldier from Massachusetts began to despair
when he heard of Scollay's changing reputation from a bawdy "bright-
light district" into something more sinister. Writing to the *Globe*, he
explained that Scollay was no longer "safe for a service man to take his
mother through." Such concern about a mother's safety pointed to the

fact that Scollay's subway station and central location in downtown Boston resulted in civilians facing the ire of inebriated sailors. Feeling "burned up by the things I hear about it," stories from navy men made the Boston GI "flatten a few guys to convince them that Boston isn't a cheap city for bums." On his own furlough, he noted seeing "a lot of things that disappointed me" and went on to warn that Scollay was "ruining the reputation of the city." He demanded that those in charge do something to stop the stories that spread throughout the armed forces.

Boston's Watch and Ward Society—an antivice group that would sometimes raid offending businesses and haul performers to jail—increasingly worried that sailors were expanding Scollay's influence and worsening the city's reputation. Originally founded as the New England Society for the Suppression of Vice, the group had won several victories in its campaigns against drinking, gambling, and prostitution, including shuttering the Old Howard for a brief period. The war undid many of its gains, and its members feared that the new military presence had introduced far worse threats to the morality of the city and its citizens. They decried Scollay as "a sink of sin" and despaired when it became apparent that their crackdowns resulted in publicity that drew sailors to the very establishments they hoped to close. A Boston judge said Scollay had become the "crossroads of hell," while the radio star Fred Allen depicted it as a "burial ground not listed in guidebooks." Under the onslaught of wartime mobilization, and with the streets filled with navy men, Boston's Watch and Ward could do little to slow the square's growth in revenue and danger, and its operations within Scollay soon dwindled.

"SHANGRI-LA OF JOE DOAKES"

While the sailors' invasion of Scollay Square made the block an area unwelcoming to civilian interlopers, the war also sparked a growth in the number of servicemen's amusement zones into new areas beyond the old boundaries. Although Central Park and Coney Island never truly rivaled Scollay's worldwide reputation among the services, both areas became defined by their military visitors. This mass influx of troops presented a formidable challenge to some of the most powerful city officials in America. Even the legendary master builder Robert Moses saw his urban renewal efforts dashed when servicemen arrived.

By the 1920s, both Central Park and Coney Island had slid into disrepair and disrepute. No longer the testament to middle-class sensibilities and proper conduct its makers envisioned, Central Park had become unkempt and neglected, large sections serving as refuges for drunks and the homeless. Moses confronted a real crisis when, as parks commissioner, he took control of the park in 1934. The mall was marred by "dust holes," potholed walks, paths "covered in dung," heaps of trash, and rows of dead trees. At the Central Park Menagerie's animal houses, armed guards were stationed and tasked with shooting carnivores that might escape the rotting cages. The few remaining attractions included "a senile tiger, a puma with rickets, and a semi-paralyzed baboon." The Harlem Meer had purportedly become a particularly unsafe section with little oversight from the Park Department and police. One visitor claimed: "You couldn't tell the difference between a park employee and the bums hanging out in the park." Moses soon moved thousands of workers into the park, reconstituting the Shakespeare Garden, creating the Great Lawn, constructing new playgrounds, evicting Jacob Wrey Mould's inbred and deformed herd of sheep, destroying shantytowns, and killing hordes of rats (over 230,000 in one week alone). He hoped to beautify and revitalize Central Park, throwing out its less reputable denizens and restoring its pastoral beauty, making it a refuge for New York's middle and upper class.

But the war brought unexpected challenges to Moses's efforts as Central Park became a "beachhead" where New Yorkers encountered the "'invasion' forces of joyous doughboys and gobs." In the unlit "shaded lanes," soldiers and women could "promenade à deux . . . until the moon glows high and most civilians are in bed." In hired rowboats and horse carriages, soldiers slipped their arms "possessively around their dates." But the lack of lighting also provided cover for a series of robberies, rapes, and murders committed by military men that hindered Moses's reforms and gave Central Park a reputation for being dangerous. One woman was found strangled in the Harlem Meer section, while a seventeen-year-old was rescued in the Ramble area from an attempted rape by a group of men that included two British sailors. Park Department officials chided women to avoid visiting certain sections of the park "day or night." But even women who stuck to the revitalized areas were not safe. One sailor abducted a thirteen-year-old girl from the mall, took her to a number of bars, and then eventually transported her to Columbus, Ohio, before she managed to escape while he was passed out. Young male civilians could likewise be targeted by servicemen. One eleven-year-old boy who interrupted a sailor "wooing a girl" was thrown into Central Park Lake. Other men who attempted to intervene between servicemen and women could face more severe consequences. In a highly publicized case, three veterans were found guilty of murdering a woman's escort—himself a former AAF man—and then raping her in the early hours of the morning. Throughout the war, Moses demanded larger details of police to manage the furloughed men who flagrantly disobeyed rules on drinking and sleeping in the park, but to no avail. At times, he took alternate—and somewhat petty—routes to excluding soldiers from his parks, such as when he barred them from free golf, claiming that the average GI "doesn't know a divot from an Attic tomb inscription."

Similar challenges hampered Moses when the war came to Coney Island. A longtime refuge for working- and middle-class New Yorkers seeking respite from the crowds of Manhattan, the piers, beaches, and parks of West Brighton and Brighton Beach had always bordered seedy areas like "the Gut" of the West End. But, during the Progressive Era, park entrepreneurs like George C. Tily had worked to cordon off these bawdier spots—such as the Pavilion of Fun—from the more respectable seaside resorts. By the 1930s, however, the arrival of subway lines, immigrants from southern Europe, and the Great Depression drove the middle class away from the "Landscape of a Vomiting Multitude," as the poet Federico García Lorca called it.

Moses despised the beaches polluted with peanut shells, shattered liquor bottles, and garbage that "jammed the beach so full on a Sunday that one could hardly see the sand." He believed: "There is no reason to perpetuate out-of-doors the overcrowding of our tenements." Coney's iconic mechanical amusements likewise, he thought, posed a threat to moral sobriety. Rather than "bemoaning the end of the Old Coney Island fabled in song and story," he envisioned "a new and very different resort" where upright patrons could "come for exercise and healthy outdoor recreation" in the model of the suburban Jones Beach on Long Island. Taking control of zoning and regulations in 1937, he instituted bans on barkers advertising shows, phonographs, the sale of food on the shore, and "using newspapers as beach blankets" while planning "a strict enforcement of police, building, fire and health regulations."

This remaking of Coney collapsed with the outbreak of war and the influx of servicemen desperate to experience the famous oceanfront. Even New York's most powerful unelected official could not stop a record forty-six million visitors from coming to the amusement zone in 1943. Servicemen and gas-rationed New Yorkers flocked "down to the sea in subways" to drink, party, and pick up girls in the revitalized "nickel empire." Like Times Square, Coney became a "rollicking playground" where "every race and tongue has a representative" and every nation "has a delegate to this turbulent convention of pleasure seekers." It was "sordid, shoddy, thin as pasteboard. . . . [a] Coney Island of the mind," the novelist Henry Miller once reveled. Elderly middle-class patrons attempting to enjoy Moses's vision of a middle-class beach did not share Miller's glee. They found "little pleasure in being jostled every five strokes in the water" or in "the tremendous vitality of the mob" that left them "cold and a bit frightened." Driven away by crowds of military visitors, the respectable beach crowd longed for "the order and lebensraum of their old haunts." Park Department employees attempting to find the families of lost children were heckled by passing sailors who yelled: "I'm lost, too. Blow that whistle and find me a momma—a young one." Along the boardwalk, men encountered a variety of attractions: the World's Fair's Parachute Jump, "tests of strength," "sideshow freaks," and caricatures of Axis leaders to be smashed with baseballs. Passersby would hear the voices of loud, often-inebriated soldiers singing "the refrains of sentimental ballads" in restaurants and bars or "periodic choruses of feminine shrieks." In the "old carnival spirit" of the Bowery, men picked up girls on roller coasters or took them into "darkened tunnels streamlined for romance." The enforced wartime dimout became one of Coney's key appeals for servicemen. Murray Schumach of the *New York Times* wrote: "Faces are in shadow except when the flame of a match curls around a cigarette." The darkness provided cover for illicit activities and a refuge from Moses's attempts to convert Coney's den of pleasure into "a more crowded Jones Beach." Rather than undergoing Moses's vision of urban renewal, soldiers drove away middle-class reform. Coney was reborn as the "Shangri-la of Joe Doakes," a place where servicemen could find "a refuge that is free from taboos and repressions." It was a place where "you enjoy risks, a little well-chosen danger."

The military also formally annexed or temporarily commandeered civilian establishments like hotels, bolstering the unofficial military takeover of other urban locales. In Miami, military officials simply seized and ran the cheap "dollar-a-night" hotels as well the "$35-a-night de luxe palaces" near the beach. In Atlantic City—another renowned amusement zone—hoteliers watched as some of the most profitable spots were "requisitioned by Uncle Sam's land forces." In addition to the Ambassador Hotel, the AAF snagged several other famous beachfront resorts, giving it control of most of the city's largest establishments. The move, *Variety* reported, left "hundreds of employees out of work" and caused several orchestras and the Ice Capades to cancel their lucrative summer tours. By midway through the tourist season, the army took nearly thirty more hotels, and Atlantic City's trade floundered. *Variety* concluded that the city was now a "militarized resort." In Chicago, the military moved into some of the most expensive hotels near the beach and amid the skyscrapers and downtown shopping districts all along the Loop. By September 1942, the *Los Angeles Times* proclaimed: "Uncle Sam turns innkeeper." The military's expansion into urban centers had made the federal government the largest hotelier in the country. This loss of property accompanied a loss of municipal tax revenue as cities struggled to collect taxes from sailors and soldiers.

WARTIME CONGESTION AND VICE IN NORFOLK

Beyond the vast numbers of servicemen hitting port cities, civilians also flocked to centers of wartime production like Hampton Roads. Encompassing cities like Norfolk, Newport News, Portsmouth, and Hampton Roads, the area had long been the nucleus of the maritime and defense industries as well as the navy. It was nevertheless unprepared for the impact of mobilization. Ramped-up war production in 1939 almost immediately led to a region seized by wartime congestion. Incoming workers and military families exacerbated a preexisting housing shortage and lack of infrastructure. The civilian population grew by over 180,000 from April 1940 to November 1943, a 46 percent increase in just over three years. The region's military personnel boomed from 15,715 to approximately 158,000 in the same time. By 1945, sixteen new military installations had been constructed, joining the ten existing sites. The lack of housing and municipal facilities was worsened by unresponsive state and local governments already in conflict with federal and military officials. Wartime congestion led to poor housing conditions, burdensome costs of living, and inefficiencies at almost every level of defense production. These conditions also led to intractable conflict between every level of civilian government and the military, with constant political infighting and grappling over who could try to control the military personnel blowing off steam in cities paralyzed by overcrowding and poor policing.

The whole area—and Norfolk in particular—faced an acute housing shortage, failures in municipal services like garbage collection and fire prevention, overworked nurses, doctors, and teachers, and an inefficient transportation infrastructure leading to seemingly endless delays in production. Defense workers with few other housing options crowded into homes far too small for the number of occupants. Twenty-one people living in one house were forced to share a single bath and one toilet "which empties through a pipe into a bucket on the lower floor." The home lacked heating as well, but the occupants still paid a significant amount of their paychecks each week. Other workers reluctantly hired surprisingly costly "hot beds," a hot bed being a bed that they owned for twelve hours while a worker on the opposite shift owned it for the other twelve. Tenants feared their landlords, who took advantage of the glut of workers moving into the area to evict any renter who might complain or cause trouble. Landlords also refused to ameliorate horrendous living conditions, their intractability bolstered by the huge demand for housing. Efforts to control rental rates floundered, and prices for a bedroom jumped by 250 percent in three months. Health workers feared an outbreak of disease as hospitals strained to treat the many workers living in filthy tenements and eating in unsanitary restaurants. Food prices spiked, and water had to be rationed. Terrible working and living conditions in concert with price jacking by local merchants led workers to quit at an unacceptable rate. Many other liberty ports also faced these conditions, but Hampton Roads saw almost unparalleled population growth in an already jam-packed zone.

Hampton Roads soon became identified as the archetypical American port beset by unchecked vice and poor civil management. The region's labor, housing, and policing problems attracted attention in the local and national papers as well as a range of publications, including *Collier's*, *Domestic Commerce*, *Business Week*, and *Architectural Forum*. Magazine reporters blasted Norfolk's "confusion, chicanery, ineptitude," while the *New York Times* covered the 115 people captured in a massive vice raid outside the city. The *American Mercury* later published an eight-page profile of the area, describing Norfolk as "our worst war town" and "a city of headaches."

Early war anti-venereal disease efforts pushed sailors out of Norfolk's established and regulated vice district in the East Main Street area, ultimately leading to a diffusion of drunk and criminal activity throughout the city. After World War I, Norfolk's municipal leaders chose to give up a fruitless antivice campaign and smartly began regulating and working with the four hundred prostitutes in this segregated zone. Women were to be regularly examined for venereal disease, to pick up customers only inside the boundaries of the district, and "to get a health certificate every week." A cop approvingly recalled that the women paid their property taxes and, "when a sailor came up with a disease, the navy told us where he got it and we took the rotten apple out of the barrel." The prostitutes working this amusement quarter were likely a mix of white and black women, though the customers were nearly 100 percent white.

This segregated vice district was hardly a model for fair and orderly pleasure, but it likely afforded the women more protection and avoided creating an underground market for sex. Early in the war, however, local police explained: "The Navy men came down and told us we had to close the district up. We had to use *suppression* for the duration. We argued with 'em but we agreed to do our damnedest. And God knows we've tried. We've put women in jail by the hundreds." The government and the navy became involved after Surgeon General Thomas Parran was made aware of an outbreak of venereal disease among bluejackets in the area. They demanded that the tolerated prostitution area be closed. Norfolk's officials initially objected, predicting that the order to break up a regulated vice district would only lead to sailors seeking delights elsewhere in the city. The city manager, however, ultimately complied with the order.

The results were predictable, with raucous sailors and defense workers scattering out into the city and straining a municipal government buckling under the stress of wartime congestion. Each night, a "sea of white caps" flocked to a nearly identical set of beer joints each featuring a main bar, hamburger stands at the back, and "a gargoyle of a juke box" playing "*Pass the Ammunition* and *Der Führer's Face* in monotonous repetition." B-girls "of all sizes, shapes, and dispositions" waited tables and flirted with the boys. Men who got lucky—or more likely negotiated a price—exited with a waitress when midnight signaled closing time and quickly flagged a taxi. The cabbies worked with the women, selling pints of whiskey or parking in an alley to give the couple in the back five minutes in the dark. In East Main's pub district, the sailors crammed the Burlesque Theater to ogle acts like Miss Rose La Rose. After the bars closed at midnight, squads of navy men crammed into taxicabs to see the "palaces of sin" in the countryside. Looking like "old frontier forts," these spots fielded their own bouncers to guard the entrances. Inside, men found areas dedicated to gambling, whoring, dancing, and drinking. Longtime Norfolk residents were rumored to be so incensed at the seemingly endless stag parties that they supposedly put up signs declaring "No Dogs or Sailors Allowed on Grass."

After touring these areas with a reporter, a cop remarked: "Now you can understand one of the things we're up against." Norfolk's chief of police acknowledged that tackling the vice problem would be impossible given the lack of space to hold women arrested for prostitution. He explained that he had requested "a concentration camp" from the government, but he claimed it would need to be able to hold two to three thousand people. The federal government proved reluctant to offer any aid, demonstrating how the FDR administration often ignored the consequences of its anti–venereal disease directives. Norfolk's officials initially ordered indicted women to leave the city, with predictably ineffective results. They also sent African American women arrested for vice violations to the city farm building and then later replaced them with white female prisoners previously crowded into the city jail. The city farm building was made up of only one room where women were forced to share toilets and showers with no curtains or privacy. The city abandoned the cruel experiment after the prisoners started a fire, fought the guards, and began rioting.

Reporters contended that the navy's seven-ocean front and the resulting mobilization had created a catastrophe in Hampton Roads and Norfolk, "unhealthy, confused, inept, and 'shocking' conditions" plaguing the area. "The plain facts are," explained the *American Mercury*, "that Norfolk is swamped and bulging with humanity—legitimate and illegitimate followers of war activity." Outside observers and municipal officials agreed that the federal government and the navy ought to remedy a situation they helped create. "Since the Government houses and supplies the sailors," the *Mercury* reasoned, "they contribute chiefly to the entertainment, transportation, and law enforcement problems." Problems like "housing, sanitation, disease control, and food and water supply" drove municipal and state officials to confront federal and military authorities over the terrible conditions and the failure to discipline troops who assaulted civilians. "We need more government help, and still more government help," implored a city official, "to assist us in combating the extraordinary conditions brought on by the tremendous influx of war workers, Navy men and transients to our city."

Before the *American Mercury* report was published, the Army and Navy Munitions Board had already taken notice of the serious challenges facing one of the key Atlantic ports and maritime industrial hubs. On October 20, 1942, the board listed Hampton Roads as the area of greatest concern and set about commissioning Robert Moses to investigate the situation and devise a set of remedies. The board explained that it also sought reports on troubled West Coast ports like San Francisco and San Diego as well as Boston's smaller subports like Portland, Maine, and Newport, Rhode Island, that also played host to sailors taking liberty. Moses somewhat cryptically explained that he was charged with analyzing "congested war production areas" that had become "suddenly overcrowded, unprepared centers where municipal functions and services were overtaxed by strains beyond their control." He and his group of engineers began by rapidly surveying Hampton Roads and found little to praise, identifying the area as facing far more problems than other defense hubs. He blasted the lack of municipal, state, or federal planning for the disruptions brought by mobilization and congestion. "No one in his right mind would establish a city of this size without community facilities," he wrote. His report singled out the navy for failing to provide recreation for its men or even an "interest in the subject," leading to widespread vice and crimes committed by servicemen. Even worse, Moses argued, the anti–venereal disease campaigns that demanded the raiding and shuttering of the regulated East Main prostitution zone had pushed the stag trade into neighborhoods throughout the city. This "pious effort to deny the existence of prostitution" failed when the bluejackets came to town.

Moses reserved his greatest ire for both federal and naval figures, lambasting their stubborn failure to grapple with what was happening in Norfolk and many other cities. He depicted ranking officers in the navy as being disinterested in the problems of congestion and drunken behavior in port. He noted sarcastically that it would be pointless to look to anyone in the navy for leadership as it was "doubtful whether such an official would have the time." Federal agencies were also cited for the inordinate demands they placed on "bewildered municipal officials who have suddenly had the war expansion thrust upon them" and "cannot be expected to cope with such a problem." Moses called on officials to use federal funds authorized under the 1940 Lanham Act to build better municipal facilities in a bid to alleviate congestion. He also demanded that there be far better cooperation between local, federal, and naval officials.

Just as with his efforts in Central Park and Coney Island, however, the power-hungry and petulant Moses confronted the limits of his influence when he came up against the military. His mocking of the admirals as being too old, conservative, and disinterested to do anything predictably led to entrenched opposition from the navy. He explained that "the navy people—the old-school-tie admirals were especially affronted," leading them to pressure the secretary of the navy to disavow the report's conclusions. The Army and Navy Munitions Board attempted to bury the report, moving quickly to prevent Virginia's governor from reading it. Knowledge of the report leaked to the papers, however, just as the scandalous *American Mercury* report appeared. One journalist revealed: "For weeks the Navy has kept the lid on a blistering report on Federal handling of wartime problems."

Responding to the outrage over the silencing of Moses's findings, a House subcommittee was convened to examine the problems of congestion and vice in Hampton Roads. The hearings ran through the long list of municipal, policing, and housing problems that made Norfolk and surrounding cities regular sites of civil-military conflict. Weary locals, war workers, police, and harried city managers all discussed the myriad problems and the failure of the navy or federal agencies to remedy the situation. The congressmen on the subcommittee, however, behaved deferentially to the admirals who testified. Rear Admiral Felix X. Gygax, for example, lazily rebutted the many well-documented issues with wartime congestion and the behavior of naval personnel. He ran through a vague list of actions that the navy had taken to improve the community. One subcommittee member, Congressman George Bates (R-MA), seized this moment to undercut Moses and his conclusions: "I am inclined to believe what you say, Admiral. It is a complete refutation of the report. We are not in sympathy with this report. We think the commandants and the naval establishments are to be commended for the records they have made under difficulties." Congressman Winder Harris (D-VA) agreed and praised Gygax by directly countering Moses's condemnation of naval inaction: "I have been in conferences with [Gygax] with representatives of Government agencies and instead of being too busy to exhibit an interest in this he has exhibited the finest sort of active interest." Harris concluded by asserting that "any criticism of him along those lines in the Moses report" was "unwarranted."

The committee's follow-up report repeated Harris's assessment that the navy displayed "initiative and alertness" and determined Moses's analysis to be "wholly unjustified." A subsequent president's committee, however, quietly followed up on Moses's report and began implementing many of the reforms that he recommended, with Hampton Roads seeing improved municipal services and housing, if not better policing of the navy. This episode at Hampton Roads demonstrates how wartime congestion could worsen already chaotic conditions in port cities. It also shows how much influence the military wielded in Washington. Even in the face of numerous damaging articles in the press and one of the more powerful municipal officials in the country attacking the fleet's leadership, the navy continued to exercise its political power to shape local communities and quash opposition.

ACCOMMODATION AND COOPERATION

As seen in Norfolk, civilians were not foolish or naive about the kinds of disruptions that war and a major troop presence brought to their midst. Some civilian businesses saw great opportunity for profit in the hordes of men and their now-plump wallets, but many more women, law enforcement figures, neighborhood associations, and religious organizations feared the crime and disorder that accompanied a military presence. Given the scale of mobilization and the stakes of the war, however, most civilians recognized that little could be done to resist the accumulation of military power in American cities. In the face of government propaganda touting civilians' duty to be "war-minded" and the complementary promotion of the combat soldier as an unassailable, almost reverential figure, few people could carve out a space for explicit public criticism of the military. Though some directly protested the disruptions caused by servicemen in liberty ports, most chose to cooperate and accommodate these special visitors.

Civilian cooperation with the military took many forms, both passive and active. In some cases, civilians simply ignored or tolerated troop misbehavior and crime. They mocked the soldier's nemesis, the Shore Patrol, calling its members "Stool Pigeons." At other times, they actively defended the apparent rights of servicemen to revel and drink while taking liberty. In multiple incidents, civilians joined troops fighting military or civilian police attempting to make arrests. The pattern was fairly simple. The police arrived after an incident or because of a complaint and moved to clear an establishment or subdue an offender. A fight would kick off, and civilians—often fellow patrons of a dance hall or tavern—might reject what they perceived as police encroachment on the right of servicemen to carouse and join the fray. Police brutality may have also sparked larger battles. In some cases, fights that started as civilian versus soldier could transform once the police arrived. In Vancouver, Washington—a liberty spot for troops across the Columbia River in Portland—city police arrived at the riverfront district to break up a fistfight between a soldier and a civilian. But, after a policeman struck the soldier, sending him to the barracks hospital with a head injury, both the assembled crowd of two thousand troops and civilian bar patrons turned on the cops. Eventually, the police broke out tear gas and riot guns, the fire department threatened to use hoses to put down the riot, and the chief of police called in the state guard. Opposition to police action, then, could unify civilians and soldiers even if they had been initially fighting each other.

In contrast to civilians who defended the liberty privileges of servicemen, others cooperated with military authorities and the government by informing on AWOL troops and deserters. Military Police records are filled with reports from informers who despised men who "shirked duty." In one letter, a "lawabiding citizen" from Brooklyn claimed it was his "duty" to notify the MPs about Mickey, a "lazy good for nothing" deserter whose family brazenly kept "the Service flag in their window." "The nerve of them," steamed the informer, who had two sons of his own serving in the armed forces. He even suggested specific times when the MPs might catch the culprit. Other civilians wrote in with similar complaints about AWOL men who were not "loyal to this country." One informant claimed that his AWOL son-in-law stated: "I would rather fight for anything but this country." In this case, MPs suspected "a family quarrel may have been the basis of his allegation." Citizens sometimes demanded furlough papers from men they suspected might be deserters and relayed their suspicions to military authorities. Occasionally, informants reported on suspected deserters because they were "continually drunk" or "the boisterous type" or played their radios so loud they woke their neighbors. To incentivize informers, the army issued films and posters imploring civilians to turn in deserters while also publishing the names and addresses of AWOL soldiers in their home newspapers.

Some civilians were driven to excuse the excesses of troops because of Roosevelt's idea that citizen and soldier had entered into a moral compact. Civilians would honor the potential sacrifice the soldier was making by committing to personal sacrifice at home. In his April 1942 fireside chat, the president declared: "There is one front and one battle where everyone in the United States—every man, woman, and child—is in action, and will be privileged to remain in action throughout the war. That front is right here at home, in our daily lives, in our daily tasks." Being a part of a war front, civilians would be expected to make sacrifices. This meant, for example, buying war bonds, tolerating servicemen getting aggressive, and not striking for better wages.

War workers were also motivated to cooperate with troops and the military because of the economic boom created by the war. By 1943, unemployment had plummeted to 1.2 percent owing in large part to the burgeoning defense plants surrounding liberty ports. In 1945, defense spending totaled 37 percent of GDP, helping produce a substantial increase in the discretionary income of many civilians. Besides hoping to appear patriotic, politicians also likely recognized that criticism of soldiers would be an especially poor electoral strategy and tended to accommodate the military. Republicans and Democrats both courted the soldier vote, and Roosevelt openly pandered to troops in his 1944 reelection campaign, suggesting that Republicans hurt morale with their campaign rhetoric. By the end of the war, some civilians even pressured the armed forces to be more lenient toward servicemen. Members of Congress, responding to constituent complaints, charged that military justice had become "unduly severe," leading the military's general council to worry that congressional criticism would present "increasing difficulty."

The challenges of a crackdown on wartime crime and a purported outbreak of juvenile delinquency left city politicians and the police stretched thin. Washington, DC, officials asked the Military Police to help "check the current wave of depraved and vicious crime," though it is unclear whether this led to any improvements. Mayor La Guardia never explicitly criticized the troops, but he did attempt both nudges and shoves aimed at stopping crime and disorder while simultaneously bolstering his own power. In early 1942, La Guardia implemented volunteer city patrols, known as the city guard, to stem the loss of members of his police force to the draft. Not content with this meager augmentation—the mayor was also forced to change the group's name after the state's adjutant general banned him from using the word *guard* to refer to a municipal force—La Guardia met with the American Legion and formed a volunteer auxiliary police brigade, beginning with a nucleus of twenty-five hundred to three thousand legionnaires, who would relieve regular patrolmen between 6:00 p.m. and midnight (and often until 6:00 a.m.).

When La Guardia first met the commander of what became known as the New York City Patrol Corps to announce the force, its members had already been drilling at an armory in Brooklyn for several weeks. Veterans crowded the Brooklyn headquarters to join what one paper described as "a quasi-military force, separate from and independent of the police department, with veterans of American Legion posts as the backbone." The legionnaires were armed with a .45 revolver and a nightstick and wore their World War I army uniforms. While the mayor assured the public that they would focus on civil defense and antisabotage efforts rather than policing civilians, the press noted that "members of the corps [would] have the power to arrest" and that the police would "have no jurisdiction over them." Ads called on volunteers to join an organization "cloaked with police authority." One pamphlet warned potential volunteers of "THE MENACE" and explained: "Our increasingly crowded city, with its countless thousands of transients encourages criminal activity." By October 1942, the force had well over seven thousand members, and La Guardia was already extolling the reduction of "crime and vice," asserting that no other wartime metropolis had done better in meeting the challenges that came with war. Speaking at a patrol corps ceremony, the mayor stated: "I, for one, do not believe it is necessary to have to lie down on law enforcement because our country is at war. There is a tendency all over the world towards crime and vice when a country finds itself at war. . . . There is no reason why that should happen in our city." The patrol corps continued to police New York into August 1945. When La Guardia finally announced that the auxiliary force would be disbanded, he said: "It has been suggested that the Patrol Corps be continued, but I will not have it. You have served your city well. You are good and honest people. Let the barflies and night-club bums come out and do something now."

Other cities copied this arrangement or implemented their own American Legion forces as part of an Office of Civilian Defense initiative. (The Office of Civilian Defense was headed by La Guardia.) Chicago began by planning for twenty-seven hundred boys in the Sons of the American Legion to be trained by legionnaires for "service in the defense of the Chicago area." Later that month, Mayor Edward J. Kelley announced that the legion would provide up to seven thousand auxiliary police officers. This program faced immediate opposition, the Chicago Civil Liberties Committee writing that it saw "decided threats to democratic processes" and that the plan was "a dangerous extension of public power to a private group." If Chicago proceeded, the committee argued, it would be endorsing a force "that smacks of the gestapo or storm troops." Chicago and other cities moved ahead with the plan anyway, seeking any means to reinforce department ranks.

PROFITEERING

The war's economic boom created a swell of soldier and defense worker dollars that bolstered businesses in liberty ports and stopover towns

THE MILITARIZED CITY   169

while also making local proprietors more beholden to the whims of the military. With the amusement and vice trades flourishing, business owners could reliably pull in significant profits with each arriving ship or train. Many tailored their businesses to the furloughed serviceman, the adventurous girl, and the war worker flush with cash.

Capturing these spoils of the war economy, however, came with constant risk. Business owners might see their establishments wrecked by the regular brawling and disorderly conduct with little chance of compensation. Soldier establishments also attracted prostitutes, B-girls, and con women, who in turn drew the oversight of vice squads, MPs, SPs, and the army-navy vice board. These antivice forces zealously attacked sources of venereal disease and leveraged their power to declare problem businesses out-of-bounds for all military personnel. Thus, the proprietors of bars, taverns, dance halls, and other businesses had to find ways of drawing in servicemen and women that prevented as many fights as possible and avoided the scrutiny of the military's antivenereal disease task force.

Military authorities routinely pressured trade groups like liquor associations to ensure that their members would self-police by keeping prostitutes out of their establishments, flexing their burgeoning political and legal power in major cities. In November 1941, after a bit of prodding from the army, the Chicago-based Illinois Association of Breweries issued a warning to the bars and saloons that it represented. Acknowledging the growing number of soldiers and sailors stationed near cities, it noted: "Many of these young men have, or will undoubtedly patronize your place." Maintaining a "high code of conduct" and ensuring that nothing would "endanger the welfare and well-being of our young service men" would, it continued, be a critical duty of every proprietor. Retailers that did not manage to uphold a high standard and "wholesome conditions" or failed to ban people "of questionable character" would face consequences. Businesses that allowed prostitutes or other unsavory characters might gain an "unpatriotic stigma" for not supporting "our country's national defense program." The association went on to spell out the real penalties of this thinly veiled threat, explaining that owners who did not maintain proper standards might have MPs stationed near their businesses, lose their licenses, or be declared out-of-bounds by military authorities.

Avoiding being designated out-of-bounds became a consistent challenge for many businesses. Even if a business owner wished to comply with military and trade regulations, ejecting women from a soldier bar was no simple task. Troops could obviously resist such efforts, and, even if those efforts were successful, a bar with no women would likely mean no trade. Proprietors, however, would be held legally responsible if they failed to eject prostitutes from the premises. Military forces and the Justice Department invoked the May Act—which made any prostitution near army camps and bases illegal and a priority policing target—to hold business owners complicit in any legal charges. Speaking to the International Association of Chiefs of Police, La Guardia argued that any owners who ignored prostitution in their establishments were "as much responsible as the pimps who bring the girls to the place."

If declared out-of-bounds, businesses lacked a clear path to redemption and could only seek the mercy of the military figures now controlling their economic fortunes. After the Hollywood Tropics, a Los Angeles restaurant on the famed Vine Street, was placed off-limits, the owner sent telegrams to both President Roosevelt and Rear Admiral R. S. Holmes pleading to have the out-of-bounds designation rescinded: "We conduct a first class restaurant . . . and only your office can prevent our closing the doors which would mean not only our entire financial loss and source of living cut off but the unemployment of forty or more people. A good many of whom have families to support." In rejecting this appeal, the Eleventh Naval District commandant noted that the restaurant was notorious for producing drunks and stragglers who "endangered the security of the Task Force." The Hollywood Tropics was just one of sixty-two establishments in Los Angeles placed off-limits to servicemen, and the city's Shore Patrol uniquely appears to have diligently reported and policed the most troublesome spots. It even recruited sailors and soldiers to record which businesses were violating regulations or generating the rowdiest and most violent situations. Shore Patrol commander Fogg publicly exhorted Los Angeles bar owners: "Run your bars in a clean, orderly, and respectable manner. This is a patriotic duty." Crackdowns on troublesome bars and taverns, however, did little to attack the source of the drunkenness and disorder. So, when one saloon was shut down, another gin joint a block away was ready to snatch up the displaced dollars.

Besides evading the attention of the military regulators, operators of military bars faced a higher risk of getting caught up in a physical altercation. Because most managers and owners were male civilians attempting to handle often-drunken servicemen, they could easily become targets. In one instance, a floor manager of the Honeymoon Lane dance hall in Midtown brawled with four GIs on Broadway after a dispute over a cab at 4:30 a.m. The manager recalled that the soldiers "had been drinking and were feeling a little tough." After a twenty-minute fistfight, witnesses claimed that Colonel Elliott Roosevelt—FDR's son—emerged from the crowd to break up the fracas, telling the soldiers "to scram." Occasionally, proprietors needed to step in and break up clashes between men. In Chicago, a tavern owner's wife ended a knife fight between two sailors by smashing a beer bottle over the head of one of the combatants. In one Louisiana boomtown, several national guardsmen wrecked a saloon after the owner announced a price jack on beer, leading the owner to shoot one of them. In another tavern, this one in Chicago, two sailors spent a night insulting and abusing the barman. One of the bluejackets, roaring drunk, hit the bartender in the face with a loaf of bread and threatened to kill him. After the bartender returned with a pistol, the sailor rushed him. The bartender fired the automatic pistol, hitting the sailor nineteen times. The sailor wound up dead on the floor and the bartender in jail. Such armed conflicts between proprietors and patrons occurred throughout the war, pointing to the regularity of civil-military conflict on the US home front.

Some businesses decided that revenue that came with the risk of dealing with the military or its men was ultimately not worth the trouble. In Washington, DC, an army lieutenant went on a rampage in the Hi-Hat cocktail lounge at the Ambassador Hotel, drunkenly swearing at guests and punching the civilian manager in the stomach before kicking and breaking a glass door. The hotel feared that this behavior would drive off its civilian clientele. Other incidents humiliated the navy and caused severe property damage. In New York, the district commandant worked with the glamorous Hotel Astor in Times Square to put on parties and dances for naval officers and enlisted men. The hotel gave the navy the space for free and made up the difference by selling men drinks and refreshments. Commanders enjoyed the arrangement because it allowed a ship's crew to take liberty in Times Square but under naval supervision. But one party in 1945 turned into what the hotel manager described as "a disastrous experience." Crewmen got smashed on the hotel's roof garden and became disorderly, leading the manager and his assistants to make a frantic attempt to clear the 350 sailors from the area. Navy men jammed themselves into elevator cars above safe capacity, while the employees begged the "absolutely ineffectual" Shore Patrol officers to help. By the end of the affair, the manager and his assistants had been knocked down by the sailors and "very nearly kicked into unconsciousness." In his letter to the New York commandant, the hotel manager explained that the Hotel Astor would never again allow the navy to use its premises. The luxury to refuse business in this way, however, proved harder in areas where servicemen's wages were such a central part of the local trade.

The war also sparked rampant price gouging and profiteering related to the liquor trade, creating disputes between servicemen looking for a drink and civilians hawking overpriced booze. Military investigators regularly scoped out establishments suspected of engaging in price gouging, an offense that could result in an out-of-bounds designation. Taverns and cafés pulled a number of tricks aimed at driving up prices, like conveniently running out of draft beer just at 7:00 p.m. on weekend and pay nights just as men began to stream in. The barman could then triple prices for bottled beer. Military Police dedicated whole units to investigating this profiteering and sought to shut down establishments that engaged in it. In one notable case, a group of soldiers sued a bar for overcharging and even won a $600 settlement. The military in Hawaii, however, also engaged in a kind of sanctioned price gouging by demanding very high fees for liquor permits. Taxi drivers, notorious for overcharging fares, sometimes worked with bar owners by picking up servicemen and then recommending the proprietor's spot. The driver received a kickback, and the bar got a customer. Other cabbies cut out the drinking establishments entirely by selling black market whiskey directly to their military fares. Barbers attempted their own rackets, giving soldiers a haircut before producing a comb with yellow flakes on it. The barber would then explain that the soldier suffered from yellow dandruff, "a contagious disease" that could be cured only by an expensive treatment the barber luckily had for sale.

In addition to these rackets, civilians ran a number of scams that specifically targeted servicemen. Some scams were simple. Young boys would wait for soldiers to arrive on "short-stop" trains at stopover points like Omaha, Nebraska, and then offer to purchase meals and other items for them so they did not need to leave the train. After receiving the cash, the boys never returned. Bases and camps attracted carnivals, roadhouses, and gambling joints where B-girls enticed troops to drink and play crooked games. Troops frequenting downtown Washington, DC, regularly encountered street photographers who would encourage them to pose, supposedly snap a picture, and then give the marks a numbered card. The soldiers simply needed to mail the card and some cash to the address given on the card, and soon they would receive a photographic memento of their time in the nation's capital. No photo ever arrived, of course. Similar photo scams existed in all the major port cities.

Other scams were quite elaborate. Horace Lancaster, a particularly inventive con artist, befriended servicemen and convinced them that he was an acclaimed portrait painter. For under $10.00, he would transform a man's photo into a large portrait. In reality, Lancaster periodically worked as a butler and handyman for a family of artists. When servicemen asked to see his work, he showed them portraits painted by the family he worked for. Convinced of his ability, they then surrendered the fee and a photo with the promise of a portrait before too long. No paintings ever arrived, and Lancaster made thousands of dollars before being caught. Nightclub operators and bootleggers also scammed troops, selling watered-down beer or dosing real beer with a chemical agent that made the men pass out. After the soldiers were helpless, the operator "rolled them for every penny."

Corruption and graft boomed on the home front with both military and civilian authorities taking part. Civilian police occasionally worked with hotel detectives, engaging in a "shakedown" routine targeting traveling troops. The hotel detective would claim that a visiting serviceman had been seen entering his room with a woman not registered at the hotel, a grave offense. Civilian police would then arrive, forcibly arrest the lone serviceman, and, while in transit to the police station, suddenly declare that the man could be freed for $15.00. Naval officers also abused their power to profit off the growing income of civilians. At worker recreation halls in Pearl Harbor, a group of ten naval officers ran "a little Tijuana gambling syndicate" where civilian employees reportedly wagered $50,000–$175,000 every night in poker and dice games. Each day, they pocketed thousands of dollars taken as protection money.

Few, however, surpassed the brazen corruption of Provost Marshal Captain Guy Taylor. As head of military policing in Tampa Bay, Taylor flagrantly abused his office throughout the war. He routinely accepted bribes from local bars and dance halls to avoid being placed on the out-of-bounds list. Establishments in his debt provided him with scotch, women, and a regular spot to hold parties. He also asked a bar owner for $250 to cover abortions for two women with whom he had had affairs. When the owner refused, Taylor began sending MPs to harass him into paying up. GIs who wished to avoid being sent abroad also sometimes paid Taylor $1,000–$1,200 to be kept at home as rear echelon soldiers. The army made some attempts to stamp out scams likes these but struggled with the formidable volume of wartime graft.

PROTEST

Before the riots, crime, and corruption, civilian authorities anticipated that the war would likely bring a high level of lawbreaking and disorder to American cities. Shortly after Pearl Harbor, one of New York's district attorneys announced that the city should expect a possible crime wave related to the onset of war. J. Edgar Hoover publicly expressed concern when the FBI reported that the first quarter of 1942 saw a 3.3 percent nationwide increase in the crime rate, with rape increasing by 8 percent. Early on, urban officials looked to London as a potential model for what might happen in liberty ports. Los Angeles's district attorney John F. Dockweiler wrote to Mayor La Guardia in 1941, explaining that their cities would need to brace for the kind of crime wave that visited wartime London. He noted that war had brought a flood of criminality to London and other urban hubs and that "our large cities cannot escape the same woeful conditions." Dockweiler established an anticrime committee and proclaimed: "Our task is not only to remove the rotten apple from the barrel, but to keep that one apple from becoming rotten."

In tackling the challenges and disruptions that thousands of troops might cause, urban officials usually chose to focus on the apparent threat of civilian juvenile delinquency, a concern that soon became coupled with the problem of troops in cities and boomtowns. In his letter to La Guardia, Dockweiler suggested that available municipal resources be directed toward diverting "the misplaced energies of young offenders into useful channels." Citing headlines from London like "London Youth Crime Grows" and "London Swept by Crime Wave," he lobbied La Guardia to use Office of Civilian Defense resources to prevent a similar fate in the United States. Other civil authorities acknowledged that mobilization could spark a rise in criminality and affirmed in warlike tones that "now is the time to formulate the grand strategy for the campaign against wartime delinquency." With fathers and mothers leaving for military service or defense jobs, more and more young people would lack supervision and the fundamental steadying structure of the family, becoming increasingly likely to engage in "juvenile and sex delinquency." When New York proposed eliminating the police department's Juvenile Aid Bureau, the Women's City Club—originally a progressive suffragette organization—protested and cautioned that similar cuts had fueled "the wave of juvenile lawlessness" in Britain. The Department of Labor's Children's Bureau seemed to confirm the fears, claiming that, in large cities across the country, juvenile delinquency cases spiked by 52 percent from 1940 to 1943. Did this reported rise in juvenile delinquency cases result from a true upswing in youth crime and misbehavior, or did the unfounded panic over potential wartime disruptions simply cause police and courts to focus more resources on youth policing? Urban officials and groups like the Juvenile Protective Association believed that, by failing to combat the supposed flood of juvenile delinquency, "the home front is losing its own war." Scholars remain more circumspect and convincingly maintain that a peripheral concern was exaggerated into a great moral panic.

Though no official or politician directly blamed juvenile delinquency on the armed forces, the battle against the misbehavior and criminal activity of girls and teenagers became a kind of proxy battle or indirect protest against the disruptions created by servicemen. Both experts and young people themselves began citing the growing presence of soldiers in nearby towns and cities as a primary cause of youth crime and promiscuity. Reporters saw the unchecked growth of boomtowns and the vice trade as factors in the rise of delinquency as well. A Department of Labor report backed this assessment by blaming the growth of businesses targeting servicemen, explaining: "Employment of younger boys and girls in places where liquor is sold, in dance halls, 'honky tonks,' 'juke joints,' on the streets, and so forth, often brings them into undesirable surroundings or into association with persons who contribute to their becoming delinquent." When these teenagers left their jobs at night, the report noted, they would be "tired and unprotected" and would face difficulty refusing "temptations."

Capitalizing on concerns over delinquency and public morality, La Guardia cleverly used the press and public events to make a subtle push against unsavory military behavior. After the millionth serviceman entered the National Catholic Community Center in New York, he greeted the sailor with several prizes, cash, and a photography crew. In his speech at the event, he remarked that "recreation is not inconsistent with wholesomeness" and sourly noted that he had yet to convince enough people of that message. Even here, however, he avoided direct condemnation of servicemen's criminality and worked within wartime limitations on what could be condemned.

Direct and open protest of servicemen's criminal behavior remained a rare but important action that politicians and civilian groups could use to pressure the military. As seen in previous chapters, some individual women and male civilians protested to military authorities or used major newspapers to condemn the unrestrained pleasure seeking in cities. These civilians could use the anonymity of telegrams and letters to the editor or simply rely on the fact that they were not public figures to avoid accusations of not being patriotic enough. City officials and organizations lacked those protections, so any public criticism of the military would have to be carefully stated. Criticizing drinking and the corruption of "our boys" proved a somewhat acceptable method of denouncing the larger problems plaguing liberty ports and boomtowns.

Prohibition groups and allied politicians employed this strategy in their fight to make all areas surrounding camps and bases dry zones. This fight to prevent draftees from readily accessing liquor started in prewar Oklahoma. When Oklahoma became a state, it wrote prohibition into its state constitution and remained dry even in 1941. As the draft expanded and recruits began arriving at Fort Sill in the southwestern corner of the state, army officers started shipping in liquor from wet states. Oklahoma governor Leon C. Phillips, a Democrat, demanded they immediately cease violating state laws, but army officers replied that the fort was actually "not a part of Oklahoma and, therefore, not subject to the State's prohibitory laws." The governor responded by threatening to use highway patrol officers to essentially blockade the fort and confiscate any incoming contraband. Federal and state prosecutors conferred and, with the assistance of the local army commandant, agreed to cease any more shipments. A subsequent federal statute made importing alcohol a felony offense, though bootlegged drink could still be found.

Senator Joshua Lee (D-OK) rekindled the conflict when he attempted to attach a dry amendment to a bill that extended the draft to eighteen- and nineteen-year-olds. The amendment would ban alcohol sales at camps, bases, and adjacent towns. Lee seized on the notion that "boys of 18 and 19" would require "some protection against liquor and vice." Prohibition groups had long campaigned for such a bill, and members of Congress claimed that they faced an unprecedented deluge of letters and telegrams supporting the measure. Civilian organizations like the Woman's Christian Temperance Union (WCTU) mobilized in support of Lee's efforts, pointing out that men in uniform during World War I were barred from drinking. Groups opposed to prohibition made wild claims that the measure was the product of "the Goebbels secret prohibition propaganda." Secretary of War Henry Stimson denounced the measure, arguing that it would incentivize bootlegging and "seriously undermine morale." Senator Scott W. Lucas (D-IL) pointed out that the army and navy already used large Chicago hotels near the Loop, making it effectively impossible to enforce the ban. Though the amendment failed to pass, military authorities took it as a serious threat—a portent of future criticism. When Chief of Staff Marshall learned of the growing problems of "soldier drinking" and the subsequent "mounting wave of criticism and resentment" on the part of civilians, he wrote that "this situation" could have resulted in "the passage of the Lee amendment in the Senate." He demanded that something be done to prevent any similar protests or legislative measures.

Challenges to drinking, however, continued to surface throughout the war, constituting the most consistent attack on the behavior of troops in public. Judges and prisoner advocacy groups both linked alcoholism to criminality, and attacking alcohol abuse became a somewhat acceptable way for civilians to criticize soldiers. Even so, most politicians wrapped any disapproval of troops in concern for their welfare. La Guardia toed this line when he denounced "debauchery and reckless drinking" spreading through the nation's cities in 1942. The *New York Times* reported that La Guardia suggested that booze and vice were "impairing the health of the men in the armed services and . . . tending to increase crime." In Los Angeles, "several hundred civic and religious leaders of Hollywood" barged into a police commission hearing to a launch a "barrage of complaints" against "amusement enterprises and night spots" catering to the unwholesome desires of servicemen. In each of these cases, civilian leaders condemned the conditions that enabled poor troop behavior, effectively suggesting that the men could not control themselves.

Other civilian groups were far more direct and less willing to tolerate the actions of military men. The Los Angeles chapter of the WCTU stands out for its forthright censure of military misbehavior. In a letter to the district commandant, it directly urged the military to honor its own policies and stop military men from frequenting "disorderly premises that are gathering places for prostitutes and sex-perverts." Though certainly more direct in tone, this type of criticism was still within the bounds of protecting the welfare of "our boys." The WCTU, however, proceeded to angrily protest that servicemen's incessant drinking and harassment were turning Hill Street and Grand Central Market—located near Bunker Hill's two-story Victorians and a middle-class shopping zone—into a "veritable 'skid row.'" Women claimed they were unable to move through the area without being annoyed, accosted, or insulted by a "horde of obnoxious drunken bums."

As WCTU president Ida B. Wise Smith put it on another occasion: "A soldier plus alcohol plus sex equals trouble—and always will."

More rarely, civilian legal authorities took a stand against the military's failure to police its men properly. In Olympia, Washington, both the local police chief and the district attorney assured commanders at nearby Fort Lewis that they would cooperate and turn over soldiers in the majority of legal situations. The district attorney politely explained, however, that "Mr. Huntamer, who is sheriff, feels differently about the matter." Sheriff Huntamer originally cooperated with army authorities, turning over GIs accused of crimes. But he soon noticed that the army did nothing to these men, crime went unchecked, and no MPs policed the dances where soldiers congregated. So he started refusing to turn over troops and prosecuted them instead in state court, leading to a reduction in the crime rate. The district attorney hoped that "we may be able to change his mind and get him to turn these violators over to you," but he also noted the sheriff would change his mind only if "men will be properly disciplined." Huntamer's protest succeeded for one critical reason: Pearl Harbor had yet to occur, meaning that the need for manpower was not as dire. The army did not yet need to be as aggressive in asserting its legal privilege to uphold adequate troop levels.

Communities also sometimes banded together to protest and resist the disruptions and dangers created by servicemen. In North Stelton, New Jersey, a small town south of Newark, women formed a committee to lobby their senator, H. Alexander Smith, a Republican, to intervene on their behalf after soldiers from nearby Camp Kilmer began to bother locals. In a telegram that Smith forwarded to military authorities, the women of the North Stelton Committee described the grim situation: "North Stelton, adjoining Camp Kilmer, has been repeatedly terrorized by acts of violence including house-breaking, burglary, molestation of women and children, rape of seven year old girl in broad daylight, brutal rape of young mother by four soldiers after repeated demands to Camp and Local authorities for protection." The women believed that their only recourse would be to "deputize the

THE MILITARIZED CITY   181

few men remaining in a Community consisting mainly of women and children." Their demands were simple. The provost marshal should immediately provide enough MPs to control the situation, and then the army should install "a manproof fence and floodlights for the boundaries between Camp Kilmer and North Stelton." The three women leading the committee bitterly concluded the telegram: "An infuriated community demands prompt action." A military investigation denied initial suspicions that this complaint might be racially motivated, noting: "The racial question was in no way involved in subject incidents." Investigators, however, blamed the sexual assaults and other crimes on the history of the area, which they claimed was originally founded "as a Trotskyite settlement" that "practiced the theory of free love" and that the whole area suffered from lax moral values. Nevertheless, the commanding officer agreed to declare the town out-of-bounds, build an iron mesh fence and install floodlights, increase the number of MPs, and establish better checks on men slipping through the current fence. The provost marshal general wrote back to Smith promising to resolve the situation. Nevertheless, the town still deputized ten residents as special patrolmen and remained on edge.

Consistent and fearless criticism came from a group of Americans who were both civilians and members of the military simultaneously: chaplains. Chaplains occupied a fascinating space within the military—they were part of a secular organization, but they were also religious figures. They lacked the authority of a commanding officer but wielded the moral authority that came with their vestments. When one George A. Turner wrote to Chief of Staff Marshall objecting to intoxication by soldiers on leave at night or on the weekends as well as the mistreatment of "young ladies" by "military men whom liquor has robbed of natural inhibitions," he was pointed to the chaplains as a force that could combat these evils. As members of the military charged with shepherding the moral and religious lives of the armed services, chaplains carved out a space for open and even fierce condemnation of sinful behavior. Some focused on the omnipresent issue of liquor and its effects on men, agitating for better military control of alcohol abuse. Chief of Chaplains William R. Arnold contested the military's lax policies on drunkenness and asserted that the armed forces were caving in to the interests of the liquor trade, which, as one of his junior chaplains remarked, amounted to "sabotage to the American people and a disgrace to the US government." Quoting Marshall, one chaplain protested: "When the soldier leaves camp, our troubles begin." Given the rampant "gambling, profanity, and sexual sins," even senior chaplains seemed to believe that "the world is imperiled today by sin": "It is the supreme tragedy of the world. The whole earth is groaning under its curse." Another chaplain with experience in the United States and the United Kingdom noted that the most troubling behavior occurred when "our thoughtless soldiers" decided to "molest nice girls on the streets who are strangers and give the soldier no reason to get familiar with them." The chaplain seethed that the MPs did nothing, even though "many of these incidents borders on 'rape conduct.'" Though such protests achieved few changes, the moral courage to challenge command openly remains noteworthy in a period defined by accommodation and cowardice in the face of authority.

All these civilian groups and officials that engaged in direct and open protest of the military were scattered voices, lacking a central, coordinated movement. Few could sustain consistent criticism in a country that militarized both the city and the civilian. By the end of the war, however, some civilian leaders could no longer contain their acrimony or disgust with the failures of policing. City councilmen in Los Angeles passed a unanimous resolution calling for the War Department to release the more than four hundred policemen who had been drafted immediately. Other cities asked for similar releases to bolster the depleted police department ranks. Council members complained bitterly that crime and unrest had been allowed to run rampant, with assaults against women going unchecked as the city became "infested with criminals." Councilman Meade McClanahan remarked: "Something is radically wrong with the Police Department from the heads down."

The most explosive and visible civil-military policing conflict occurred in 1945 on Staten Island, where Richmond County's district attorney, Farrell M. Kane, railed against "a crime wave" caused by soldiers on the east shore. After months of robberies, thefts, and assaults,
he threatened to usurp the military's legal authority in the district: "It
is primarily a military matter and I wish to give the military authorities the opportunity to handle it. However, if they fail to correct the
condition, steps will be taken by civil authorities." Kane's proclamation was a remarkable challenge to wartime governance and law enforcement norms, but it was prompted by what citizens claimed was
a wave of "stick-ups, muggings, assaults, store robberies, and the mo-
lesting of women and young girls, committed by uniformed soldiers."
Tensions deepened after a civilian was apparently set on and stabbed
by six GIs and a policeman attempting a rescue was shot at with his
own pistol. Kane demanded that the army put "an end to the reign
of terror," and local businesses suggested that they might begin closing before dusk. Civilian complaints to city and federal officials—as
well as petitions to Stimson and New York governor Thomas Dewey to
close the local cantonment that housed over three thousand soldiers—
led to an armed guard, two hundred men strong, patrolling the area
throughout the night. Robberies and assaults persisted, however, and
few women dared to walk in the dark. La Guardia requested greater
cooperation from the army but admitted that "the situation has not
been good for several days." A grand jury investigated the disturbances and pinpointed the "breakdown in military discipline and morale" as the key cause, recommending better security, an end to "Army
laxity" in policing, and improved recreational facilities.

Why did Kane and the citizens of Staten Island become so willing to denounce soldiers and the army when other communities experiencing similar incidents remained mostly silent? While wartime
dictates prevented most city officials from publicly criticizing the
military or its men, the factor of race compromised this stricture. Indeed, the local GIs on Staten Island were predominantly black troops

working as stevedores and longshoremen. Given their race, black troops lacked the same privileges bestowed on white troops, so their crimes, real, exaggerated, or more likely fabricated, became acceptable targets of civilian protest. While it is ultimately impossible to determine whether the black troops on Staten Island committed these crimes or whether their crime rates significantly differed from those of white servicemen, the accusations should be looked on with a great deal of suspicion. The descriptions of the crimes contain similarities to accounts of crimes committed by white troops, but inconsistencies in eyewitness testimonies and the fact of rampant racism undercut the reliability of the evidence. Rape accusations against black men remained a powerful and terrifying tool with which to maintain white supremacy, and the black soldiers on Staten Island may well have been innocent men targeted by a racist community, press, and local government. The *Chicago Defender* considered the whole affair a "wide-spread smear campaign against Negroes" that predictably culminated with "the charge of rape lodged by a white woman." It blamed the *Times* and the *New York Post* for provoking a "rape hysteria" with little basis in fact. Whether the crime wave was genuine or more likely prompted by racial panic, military authorities responded by transferring one thousand black soldiers to other parts of the country, giving civilian officials and local citizens a rare victory.

The military rarely assented to civilian attempts to regulate its men, but, when Office of War Mobilization director James F. Byrnes issued a midnight curfew for all major American cities in February 1945, military authorities curiously agreed to enforce the order. Byrnes sold his order as a move to reduce coal consumption by night clubs, bars, and other places of entertainment, though he admitted: "It will also be helpful in the fields of transportation, manpower, and in other ways." Congress launched an inquiry to determine the true motives for the curfew, asking whether Byrnes and the military intended the order as a check on vice. One congressman described Byrnes as "power drunk" and suggested that the curfew was an act of "dictatorship," dismissing the "alleged coal saving."

No smoking gun exists, but the Byrnes order appears to have been intended to curtail drinking and disorderly conduct in liberty ports. It notably allowed some establishments to stay open past midnight if they stopped serving alcohol, undercutting Byrnes's ostensible desire to cut back on coal usage. The military also chose to enforce the order, suggesting that it hoped doing so might quell some of the outstanding issues created by men on leave. Though La Guardia attempted to overrule Byrnes and set New York's curfew at 1:00 a.m., both the army and the navy sent squads of MPs and SPs charging into midtown bars in New York to eject troops violating the midnight order. Alexander Feinberg argued that the order resulted only in earlier and more hurried drinking, fistfights, and angry troops. Commanders cleared Scollay Square at midnight as well, a rare show of determined military policing. Earlier in the war, the army imposed an ordinance preventing liquor sales after midnight in San Francisco, so the Byrnes order functioned as an extension of that rule. Though some entertainers and supper clubs believed the order would shutter their businesses, other establishments agreed that speakeasies would replace the closed spots and that most clubs would simply open an hour earlier to cover the loss of late-night revenue. Nevertheless, the military's compliance with the order signals that army leaders may have begun to think that concessions should be made to better control the roiling situation in stateside ports.

Other protests occurred in everyday civil-military clashes, especially on trains where civilians and soldiers were placed in close proximity with booze and boredom. Because the military required a significant number of railcars for troop and freight transportation, civilians faced chronic delays. Given the endlessly interrupted service, overcrowded cars, and number of trains transporting both civilians and servicemen simultaneously, conflict proved inevitable. In one example, an MP and a civilian began hurling insults over a delay, with each side soon reaching for their hips and drawing pistols before cooler heads prevailed. Delays frequently provoked similar incidents as antsy soldiers on interminable train journeys got increasingly drunk. Train bathrooms were regularly ruined when intoxicated men vomited in the sinks and the toilets, leaving the facilities unusable for the remainder of the journey. Other civilians complained about the singing and loud banter, while the chief of the Military Police Security and Intel Division argued that officers on trains commonly failed "to exercise proper control," leading to "misconduct and other incidents in civilian communities which reflect unfavorably on the military establishment." He also reiterated that troops should not detrain unless "under proper supervision." Riots occurred when the army attempted to send too many men through on overstuffed, boiling-hot cars, causing further delays with the whole railroad system threatening to buckle. Civilians resented the preferential boarding treatment given to soldiers, often finding no available seats when they were eventually allowed into the cars. Trains thus became another place where civilians were exposed to the risks and hardships that came with mobilization.

Young, male civilians classified as 4-F—4-Fs were essentially registrants who could not be accepted for military service owing to physical, mental, or moral limitations—suffered the ridicule of both society and military men, though they also engaged in their own protests. These men generally suffered from physical ailments that prevented service, but they lamented that they were given "the same rating as imbeciles and criminals." Regularly seen as cowardly, effeminate, and worthless, 4-Fs spoke of experiencing the war as an endless succession of humiliations when civilians suspiciously questioned why they were not in uniform or soldiers mocked their inability to serve. GIs particularly targeted 4-Fs to emphasize their own masculinity and confront obvious sexual rivals, leading one factory owner who relied on these essential war workers to plead with the army to recognize their value. *Four-effer* became its own epithet, wielded by military men but also by "young girls who make a boast that they wouldn't date a 'Four-effer.'" In Schiff's *Scollay Square*, a male civilian is mocked for being jealous because women would not give him "a tumble without a uniform." Radio programs piled it on, routinely making 4-Fs the butt of jokes. The *Chicago Daily Tribune* admonished readers that, though many 4-Fs might be young and lack "the appearance of a cripple," many had legitimate medical reasons for rejection and that "most of them would mortgage their lives for the privilege of wearing a United States battle uniform." Emily Post offered a similar reprimand, telling soldiers to stop shouting "slacker" at 4-Fs.

Occasionally, civilian men confronted the soldiers who tormented them, with one notable 4-F beating up four soldiers who had taunted him. "I've been taking that kind of guff from soldiers too long," he said. 4-Fs were also seen as men who "hate uniforms" and pick fights with those who wear them. Others protested by appropriating the coveted military uniform, leading to civil-military conflict. One 4-F in Los Angeles posed as an army captain before being caught by suspicious MPs. Conflicts over who was allowed to wear a uniform could become violent. In a nightclub, MPs confronted a male civilian wearing a military jacket. He explained it was a purchased "reject" jacket and an argument ensued. A brawl between the MPs and the jacketed civilian and his friends soon turned into a shoot-out during which the participants as well as bystanders were wounded.

PERPETUATING THE WARFARE STATE

When victory arrived, civilians celebrated, but they also dreaded what would happen when the troops returned to their communities. During the war, fears proliferated that, "when GI Joes lay down their guns for Uncle Sam, many will pick up new ones and run amuck." The prominent businessman Harvey S. Firestone Jr. predicted an unparalleled postwar crime wave brought on by "soldiers, schooled in the use of lethal weapons and accustomed to living intimately with death." Criminologists at the Harvard Law School joined this chorus of warnings, arguing that both delinquency and criminality would rise because of the "wartime experiences of soldiers and civilians." Hoover admitted similar concerns, suggesting that demobilizing troops might fall into "protest and perhaps violence." Some of these fears derived from the memory of returning World War I veterans, some of whom had been implicated in shocking and highly publicized crimes. Reports of American troops looting and committing rape in contemporary Europe, along with firsthand experience with troop disorder in stateside hubs in the immediately preceding years, exacerbated these concerns. To quell the growing apprehension over demobilization, Brigadier General E. C. Betts issued statements to the papers, assuring the public that there was no cause for worry because the military had instilled a rigorous self-discipline in each man that would surely curtail any surge in criminal behavior. Still, lurid stories made the front pages, reinforcing civilian anxieties. In one report, the separated wife of a GI told a New York court how her husband promised: "I'm going to put a knife in you and twist it. The Army taught me that."

Military authorities certainly feared that the misbehavior of returning servicemen might further damage the image of the armed forces as well as endanger efforts to institutionalize universal military service in postwar America. Their fears grew as soldiers began to grumble about the extremely slow rate at which they were discharged. As boredom and waiting time increased, chaplains reported that morale plummeted and misbehavior flourished. Even before the end of the war, the provost marshal general had been preparing for the potential disruptions that might visit postwar America. He suspected that the effort to police returning GIs would prove as difficult as it had been in wartime and that it was also "probable that serious criticism of the War Department will arise as a result of the conduct of many of these servicemen." Civilians, he thought, would particularly object to soldiers using their uniforms to obtain "tacit exemption from minor ordinances applicable to civilians." If the War Department permitted the uniform to be "debased" by unchecked misconduct, he admonished, civilians would react by rejecting postwar universal military training.

As the nation returned to peace, the military consolidated its accumulated power. Some scattered voices rejected the militarization of the city, civilians, and the nation. Writing in January 1946, the *Boston Globe* writer Charles A. Merrill argued that Americans were loath to "continue in [their] wartime roles as puppets of the state." Wartime necessarily induced "the military and naval establishments, even in a democracy like ours," to be "invested with vast authority" and "be tempted to usurp and perpetuate their powers." Merrill suggested that, moving forward, no American "be compelled to serve in the Army" and that the military reduce its footprint. Abroad—and also at home—the augmentation of military power would continue to expand in the coming decades at unforeseen levels to create the American Century. Civilians had been made part of a warfare state through the use of extensive propaganda, economic contributions, and personal sacrifice. But the militarization of American life also took place in the daily interactions and conflicts between civilians and servicemen in urban centers. In the postwar era, the imprint of the military on American cities remained, continuing to influence lives of the civilians in liberty ports.

POSTWAR INVASIONS AND OCCUPATIONS

AFTER THE CHRONIC MISBEHAVIOR, absenteeism, and insubordination that had plagued the military during World War II, generals and other top brass became determined to remake the postwar army as a disciplined, technologically adept, and professional fighting force. They offered an array of incentives for skilled technicians, engineers, and craftsmen to enlist, including half pay for life following two decades of service. The army would become more mobile, efficient, and intelligent. The infantryman was to be "tomorrow's armored Pegasus"—a warrior ready to fly into battle with "pilotless aircraft, guided missiles, with atomic warheads, [and] super-sonic planes." Talk of abandoning traditional fronts abounded, with planners imagining highly trained soldiers launching airborne assaults even a thousand miles into an enemy's territory. The army expanded its elite ranger program—which specialized in commando tactics—especially after rangers' early successes in Korea. One lieutenant general argued that a better training system might eliminate the military's caste system, heralding an end to chickenshit while bringing in enthusiastic, talented young men.

Command also understood that the regular, uncontrolled weekend benders had only worsened the prewar view of the army as a place for navy and marine rejects. The force's poor image was further cemented when across the globe GIs rioted and mutinied against the laborious and sluggish pace of demobilization. Widespread boozing and epidem-

ics of venereal disease even after 1945 seemed to confirm the army's per-
petual lack of discipline. Major Louis Altshuler, chief of the venereal
disease control division, argued: "One of the greatest criticisms of the
Army by the parents is that the Army encourages and condones immorality, drinking, and gambling. . . . If we are to get the skilled technicians required in a modern Army, we must show that the Army is a
character building organization and not one that breeds immorality."
Command took small steps to disincentivize misbehavior on liberty
like urging noncommissioned officers to get married and bring their
families to live near base.

Remaking the Old Army with its tradition, discipline, and un-
abashed love of a military world cordoned off from and starkly contrasted to civilian life would be impossible in a new international
order that required permanent and sizable armed forces. Planners
therefore envisioned a new training program that might bring in
more skilled recruits while also abandoning the rough, aggressive
barracks culture that defined wartime training. The new GI would
be technically skilled and morally sober. Training would utilize more
carrots than sticks and focus on technical education as much as on
hikes and target practice.

The "Umtees" (short for universal military training [UMT] demonstration units) epitomized the new approach. In 1947, the army
brought a battalion of seventeen-year-old recruits to Fort Knox and
showcased them as a potential model for the postwar army. Abandoning the old model of "beat 'em down, cuss 'em out, and keep 'em
squirming," commanders saw to it that these trainees received demer-
its instead of a dressing-down. Liquor was strictly prohibited, officers
organized educational trips to sites like Mammoth Cave and Lincoln's
birthplace, and the fort offered courses on subjects like rocket launching. Barracks were now built up and practically luxurious by World
War II standards. Boys were even given their own lockers, plugs for
radios, a reading area, and an entire room devoted to listening to clas-
sical music. Dances were offered several times a week, with local female chaperones in charge, no MPs required. The army highlighted its

coordination with a board of prominent citizens in Louisville to "foster better relations between the civilian community and the Army" so that "the boys feel at home on liberty hours." The *New York Times* promised that the army would keep each "beardless wonder" out of trouble by "hovering over him like an anxious parent." The cutback on swaggering masculinity continued when one commanding general even pledged to cut back on swearing, a key element of the World War II GI's vernacular. "We don't intend to stop anyone from using a healthy 'damn,'" he explained, "but this stream of obscene, vulgar stuff, it's too much." The Umtees were given the power to run courts-martial for each other, delegating legal responsibility to peers rather than commanders and the legal branch. The officer corps even solicited them for advice and feedback on their training.

After several months, the army pronounced the pilot program a success, specifically citing the low levels of drunkenness, venereal disease, and instances of men going AWOL as well as the higher rates of church attendance as evidence of more skilled, well-adjusted recruits ready to form the core of the modern army. The service, at least publicly, seemed to be on its way toward a more effective and better-behaved force.

Old Army regulars remained skeptical. They saw the Umtee boys as the "Lace Pantie Brigade," "senior boy scouts," or "male Wacs," arguing that their unit was little more than a cute experiment or a publicity stunt for Congress. One veteran sergeant cautioned: "In the old days the army either made men or broke them; this way doesn't do either." That many army recruits were still poorly educated only added to the misgivings of the regulars. The young recruits of 1946 and 1947, often labeled *GI Joe Jr.*, offered little cause for optimism among army planners gunning for technically skilled and tactically sharp units. The average man entering training recorded lower scores on the army's general aptitude test compared to recruits in World War II, and few brought a university education or trade or engineering skills. Many could not read, remained undisciplined, and/or engaged in misbehavior. Studies of camps and forts revealed that instructors also lacked education and ability, leaving most men to struggle through a training process that was described in an army investigation as "poorly planned, insufficiently executed, and hopelessly obsolete."

The army's first forays in Korea revealed that the training reforms failed to produce a more effective combat soldier. The grandiose plans for bright, morally upright GIs floundered when the brass chose to slash the training period from seventeen weeks to eight to solve yet another manpower shortage. Troops arrived not knowing how to fire their rifles, mortars, or artillery. Most dangerously, very few understood how to use their radios, leaving units cut off and uncoordinated. One veteran officer explained that the United States was fielding "a cream-puff Army, not an Army of soldiers." The main problem, he argued, was that the Umtee system of more democratic and less harsh training had resulted in "damned coddling and babying of troops." "Let the Army make soldiers," he implored. "We've got to teach 'em how to fight, get rid of the nonessentials, and get down to tough, hard bed-rock training." Mean, tough GIs would be needed in order successfully to meet "the hordes of Asia or armies of barbarians." General Mark Clark, the commander of US Army Field Forces, already made the move to turn away from producing the "G.I. gentleman" in favor of what Major General Lewis B. Hershey called "young 'killers' ready for grim war." The virile, aggressive soldier was quickly back, as was the rough approach to basic training that so often spilled over into violent carousing on liberty.

Ending or limiting the effects of a hyperaggressive, martial masculinity proved impossible for the military. For civilians and cities, too, the war's legacy loomed large, and in the postwar United States the culture of wolfish carousing both lingered and evolved in subtle ways.

INVASIONS

Before making their assault on the building, they made plans. They waited for the cover of night, and, while the sun set, the leaders of a

250-man "army" drew up coordinated lines of attack. A little before
12:45 a.m., the leaders ordered four "squads" of scouts to move ahead
and enter the building via a heating plant tunnel. There they found a
power switch and quickly cut the main telephone cable and the lights.
With the building now darkened and having no access to external
communication, a spearhead force donned masks and moved to designated attack points. The scouts crept through the tunnels leading into
building and silently unlocked the front door, "admitting the main assault force." Quickly and quietly, the men charged through the doors
and began their raid.

Though the men acted like an organized military unit—and their actions were consistently described in those terms in the newspapers—
this was no army assault on a hostile encampment. This was the first
panty raid, a hallmark of postwar campuses beginning with this incident in 1949. Before entering the women's dormitory, the male undergraduates of Augustana College in Rock Island, Illinois, dispatched a
sortie to lock the housemother in her room. The "masked prowlers"
then ran through the unlit hallways, barging into each woman's room.
The *Chicago Daily Tribune* reported that "pajama clad girls were tossed
to the floor as beds were tipped over." The invaders splashed sleeping
girls with water and threw others into the showers. For ten minutes,
"feminine screams came from all quarters of the building." The "night
prowling squadron" targeted dresser drawers, emptying or breaking
furniture in pursuit of women's panties, bras, and other lingerie. The
women later told the *Washington Post* that the men had "wrecked the
place," leaving some struggling to find more clothing. The police soon
arrived, prompting "a leader of the raiders" to sound the "retreat on a
trumpet," after which the men scattered into the night. Given that the
police report recorded that the station had been notified of the raid
six minutes before it began, a rumor flourished that "there had been
a 'leak' in the invading forces." The reaction of the women to the raid
was mixed. Some responded by grabbing whatever makeshift weapons they could, with one co-ed smashing one of the men on the head
with a chair and others wildly swinging their fists at interlopers. The

women also grabbed water buckets, waiting to drench the invaders, while those who heard the commotion attempted to lock their doors and hold out for the cops. Others, however, could be heard yelling, "Help! Police! Isn't this wonderful?" One senior woman claimed that "it was really more fun than anything else" and then coyly said: "We had an inkling they were coming." Once the cops had ejected the men, the women began picking up their clothing and restoring their rooms. The dormitory remained abuzz throughout the night, with some girls reported to be "hysterical." The college's president later disputed much of the reporting, noting that the men had apologized, and downplayed the raid as little more than a "thoughtless, 10 minute aberration" and a "serenade."

Throughout the 1950s and the 1960s, panty raids marked some of the first stirrings of teenage rebellion, sexual experimentation, and rejection of authority. In one sense, these volatile campus disturbances stand as a harbinger of more revolutionary changes to come in the late 1960s. But, in many ways, they were a connection not to the future but to the past. Indeed, panty raids mimicked much of the behavior seen in liberty ports and boomtowns during the war. College men moved, acted, and explained their exploits in the same ways as GIs had. The planning and execution of these raids and the ultimate prize of a co-ed or her underwear matched the rough, coercive heterosexuality that soldiers performed in wartime. Like troops, undergraduates resisted and fought with police attempting to contain or stop these incidents. And the women who were the subject of these invasions often mirrored the reactions that wartime women exhibited when subject to the advances of servicemen. Panty raids, then, point to how the World War II culture of carousing on liberty may have influenced postwar youth sexuality and masculinity.

Similar incidents preceded Augustana's raid. For example, when Harvard men charged into Radcliffe dorms in 1947, "they grabbed protesting, kicking, squealing girls" and "heaved them ungently into the waiting and expectant arms" of their partners in crime. A year later, Colorado's Women's College banned the men of the School of Mines after three hundred of them "invaded" the dorms "garbed only in towel loincloths and hairy chests" and then absconded with several women. Following the 1949 incident at Augustana College, however, these invasions became more violent, organized, and focused on capturing undergarments. The panty raids were explicitly identified as military-like operations conducted by draft-age men and some veterans attending college on the GI bill. In 1950, for example, two thousand Harvard men took advantage of a blackout in Cambridge. Assembling outside their dorms, the men, "armed with flashlights," exclaimed, "On to Radcliffe," and began a march that created a traffic jam snarling up Harvard Square. The *Globe* maintained: "The imminent threat of an invasion by the Harvards did not throw fear into the hearts of the Radcliffe girls who quickly mustered their forces." As the Harvard men surged through the doors and windows of Cabot and Moor Halls, overturning furniture, the women threw water bombs in an attempt to repel the attackers. Police and the fire brigade soon arrived to help expel "the hordes of Attila." Several officers described getting into scuffles with those students who ran or resisted arrest. Reports routinely utilized military language to understand these raids. Papers referred to "surprise sorties" or "undie sorties" and characterized women's dormitories as "under siege." Besides imitating small-unit tactics and army command structures, the undergraduates invoked other symbols of military service. Bugle calls, for example, drove men to besiege the women's dorms at the University of Wisconsin. Rioters sometimes attached panties or skirts to sticks, creating makeshift battle flags just as riotous troops had done on V-J Day. And, as the Korean War became mired in stalemate in 1952, these mock invasions spread throughout the country.

Raids reached a fever pitch during the first half of the 1950s, in terms of both frequency and levels of violence against women and the police. At the University of California, Berkeley, three thousand men invaded a dozen or so sorority houses as part of a "panty raiding party." The *Daily Californian*, the student newspaper, described how the female undergraduates had been "knocked around, assaulted, carried outside in pajamas or nude." At the University of Missouri, over twenty-five hundred male students raided several dorms and sororities, stealing cash, jewelry, and lingerie. The riotous group formed after the leaders left notices on bulletin boards urging men to assemble at 10:00 p.m. They began by marching on Stephens College, which housed girls aged fourteen to nineteen. Reports indicated that "they stormed into several of these dormitories, splintering doors, and roamed thru corridors, forcing their way into girls' bedrooms." There they sought panties, dresses, hose, or any other trophy. A *Columbia Tribune* reporter luridly described "a screaming girl stripped of her panties." Similar assaults occurred at the University of Kansas, where six male students ripped robes from three women. Women also fought back, with co-eds biting an assailant who attempted to grab them from their hiding spot. One female University of Missouri employee held off several raiders with a blackjack. The governor eventually mobilized a field artillery company in an effort to put down the riot after police failed to disperse those men who resisted the officers.

Like the furloughed GI taking over a liberty port, raiding undergraduate men often took to the streets to party, riot, and directly challenge the authority of police. Just as troops on liberty almost seemed to parade in their uniforms—preferably with a girl at their side—undergraduates displayed captured panties as a token of their virility. With "sexy souvenirs" in hand, men routinely tore out into the street, the raiders turning rioters, smashing police cruisers, ripping up street signs and parking meters, and flooding streets after cracking open fire hydrants. Not wishing to harm what was generally a white, middle- to upper-class population, police typically followed an incremental response, starting with calls to disperse or attempts to block entrances to threatened dorms. When those tactics failed, officers sometimes engaged the panty raiders directly. The resulting melees lasted hours and involved hundreds of police and students. Sometimes riot squads were even dispatched. Battling against a hail of rocks thrown by the undergraduates, they resorted to tear gas or fire hoses to drive away the mob.

As the raids continued, however, police forces increasingly favored passive responses, allowing the raiders to have at it. One police sergeant explained: "Officers have been instructed to stand by. The great number of them are afraid to make any arrests for fear of starting a riot." This may have been a prudent tactic in some circumstances given the disparity in numbers between local police units and the multitude of undergraduates. In one instance, an officer who attempted to block a surge of invaders was knocked over and stripped of his clothes. At Northwestern University, a co-ed remembered panty raiders simply picking up a sergeant and carrying him into the dorm, where "they stole just about every piece of underwear in sight." The *Daily Boston Globe* tersely explained that "police were powerless." At other times, however, policemen's passive response gave male students free rein to pillage women's dormitories. Cops responding to a University of Kansas raid advised women "to leave the doors open and not to resist." They also argued that officers should avoid the scene because the raiders' aggression would only be inflamed by the sight of the police. Cops regularly stood by and watched as students broke windows, set up ladders to make second-floor forays, and even used huge battering rams to break down locked doors. Though the police were more willing and able to arrest panty raiders than they were to arrest soldiers, cops still regularly adopted the attitude of letting the boys have their fun at the expense of women's welfare.

Like women in wartime port cities, female undergraduates engaged in active resistance to these assaults on their residences, property, and bodies. During almost every raid, women rained water bombs and eggs down on the approaching attackers, though this could be a sign of both genuine resistance and playfulness. When men managed to break into the dormitories, women grabbed fire hoses and turned them on the raiders. Others favored baseball bats and makeshift blunt weapons as often-necessary defenses against the men threatening physical and sexual assault.

But, even when covering raids during which women were assaulted, reporters consistently found female conspirators who encouraged and abetted the invaders. Tulane's raid captured this complex dynamic when some women at one dorm conspired to let a raiding group in while others desperately locked their doors. Co-eds regularly taunted the men assembled outside their buildings, shouting, "Come on in fellows." Whether to entice or to placate the approaching invaders, some women decided to simply toss lingerie out the window to the howling men below. Women also regularly rejected the aid of police and university officials, booing them, calling them "party poopers," or demanding that the cops step aside and "let 'em in!" In rarer instances, female students attacked police officers who had arrested particularly belligerent raiders. At Missouri's violent raid, during which women were assaulted and forcibly stripped, a group of co-eds nevertheless fought with a policeman who had arrested three men, eventually freeing them. Some raiders found themselves actually cornered by women, who tore their trousers off. Co-eds even began undertaking "reverse panty-raids," storming into the men's dorms while chanting "we want short shorts" and ransacking dressers for the men's underwear. In these instances, women seemed to be accepting and even mirroring the forceful, wolfish masculinity that had flourished during World War II.

Panty raids appear to have reached their zenith just as the Korean War ground to a deadlock, with the action at times seeming more like the trench warfare of Verdun and Ypres than the mobile tactics that defined the Battle of the Bulge and the German advance through the Ardennes. Though college men seemed to be aping military tactics and the rough, aggressive behavior that defined liberty in wartime cities, GIs stuck in rat-infested trenches had little sympathy for the raiders. After *Stars and Stripes* published an article about the "spring fever" spreading throughout campuses, a soldier wrote in to the civilian papers with utter disdain. Angrily attacking college men who appeared to "have nothing else to do besides going around collecting panties and bras," this "Disgusted G.I." suggested they be drafted immediately. Representing the men at the Central Front, he bitterly explained: "We, too, have 'spring fever,' but our kind is a little different than theirs. It makes me boil inside when I read about such trash going on." A civilian concurred, asking why these young men were allowed to avoid service only to end up "swiping girls' underwear." Senators demanded the boys be drafted, while one judge argued the undergraduates were sabotaging morale in Korea.

To soldiers in Korea, the panty raiders likely seemed little more than boys playing soldier. Their obsession with taking underwear— and not the women it belonged to—suggested an almost adolescent and undeveloped sexuality rather than the swaggering masculinity of a GI, leatherneck, or sailor. It seems probable that criticism of the college men was partially driven by jealousy and antipathy toward civilians. Stuck in a dirty trench, enduring conditions that alternated between frostbite and sunburn, and lacking any clear objective, soldiers understandably despised the civilian boys who seemed to be getting the girls while shirking duty. Others likely objected to the undergraduates who seemed to be claiming the markers of military identity and the spoils of war without any of the sacrifices. Nevertheless, a militarized sexuality took hold at America's colleges and universities even while the actual troops toiled away in "The Forgotten War."

OCCUPATIONS

The legacy of liberty in wartime also endured in the geography of vice imprinted on postwar cities. Though never reaching the same levels of debauchery and danger, postwar hubs retained and expanded the militarized districts that had catered to the men passing through port or the shiploads of sailors arriving for fleet week. The war made fun zones like Scollay Square a more menacing, sordid area less welcoming to civilians. In the postwar era, Scollay's reputation continued to decline even as the military man's nostalgia for the block grew. The square's now-infamous status as "Boston's Barbary Coast" drew the attention of concerned civilians and politicians looking to revitalize the city's downtown. Scollay had become so notorious for wartime excesses that an ultimately failed movement commenced in 1945 to rename the district "Eisenhower Square." In 1951, a judge claimed that the military was still failing to control its personnel in downtown Boston, demanding that certain areas "be classified as a combat zone" and out-of-bounds. When the Old Howard Theatre closed in 1953 owing to the resurgent efforts of vice squads, the last vestiges of the old Scollay Square seemed to go with it. Boston's upper class increasingly hoped the square might be "purified." Just as Robert Moses seized his chance to tear up Coney Island's parks in the late 1940s and the 1950s, the Brahmins and proponents of urban renewal sought an end to what one paper called Scollay's "honky-tonk reputation for evil."

In 1962, Old Boston got its wish when the city declared that Scollay would be destroyed to make way for Government Center, an area positively sterile in both name and appearance. "Proper Boston is standing death watch over an aged and roguish black sheep relative," declared the *Chicago Tribune*. "Brazen Scollay Square, long the stomping ground of millions of seamen and service men is breathing its last raspy breaths as a rowdy oasis in the midst of Puritan virtue." It seemed as if Boston's officials hoped to build the direct opposite of Scollay's sleazy, hodgepodge mix of burlesque, sailor bars, hot dog stands, fleshpots, and tattoo parlors, for they chose a massive, brutalist city hall and a stark plaza defined by the coldness, uniformity, and order of brick and concrete. With offices soon to populate the area, the *Globe* predicted that "only the ghosts of the crews ashore for a night on the town will loiter." Crews and trucks soon arrived, ejecting the square's denizens, and carrying the old buildings—and, with luck, the dodgy reputation—away from the center of Boston. With the square razed, Boston might move beyond the vice and mayhem that had accompanied men when they hit port. As did the army's leadership, urban officials hoped that the vestiges of the war might be erased in a modern, technocratic redesign.

Boston's elite could destroy Scollay, but they could not stop what caused the square to become what it was. Robert Levey—eventually the *Globe*'s restaurant critic—understood this when he explained that the city had merely displaced the desires and suppliers of militarized vice. "Scollay Square was called a bad thing by lots of people," he wrote, "but like television, it was as it was because there were many people who wanted it to be that way." For the moment, however, urban renewal evangelists and proper Bostonians hailed the end of Scollay and its worldwide reputation as the "place where a sailor, weary of the sea, could catch up on shore sins in jig time." For navy ensigns and other troops passing through, Boston remained a key liberty destination. With the destruction of Scollay, they simply sought out new hangouts, and they did not need to look far.

The reconstituted military zone for carousing became appropriately known as "the Combat Zone," demonstrating the degree to which liberty in World War II changed cities for decades to come. Spread over four blocks along Washington, Stuart, Boylston, and Tremont Streets, the reestablished center for sin featured some of Scollay's key hallmarks—sailor bars, hot dog stands, movie houses, strip clubs— but it ditched the old-style burlesque and charm for a grimier jungle of prostitution, pornography, and crime. The Combat Zone built on the sinister and dangerous turn Scollay took during the war, embracing a vision of vice that conjured *Taxi Driver*'s Times Square. In contrast to the broad boulevard of Scollay, the Combat Zone featured tighter, darker streets packed with wandering sailors, streetwalkers, and a jarring mix of curious interlopers, drunks, and social outcasts. Darkness defined the zone—only the flickering neon afforded a brief, hazy glimpse. The area similarly existed in a kind of legal darkness. City cops and the police vice squad with their paddy wagons lingered on the outskirts. But, once inside the heart of the Combat Zone, sailors were largely left to "blow off steam." The *Globe* acknowledged that most police took the view that visitors were committing crimes only against themselves. "If he wants to be a chicken," some officials thought, "he will be plucked." The police department opted merely to contain crime to the zone, forming a perimeter to keep the drinking, fighting, and vice separated from Boston's respectable neighborhoods and businesses. Officials admitted that even attempting to enforce the law would require a hugely expanded police force working around the clock for months just to make the arrests. And, as they learned with Scollay, shutting down a red-light district only pushed servicemen to seek out their desires elsewhere.

The Combat Zone exemplified the dirty, dangerous hubs of vice and delight often found in American cities that attracted troops, such as Times Square and Hollywood Boulevard. The sensory experience and rhythms of the Combat Zone captured the degree to which such areas were born out of the militarization of red-light districts during World War II. Like Scollay, the Combat Zone seemed almost abandoned and decaying in daylight. Without the chiaroscuro effect of neon light, the crumbling exteriors of buildings became readily apparent. The billboards promising strip dancers fared worse in brightness: "Half plucked fowls, with thigh fat," wrote one journalist. Bookshops peddled nudie magazines tightly wrapped in cellophane to prevent casual peaks from the punters. Others pushed expensive books wrapped in brown paper, suggesting that their contents were not fit to be seen publicly. Quite often, however, the purchaser soon discovered he had just bought an edition of *The Great Gatsby*. The B-girl also survived World War II, continuing to ply her trade in the sailor bars that dominated Washington Street. The smells remained the same too. Vomit, piss, smoke, and rye whiskey suffused the area, making it seem sticky and permanently filthy. "White Hunters"—men cruising the area for pickups—blocked up the streets and made easy marks for muggers and con women. Young male civilians and troops frequently brawled, with groups of roaming bluejackets clashing with civilian motorcycle gangs. "The usual fights are between men who feel their masculinity is in question, over a girl," the *Globe* explained, "and between girls, one of whose professional standing is in question." With its heady mix of boozing, whoring, and fighting, the Combat Zone continued the traditions of wartime Scollay and, really, all liberty ports. "Yeah, this is the Combat Zone all right," explained a bartender. "When they tore down Scollay Square, everybody moved down here. The joints, the sailors, the hustlers, everybody. It even smells the same."

Admitting defeat, Boston chose to make the Combat Zone an official "adult entertainment district" in 1974. Attempting to contain the misbehavior and crime of the furloughed sailor proved simpler than directly challenging it. It was the same conclusion that military authorities and politicians had come to during World War II.

TAKING LIBERTY

The seemingly endless sequences of drinking, fighting, and sexual violence capture how the militarization of civilian lives for the warfare state was driven not merely by propaganda, fireside chats, and economic restrictions. Militarization also arrived in the physical, visceral disorder and danger that came with servicemen hitting port. Civilians and troops traveled, worked, and sought bawdy fun in close proximity, and each group battled and collaborated throughout the war. The wartime lives of both groups were intertwined, with servicemen bringing the military dollars to civilian businesses and industries. Troops also brought their own desires into civilian spaces, transforming those spaces and extending the military's power in American metropolises. The story reminds readers that little separated the home front and the war front and that the home front was not a mostly safe oasis shielded from the effects of war and militarization. The history of liberty ports should push scholars to avoid the temptation of artificially segmenting the United States from international zones of occupation and invasion.

The public and scholars should also no longer imagine that the home front somehow avoided civil-military conflict. The Korean War and Vietnam stand out as remarkable instances in which civilian interests and military aims clashed. Neither conflict, however, saw the recurring battles in cities and boomtowns between troops and civilians that made civil-military conflict a defining element of the history of the home front. Legally, the military challenged and undercut the ability of civilians and especially women to seek justice. Troops assumed an aggressive, heterosexual masculinity that mocked civilian life as effeminate and weak from the barracks to their first furloughs. Once on furlough, white military men discovered that the aggrandizement of the military's legal purview allowed them to exercise incredible legal privileges that made them mostly immune to the legal repercussions of civil courts and cops. Brawls, riots, assaults, and murders marked the most troubling signs of a roiling civil-military conflict. FDR preached that citizens ought to sacrifice for the state and the war effort, and the war certainly saw the welfare of civilians ignored when troops needed to take liberty in stopover cities. The American empire was partially built through military conquests establishing legal power over foreign locales and peoples. The military's projection of legal power back into the metropole and the bitter civil-military conflicts that that projection created should form an important part of how the history of World War II in the United States is told.

This history was rendered almost invisible to most observers, and this should remind us how the military, politicians, and intelligence agencies have easily succeeded in making the costs and the damages of war almost unnoticeable today. The often-total cloistering of military lives from the civilian world in the contemporary United States contrasts with the civil-military conflict that defined payday in Norfolk, the Battle of Astoria in Queens, or the deadly riots and rapes in San Francisco at war's end. In that sense, civil-military relations are far better, but only because civilians no longer face the consequences of obsolete processes like mobilization and conscription.

Rather than a civil-military conflict, the United States now faces a civil-military divide that insulates civilians from what wars do. Perhaps the end of the all-volunteer force began an inexorable process whereby the military class became fully separate from the rest of the country. The long wars in Iraq and Afghanistan seem to confirm the reality of a civil-military divide as these grinding conflicts were and are fought by a relatively tiny percentage of Americans, many of whom come from military families. Civilians, for their part, still hold the military as one of the few institutions they remain confident in.

Members of the military were recently ranked the occupational group that contributed the most to society's well-being, beating out teachers, doctors, scientists, and engineers.

But, as Andrew Bacevich has pointed out, this public reverence for military service papers over the divide between civilians and the armed forces. Empty phrases like *thank you for your service* and ostentatious performances of reverence for the military like giving up one's first-class seat to a person in uniform mark what Bacevich calls "a conspiracy of silence, or perhaps a clamor of hollow cheerleading," that "shields our prevailing military system from critical scrutiny." Americans—especially white men—tend to idolize and venerate elite, hypermasculine units like the SEAL teams that proffered a few compelling but mostly symbolic victories in a global war often short on any meaningful triumph or decisive battle. This public, almost religious reverence for the military meant little, however, when troops returned looking for education or work or to repair their bodies and minds. Expediency, drone warfare, and exhaustion inure civilians to the nebulous, sprawling War on Terror. The bloody maintenance of a sluggish empire is bought with the promise that we Americans will not have to think too much about what happens to the people in faraway places we bomb and only a few soldiers will come home in boxes.

Just as in Eisenstadt's iconic *Kissing Sailor*, a history of sexual harassment and assault can be hidden in plain sight. Even now, the images of the war seem fixed in our shared cultural memories and imaginations. *Kissing Sailor* appears to encapsulate romance, ecstasy, and a relief from an all-consuming total war—it is a manifestation of the good war mythology. It seems to promise a coming era of postwar growth, security, social mobility, and economic possibility. Those illusions conceal what actually happened to Greta Friedman and so many other women supposedly safe on the home front. It is a finely crafted image and a false one.

One of the most remarkable parts of the research for this book was how regularly men and women discussed the street harassment and rape occurring every day in liberty ports as if it was a normal, obvious part of their wartime lives. More work needs to be done to uncover the history of sexual assault, and researchers ought to take up Mary Louise Roberts's point that they "dismiss at their own risk sexual relations as an ahistorical sideshow of combat." Indeed, sexual assault and crime in liberty ports point to a fundamentally different story about the aggrandizement of military power in the United States as it relates to the lives of women in wartime. We might also wonder how many other histories of sexual relations and violence are hidden in plain sight, waiting to be uncovered.

It is easy to understand why Americans remain hesitant to imagine "the greatest generation" leaving a legacy of sexual coercion, drunken violence, and seedy vice districts. Few periods of American history still offer the kind of "victory culture" that that this moment continues to evoke. The standard story of World War II tells a tale of triumph, justice, and the ascension of American power, all of it built on the actions and sacrifices of soldiers and sailors fighting outside the United States. The move from the tragedy of Pearl Harbor to the hard-won victories at Normandy and Iwo Jima creates a satisfying narrative arc even for those who use the idea of the good war only ironically. But rethinking the history of the American home front—recovering the central role of troops in that story—reveals a strange and unsettling world where military goals prevailed over the well-being and security, not just of foreign populations, but of American civilians. Chronicling the transformation of cities and civilian life captures the precise ways in which growing federal and military power affected American society. The stories of the people who populated American liberty ports are worth recovering, from the lives of women running the GI gauntlet to troops snatching hard-earned excitement, all the while wondering whether this youthful foray might be their last.

ACKNOWLEDGMENTS

THERE WERE SEVERAL TIMES that I was tempted to stop writing this book. After the tenth day in a regional archive slogging through thousands of army and navy memoranda (and surviving on stale bagels pilfered from a dingy motel's breakfast bar), quitting looks very attractive. I am incredibly grateful to the many people who contributed so much to this project and helped me head back into the archives so I could find this story.

I must start by thanking my adviser, Brooke L. Blower. This book would not exist without her ideas, thoughtfulness, humor, and untiring encouragement. She offered excellent criticism and guidance throughout the process of writing, and she kept me going when I missed deadlines, hit dead ends, or did not know what to do next.

Christopher Capozzola, Marilyn Johnson, and Bruce Schulman also gave generous advice and feedback that helped sharpen the book's argument and attention to the broader history. John Hall, Jennifer Ratner-Rosenhagen, and Mary Lou Roberts all offered their help when I came to the University of Wisconsin-Madison to continue working on the manuscript. Beth Bailey and Andrew Preston offered useful advice as I edited the book, and I greatly appreciate the time they gave me. I would also like to thank the History Departments of Gustavus Adolphus College, Boston University, the University of Cambridge, and the University of Wisconsin-Madison.

Archivists regularly saved me from wasting valuable research hours while patiently putting up with my often-vague requests. The staff at the National Archives and Records Administration in Waltham, Riverside, and San Bruno all devoted many hours to chasing down long-ignored naval records and dusty (and sometimes moldy) boxes. Randy Thompson, Matthew Law, and Henry Mac all stayed persistent while producing useful recommendations and showing interest in the topic. I am also indebted to the staff who keep the National Archives at College Park and the National Archives at Kew working despite the deluge of historians, researchers, and wide-eyed graduate students.

The editors at the University of Chicago Press provided insightful feedback and tireless support as the manuscript developed. Tim Mennel gave me countless hours of advice, editing, and encouragement, making the book's argument much sharper. I would like to thank the two readers who made excellent argumentative and stylistic criticisms that shaped my understanding of military culture and this story's legal history. Thanks as well to Susannah Engstrom and Christine Schwab. My copyeditor, Joseph Brown, offered careful editing and useful suggestions.

My colleagues at the University of Wisconsin–Madison gave me a place to write and a chance to discuss the book so I could better understand it. Thank you to Laura Grossenbacher, Tom McGlamery, Cynthia Poe, Mike Shapiro, Bart Skarzynski, and Steve Zwickel. Bart regularly helped when I needed to complain about the writing process or develop a new idea. I am indebted to his support, guidance, and friendship.

Friends regularly provided excellent feedback and camaraderie. I would like to thank Amy Noel Ellison and Zach Fredman for their insights as the book took shape. Andrew David has been a stalwart and generous friend, and I cannot imagine writing and researching without his help. He and his assistant, Kylie Nelson, did the research to produce the Scollay Square map, for which I am grateful. Cady Steinberg did superb work indexing the manuscript. Thank you to Elizabeth Ansfield, Matt Beachey, Andrew Byron, Glenn Carnahan, Keegan

Fraley, Janie Hynson, Warren Hynson, Jon Lager, Lauren Bennett McGinty, Ryan McGinty, and Steve Palmer for their kindness, humor, and willingness to put up with me. Kevin and Julie Byrne have always been there for excellent conversations, especially when I needed them. Thanks as well to Grace and Keri back home. Thanks to Daisy, James, Jessica, Richard, and Sebastien in our other home. Laura has been a great friend, intrepid, and guide to a family and country I love. Back in Minnesota, my mom has never stopped being the woman I have always looked up to, and she still looks out for me.

Tessa remains an inspiring person who somehow manages to keep getting smarter and funnier. I thank her for her wit, grace, intelligence, and knowing how to make our family better every day.

ABBREVIATIONS

CD   *Chicago Defender*
CDT   *Chicago Daily Tribune/Chicago Tribune*
DBG   *Daily Boston Globe/Boston Globe*
LAT   *Los Angeles Times*
NA   The National Archives of the United Kingdom
NAB   The National Archives Building, Washington, DC
NACP   The National Archives at College Park, Maryland
NARA   The National Archives and Records Administration
NYT   *New York Times*
SFC   *San Francisco Chronicle*
WP   *Washington Post*

NOTES

INTRODUCTION

(1) On August 14, 1945, American troops . . . "Victory Reports around the World: U.S. Fighting Men Lead Wild Celebrations at Japs' Surrender Offer," *Life*, August 20, 1945, 38–38A.

(1) In one Pacific "liberty port," . . . "Navy Clears Bay City Streets Following Riot," *LAT*, August 17, 1945, 8; "Boisterous Celebrants Loot Bay City Stores," *LAT*, August 14, 1945, 6.

(1) The city crackled . . . "Boisterous Celebrants Loot Bay City Stores."

(1) Local civilians and police watched . . . *San Francisco Chronicle* reporter quoted in Carl Nolte, "San Francisco/The Dark Side of V-J Day/The Story of the City's Deadliest Riot Has Been Largely Forgotten," *SFGate*, August 15, 2005, https://www.sfgate .com/g00/bayarea/article/SAN-FRANCISCO-The-dark-side-of-V-J-Day-The-2647870 .php?i10c.encReferrer=aHR0cHM6Ly93d3cuZ29vZ2xlLmNvbS8%3d&i10c.ua=2&i10c .dv=6.

(1) Drunken rioters overturned cars . . . "Riots End Liberty for 100,000 in Navy"; "Riots and Looting Mark Bay City's Celebration."

(1) Some climbed atop their vehicles . . . "Photo Caption to Waves Pillow-Fight," *Life*, August 27, 1945, 24.

(1) Soon, the men were fighting each other . . . "Weekly Intelligence Summary no. 86," August 18, 1945, 319.1 (Weekly Intelligence Summary) 9th SC., Administrative Division: Mail and Records Branch, Classified Decimal File 1941–1945, box 78, RG 389 (Provost Marshal General), NACP.

(2) GIs also brawled . . . "Navy Clears Bay City Streets Following Riot."

(2) GIs, one woman recalled, . . . Quotes from Brooke L. Blower, "V-J Day, 1945, Times Square," in *The Familiar Made Strange: American Icons and Artifacts After the Transnational Turn*, ed. Brooke L. Blower and Mark Philip Bradley (Ithaca, NY: Cornell University Press, 2015), 70–87, 85 (quoting Archie Satterfield, *The Home Front: An Oral History of the War Years in America, 1941–1945* [New York: Playboy, 1981], 366).

(2) At least six rapes . . . "Peace Rioting," *SFC*, August 17, 1945, 1, 6. See also "The People," *This World* (*SFC* magazine insert), August 19, 1945, 5.

(2) "You put young girls . . . Quoted in Nolte, "San Francisco."

(2) **Rather than ordering Shore Patrol** . . . Gary Kamiya, "S.F. Whitewash Covered Up 'Peace Riots' at End of WWII," *SFGate*, August 22, 2015, http://www.sfgate.com /bayarea/article/S-F-whitewash-covered-up-peace-riots-at-6458585.php.

(2) **When the police failed** . . . Health director quoted in Kamiya, "S.F. Whitewash Covered Up 'Peace Riots' at End of WWII."

(2) **Finally, after the authorities** . . . "Riots End Liberty for 100,000 in Navy"; "Riots and Looting Mark Bay City's Celebration."

(2) **Three days of "peace riots"** . . . Sources differ over whether eleven or thirteen people died. "Navy Clears Bay City Streets Following Riot"; "Peace Rioting"; Kamiya, "S.F. Whitewash Covered Up 'Peace Riots' at End of WWII."

(2) **The grand jury supposedly** . . . Quoted in Blower, "V-J Day, 1945, Times Square," 85 (quoting "Riot Prevention Plans Made," *SFC* September 1, 1945, 5).

(2) **The army's intelligence summary** . . . "Weekly Intelligence Summary no. 86."

(2) **When asked about the riot** . . . Quoted in Nolte, "San Francisco."

(2) **New York, Boston** . . . *Life* provided a rosy overview of other V-J Day incidents. See "Victory Celebrations," *Life*, August 27, 1945, 21–27.

(3) **Sixteen million Americans** . . . Michael Adams, *The Best War Ever* (Baltimore, Johns Hopkins University Press, 1993), 70.

(3) **During the war, over three million** . . . Chester Wardlow, *United States Army in World War II: The Technical Services, the Transportation Corps; Movements, Training, and Supply* (Washington, DC: Center of Military History, US Army, 1990), 100, 332.

(3) **Before the spring of 1944** . . . "Strength of the Army Reports," 319.1 (Weekly Intelligence Summary) 8th SC, box 78, Administrative Division: Mail and Records Branch, Classified Decimal File 1941–1945 (RG 389), NACP.

(4) **This "good war" story** . . . For examples of this type of combat history, see Stephen E. Ambrose, *Band of Brothers, 506th Regiment, 101st Airborne: From Normandy to Hitler's Eagle's Nest* (New York: Simon & Schuster, 2001); Robert Leckie, *Delivered from Evil: The Saga of World War II* (New York: Harper & Row, 1987); and Tom Brokaw, *The Greatest Generation* (New York: Random House, 2001). Films have also been critical in defining the usual history of the combat soldier. For the most influential, see *Sands of Iwo Jima*, dir. Allan Dwan (1949, Republic Pictures); and *Saving Private Ryan*, dir. Steven Spielberg (1998, Amblin Entertainment). The marine corps played a significant role in pushing Hollywood to make marines the central figures of American victory in World War II. See Aaron O'Connell, *Underdogs: The Making of the Modern Marine Corps* (Cambridge, MA: Harvard University Press, 2014). For works that cut against this romantic narrative of the combat soldier, see, e.g., John Ellis, *Sharp End: The Fighting Man in World War II* (New York: Scribner, 1980); and Paul Fussell, *Wartime: Understanding and Behavior in the Second World War* (New York: Oxford University Press, 1990). For histories that examine and challenge the good war myth, see Studs Terkel, *"The Good War": An Oral History of World War II* (New York: New Press, 1984).

(4) **Those who fought** . . . For a selection of the most influential combat memoirs, see Eugene B. Sledge, *With the Old Breed: At Peleliu and Okinawa* (New York: Ballantine Books, 2010); Robert Leckie, *Helmet for My Pillow: From Parris Island to the Pacific* (New York: Random House, 1957); and Chuck Tatum, *Red Blood, Black Sand: Fighting alongside John Basilone from Boot Camp to Iwo Jima* (New York: Berkley Caliber, 2012). Histories of American GIs initially portrayed servicemen as fundamentally ordinary and somewhat

provincial men transformed by the war into heroic and romantic vanguards of the American Century. This good war narrative faced mounting criticism in the 1980s in books like Terkel's *"The Good War,"* Fussell's *Wartime,* Adams's *The Best War Ever,* and John Bodnar's *The "Good War" in American Memory* (Baltimore: Johns Hopkins University Press, 2012). See also John Dower's influential *War without Mercy: Race and Power in the Pacific War* (New York: Pantheon, 1986); early works by Saburo Ienaga like *The Pacific War, 1931–1945: A Critical Perspective on Japan's Role in World War II* (New York: Pantheon, 1978); and Mark Selden and Kyoko I. Selden, eds., *Atomic Bomb: Voices from Hiroshima and Nagasaki* (Armonk, NY: M. E. Sharpe, 1989).

(4) **Estimates vary as to how many** . . . Adams, *The Best War Ever,* 70, 97.

(4) **In the European Theater of Operations** . . . John J. McGrath, *The Other End of the Spear: The Tooth-to-Tail Ratio (T3R) in Modern Military Operations* (Fort Leavenworth, KS: Combat Studies Institute Press, 2007), 105.

(4) **This small tooth-to-tail ratio** . . . By contrast, combat troops made up 28 percent of the American Expeditionary Forces in World War I. See McGrath, *The Other End of the Spear,* 105.

(5) **By 1942, for example,** . . . For the Battle of Brisbane, see Peter A. Thompson and Robert Macklin, *The Battle of Brisbane: Australians and the Yanks at War* (Canberra: BWM, 2000).

(5) **In Sydney, women** . . . "Sydney Girls Arm: To Deal with 'Romeos,'" *Cairns Post,* May 8, 1942, 1.

(5) **In Britain, Americans** . . . Neil Tweedie, "How Our Piccadilly Commandos Had the GIs Surrounded," *The Telegraph,* November 1, 2005, http://www.telegraph.co.uk/news /uknews/1501961/How-our-Piccadilly-Commandos-had-the-GIs-surrounded.html.

(5) **Across the Channel** . . . Mary Louise Roberts, *What Soldiers Do: Sex and the American GI in World War II France* (Chicago: University of Chicago Press, 2013).

(5) **And, in China,** . . . Several works have been particularly influential in driving scholars to examine the consequences of America's military presence abroad. See esp. Cynthia Enloe, *Bananas, Beaches and Bases: Making Feminist Sense of International Politics* (London: Pandora, 1989); and Beth Bailey and David Farber, *The First Strange Place* (Baltimore: Johns Hopkins University Press, 1994). See also David Reynolds, *Rich Relations: The American Occupation of Britain, 1942–1945* (New York: Random House, 1995). For works on American soldiers in Australia and New Zealand, see, e.g., Anthony Barker and Lisa Jackson, *Fleeting Attraction: A Social History of American Servicemen in Western Australia during the Second World War* (Nedlands: University of Western Australia Press, 1996). For France, see Roberts, *What Soldiers Do.* For Japan, see Sarah Kovner, *Occupying Power: Sex Workers and Servicemen in Postwar Japan* (Stanford, CA: Stanford University Press, 2012). For Okinawa, see David Tobaru Obermiller, "The US Military Occupation of Okinawa: Politicizing and Contesting Okinawan Identity, 1945–1955" (PhD diss., University of Iowa, 2006). For China, see Zach Fredman, "From Allies to Occupiers: Living with the U.S. Military in Wartime China, 1941–1945" (PhD diss., Boston University, 2016).

(5) **Of course, historians** . . . See, e.g., Dominic J. Capeci Jr., *The Harlem Riot of 1943* (Philadelphia: Temple University Press, 1977); and Michi Weglyn, *Years of Infamy: The Untold Story of America's Concentration Camps* (Seattle: University of Washington Press, 1976). For a more recent study, see Dominic J. Capeci Jr. and Martha Wilkerson, *Layered Violence: The Detroit Rioters of 1943* (Jackson: University Press of Mississippi,

2009). For the historiography of women on the home front, see, e.g., Bailey and Farber, *The First Strange Place*; and D'Ann Campbell, *Women at War with America: Private Lives in a Patriotic Era* (Cambridge, MA: Harvard University Press, 1984). For a history of gay men and women during the war, see Allan Bérubé, *Coming Out under Fire: The History of Gay Men and Women in World War Two* (New York: Free Press, 1990). For more recent histories, see Margot Canaday, *The Straight State: Sexuality and Citizenship in Twentieth-Century America* (Princeton, NJ: Princeton University Press, 2009); and Marilyn Hegarty, *Victory Girls, Khaki-Wackies, and Patriotutes* (New York: New York University Press, 2007).

(6) **Soldiers and sailors are absent** . . . Eduardo Obregon Pagan, *Murder at the Sleepy Lagoon: Zoot Suit Riots, Race, and Riot in Wartime L.A.* (Chapel Hill: University of North Carolina Press, 2003).

(6) **"The continental United States** . . . Lewis H. Lapham, "America's Foreign Policy: A Rake's Progress," *Harper's*, March 1979, 43-84. This quote from Lapham appears in many works. See, e.g., Terkel, *"The Good War,"* 8.

(6) **David M. Kennedy's** . . . David M. Kennedy, *Freedom from Fear: The American People in Depression and War, 1929-1945* (New York: Oxford University Press, 2005), 856.

(6) **Even leading military historians** . . . O'Connell, *Underdogs*, 182.

(6) **Mary Louise Roberts's gripping** . . . Roberts, *What Soldiers Do*, 20.

(6) **In this conception** . . . Roberts, *What Soldiers Do*, 190.

(6) **The home front is made** . . . Roberts, *What Soldiers Do*, 4.

(7) **But civilians in stateside ports** . . . For examples of works that mostly exclude servicemen from the home front, see Doris Kearns Goodwin, *No Ordinary Time: Franklin and Eleanor Roosevelt; The Home Front in World War II* (New York: Simon & Schuster, 1995); and Allan M. Winkler, *Home Front U.S.A.: America during World War II*, 3rd ed. (Hoboken, NJ: Wiley-Blackwell, 2012). Some works, however, have adeptly analyzed how war disrupted urban areas. See, e.g., Marilynn S. Johnson, *The Second Gold Rush: Oakland and the East Bay in World War II* (Berkeley and Los Angeles: University of California Press, 1993); and Pippa Holloway, *Sexuality, Politics, and Social Control in Virginia, 1920-1945* (Chapel Hill: University of North Carolina Press, 2006).

(7) **While some people are aware** . . . For venereal disease campaigns, see Hegarty, *Victory Girls, Khaki-Wackies, and Patriotutes*.

(8) **With this idea came** . . . On the amalgamation of federal and military power during wartime and its consequences, see Christopher Capozzola, *Uncle Sam Wants You: World War I and the Making of the Modern American Citizen* (Oxford: Oxford University Press, 2008); and James T. Sparrow, *Warfare State: World War II Americans and the Age of Big Government* (Oxford: Oxford University Press, 2011). See also Fred J. Cook, *The Warfare State* (New York: Macmillan, 1962); Allan Winkler, *The Politics of Propaganda: The Office of War Information, 1942-1945* (New Haven, CT: Yale University Press, 1978); Alan Brinkley, *The End of Reform: New Deal Liberalism in Recession and War* (New York: Knopf, 1995); Eric Foner, *The Story of American Freedom* (New York: Norton, 1999); Robert Westbrook, *Why We Fought: Forging American Obligations in World War II* (Washington, DC: Smithsonian Books, 2004); and Paul A. C. Koistinen, *Arsenal of World War II: The Political Economy of American Warfare, 1940-1945* (Lawrence: University Press of Kansas, 2004).

(8) **Their streets, bars, parks** . . . Alexander Feinberg, "Soldiers Tour City in Vain for Rooms," *NYT*, August 6, 1944, 1.

(8) **The FBI reported crime spikes** . . . "1941 Shows a Rise in Violent Crime," *NYT*, November 28, 1941, 25; "FBI Reports 3% Rise in Crime," *NYT*, May 13, 1942, 6; Lee Carson, "Gangster Era Is Reborn, FBI Reveals," *WP*, December 5, 1943, M12; "FBI Crime Report Reveals 49.9% Jump in Girl Arrests," *WP*, March 6, 1944, 3; "Crime Rose 8.4% in Year Survey by FBI Reveals," *NYT*, July 28, 1945, 16; "FBI Chief Reports 1946 Rise in Crime," *NYT*, November 10, 1946, 53.

(8) **J. Edgar Hoover also noted** . . . "Female Arrests Rise 18.4 Per Cent," *NYT*, September 17, 1943, 18.

(8) **In major cities, a 46 percent** . . . "Crime Rose 8.4% in Year Survey by FBI Reveals," *NYT*, July 28, 1945, 16.

(8) **As is still the case** . . . Candace Kruttschnitt, William D. Kalsbeek, and Carol C. House, eds., *Estimating the Incidence of Rape and Sexual Assault* (Washington, DC: National Academies Press, 2014).

(9) **Putting young men into barracks** . . . Numerous contemporary studies link sexual aggression and violence to misogynistic views, antisocial behavior, and hostility toward women. Alcohol consumption appears to be a more minor factor, though not inconsequential. For an overview of the literature, see Maggie Koerth-Baker, "Science Says Toxic Masculinity—More Than Alcohol—Leads to Sexual Assault," *FiveThirtyEight*, September 26, 2018, https://fivethirtyeight.com/features/science-says-toxic-masculinity-more-than-alcohol-leads-to-sexual-assault.

(9) **The specter of death** . . . Robert Westbrook, "'I Want a Girl, Just Like the Girl That Married Harry James': American Women and the Problem of Political Obligation in World War II," *American Quarterly* 42, no. 4 (December 1990): 587-614.

(9) **Army leaders like General George C. Marshall** . . . "G. C. Marshall to General Gullion," November 17, 1942, Administrative Division: Mail and Records Branch, Classified Decimal File 1941-1945, 250.1 General #1, box 65, RG 389 (Provost Marshal General), NACP; "Memorandum for General Gullion, from Marshall," n.d., Administration Division: Mail and Records Branch, Classified Decimal File 1941-1945, 250.1 General, box 65 (RG 389), NACP.

(9) **rear admirals** . . . "Misconduct of Service Personnel," January 1, 1945, box 178, [Restricted] P13 Misconduct and Discipline Restricted [2 of 2] THRU [Restricted] P14 Appointment #2, Commander in Chief, Atlantic Fleet (CINCLANT)/(RED 7), Entry #P 110 Confidential and Restricted General Administrative Files, 1945-1945, RG 313 Naval Operating Forces, NACP.

(9) **MPs** . . . "Conduct of Military Personnel on All Public Carriers," April 12, 1942, "Misconduct of Military Personnel Resulting from Drinking," November 23, 1942, and "Allen W. Gullion to International Association of Chiefs of Police," November 21, 1942, all in 250.1 General, box 65, Administrative Division: Mail and Records Branch, Classified Decimal File 1941-1945, 250 to 251, RG 389 (Provost Marshal General), NACP.

(9) **servicemen** . . . See, e.g., LeRoy Neiman, *All Told: My Art and Life among Athletes, Playboys, Bunnies, and Provocateurs* (Guilford, CT: Lyons, 2012), 28-41.

(9) **municipal officials** . . . Kamiya, "S.F. Whitewash Covered Up 'Peace Riots' at End of WWII" (where he quotes a health director).

(9) **writers** . . . Pearl Schiff, *Scollay Square* (New York: Rinehart, 1952), 256, 258-59.

(9) journalists . . . "Navy Clears Bay City Streets Following Riot"; Meyer Berger, "Times Square Diary," NYT, September 3, 1944, SM16; "Festal Mode," WP, August 16, 1945, 8; Alexander Feinberg, "All City 'Let's Go,'" NYT, August 15, 1945, 1.

(9) political organizations . . . "Woman's Christian Temperance Union to Eleventh Naval District," March 2, 1942, P 13 Misconduct 1942, Eleventh Naval District, Commandant's Office, Central Subject Files, RG 181, NARA, Riverside.

(9) civilians . . . "John L. MacNamara to Admiral L. J. Hiltse," September 21, 1946, P8-5 Protests, Petitions, and Complaints 1946 Eleventh Naval District, Commandant's Office, Central Subject Files, RG 181, NARA, Riverside.

(9) and, most importantly, women . . . Knox Memos and SP Reports, P13-2 Conduct—Offenses folders, HQ, Third Naval District, NARA, New York; "Anonymous to Admiral in Command 11th Naval District," n.d., P8-5, box 297, Eleventh Naval District, Commandant's Office, Central Subject Files, RG 181, NARA, Riverside; "Protest Letter to the Commandant," February 19, 1944, Eleventh Naval District, Commandant's Office, Central Subject Files, RG 181, NARA, Riverside.

CHAPTER ONE

(10) By the end of World War II . . . Adams, The Best War Ever, 70.

(10) In early 1939 . . . "Research Starters: US Military by the Numbers," National WWII Museum, n.d., http://www.nationalww2museum.org/learn/education/for-students /ww2-history/ww2-by-the-numbers/us-military.html.

(10) The United States was not . . . Brooke L. Blower, "From Isolationism to Neutrality: A New Framework for Understanding American Political Culture, 1919-1941." Diplomatic History 38, no. 2 (April 2014): 345-76.

(11) Fighting for girls and brotherhood . . . As other historians have explored, men often spoke about fighting for their fellow soldiers or for women they knew or imagined. Mary Louise Roberts, e.g., captures how GIs were driven to think of the liberation of France as a sexual conquest. See Roberts, What Soldiers Do, 59-67.

(11) San Francisco's Peace Day Riots . . . Three key histories focus on the way in which the United States used war and mobilization to equate citizenship with serving the state. Christopher Capozzola's study of World War I remains a highly influential examination of how the state used coercive voluntarism. See Capozzola, Uncle Sam Wants You. Benjamin Alpers's work demonstrates how military service was reclassified as "an extension, or even fulfillment, of one's civilian existence" rather than a burden. See Benjamin Alpers, "This Is the Army: Imagining a Democratic Military in World War II," Journal of American History 85, no. 1 (June 1998): 129-63, 130. Finally, James Sparrow extends Capozzola's argument about civilians serving the state to World War II while assessing how servicemen became first-class citizens. See Sparrow, Warfare State. The definitive portrait of the American soldier—and a key collection of primary sources on mobilization—remains Lee Kennett, G.I.: The American Soldier in World War II (New York: Scribner, 1987). For other works on military and economic mobilization, see George Q. Flynn, The Mess in Washington: Manpower Mobilization in World War II (Westport, CT: Greenwood, 1979), and The Draft, 1940-1973 (Lawrence: University Press of Kansas, 1993); Maury Klein, A Call to Arms: Mobilizing America for World War II (New York: Bloomsbury, 2013); Koistinen, Arsenal of World War II; Waldo Heinrichs, Threshold of War: Franklin D. Roosevelt and American Entry into World War II (New York: Oxford

University Press, 1988); Christina S. Jarvis, *The Male Body at War: American Masculinity during World War II* (Dekalb: Northern Illinois University Press, 2004); and Steven J. Taylor, *Acts of Conscience: World War II, Mental Institutions, and Religious Objectors* (Syracuse, NY: Syracuse University Press, 2009).

(11) **Fan mail to Charles Lindbergh** . . . Blower, "From Isolationism to Neutrality," 357–59.

(12) **Some Americans still felt** . . . Arthur Miller, *Focus* (New York: Penguin, 2001).

(12) **Aware of the lukewarm** . . . "President Plans Military Draft," *LAT*, June 19, 1940, 1.

(12) **The bill called for** . . . "Seeks Authority to Order Year's Training for All Units, Reserves," *WP*, July 30, 1940, 1; Carlyle Holt, "What Shall We Call Them? Draftees?—Selectees?—What's the Matter with 'Soldiers'?," *DBG*, December 4, 1940, 13; Kennett, *G.I.*, 4–5.

(12) **Military leaders and the Roosevelt administration** . . . For the poor state of the US Army, see Goodwin, *No Ordinary Time*, 23.

(12) **The army sought to eliminate** . . . O'Connell, *Underdogs*, 13.

(13) **Prior to the introduction** . . . For the May 1940 maneuvers and the *Time* quote, see Goodwin, *No Ordinary Time*, 48–53.

(13) **"It was a successful experiment,"** . . . Joseph Alsop and Robert Kinter, "America's Top Soldier," *LAT*, December 29, 1940, G10.

(13) **Influential military figures** . . . "Pershing, Conant Back Training Bill," *NYT*, July 4, 1940, 9.

(14) **Pershing's comments** . . . For more on the use of democratic appeals to reinforce the goals of the state, see Sparrow, *Warfare State*.

(14) **In May 1940, anticipating** . . . "4 Students Seized at Military Drill," *NYT*, May 18, 1940, 8.

(14) **Methodist leaders protested** . . . "Church Leaders to Protest Bill on Conscription," *CDT*, July 11, 1940, 13. Catholic bishops and archbishops joined the Methodists, proclaiming that emergencies should not be used to justify totalitarian measures. Assailing the administration's claims about the necessity of preparation, the bishops warned that the supposed danger posed by the situation in Europe did not justify the draft. See "High Catholic Leaders Blast Conscript Bill," *CDT*, July 19, 1940, 10. A California conference of churches similarly condemned Burke-Wadsworth because it failed to meet the "basic principles of democracy." See "Church Opposes Military Plan," *LAT*, July 20, 1940, 2.

(14) **Others wrote to papers** . . . Eugene Hudgins, "Anti-British," letter to the editor, *WP*, August 20, 1940, 6.

(15) **In late July, three people** . . . "Draft Foes Carry Peace Message to Public via Bed-Sheet Signs," *DBG*, July 30, 1940, 2.

(15) **In Los Angeles, the American Peace Crusade** . . . "Peace Pickets Protest Draft," *LAT*, September 6, 1940, 3.

(15) **Some twelve hundred protesters** . . . "Draft Bill Fight Staged in Turner's Arena Ring," *WP*, September 5, 1940, 13.

(15) **The next day, DC police** . . . "Demonstrators on Draft Arrested," *DBG*, September 6, 1940, 17.

(15) **The Democratic and Republican offices** . . . "Young Pickets Here Protest Draft Bill," *NYT*, September 15, 1940, 33.

(15) **Three thousand members** . . . "House Chiefs Expect Fight on Plant Draft," *WP*, September 1, 1940, 4.

(15) **The protests soon reached Congress** . . . Kennett, *G.I.*, 4.

(15) **Agreeing that peacetime conscription** . . . "Draft Evader Penalties Set by Senators," *LAT*, July 27, 1940, 1.

(15) **Perhaps the most notable protest** . . . "Mothers Hang Pepper Effigy on Capitol Hill," *CDT*, August 22, 1940, 6; Kennett, *G.I.*, 4.

(16) **At an August 6 session** . . . Frank L. Kluckhohn, "Clash on Draft: Holt Attacks Sponsors of Bill Who Met Here at Harvard Club," *NYT*, August 7, 1940, 1.

(17) **Tensions also grew in the Democratic-controlled House** . . . "House Cuts Draft Debate; Hundred Million for Planes," *DBG*, August 31, 1940, 1.

(17) **On September 4, two congressmen** . . . "Fist Battle Stirs House in Draft Row," *LAT*, September 5, 1940, 1; "Representative Calls Another Traitor over Draft—Fists Fly," *WP*, September 5, 1940, 1; Kennett, *G.I.*, 4.

(17) **Roosevelt called in powerful Republicans** . . . "Draft Evader Penalties Set by Senators."

(17) **Members of the National Education Association** . . . "Educators Urge Forced Military Drill in Schools," *CDT*, July 3, 1940, 23.

(17) **In the Los Angeles Times** . . . Walter Lippmann, "Today and Tomorrow," *LAT*, August 20, 1940, A4.

(18) **Back in June, a week before** . . . Alsop and Kinter, "America's Top Soldier."

(18) **Leaders like Pershing** . . . Col. W. A. Graham (Ret.), "Compulsory Military Training," *LAT*, July 27, 1940, A4.

(18) **FDR's allies smartly passed** . . . "Age Limits in Draft Bill Set at 21–30," *LAT*, August 1, 1940, 1.

(18) **He warned: "In another 30 days** . . . "Age Limits in Draft Bill Set at 21–30."

(19) **One supporter of conscription noted** . . . Kennett, *G.I.*, 3.

(19) **Peace Mobilization League members** . . . John G. Norris, "Signature of Roosevelt Due Quickly: 4,500,000 Will Be Trained in 5 Years; Age Limits Fixed at from 21 to 35," *WP*, September 15, 1940, 1.

(19) **Often, it was the first federal form** . . . For more on federal forms, tax expansion, and the way in which people interacted with the federal government, see Sparrow, *Warfare State*, 122–25.

(19) **Protests at New York's Union Theological Seminary** . . . For a description of October 16 and the protests, see John G. Norris, "Duty Forced on Us, Roosevelt Tells Selects; Few Protest," *WP*, October 17, 1940, 1. See also Kennett, *G.I.*, 7.

(19) **By this point, Americans** . . . Kennett, *G.I.*, 6.

(19) **One father of a selectee** . . . Benjamin Russell, "The Swiss Make it Work: . . . How Selective Service Builds Democracy . . . ," *LAT*, November 17, 1940, J8.

(19) **Lieutenant Colonel Lewis Hershey** . . . Norris, "Duty Forced on Us, Roosevelt Tells Selects."

(20) **Chief of Staff Marshall faced** . . . Alsop and Kinter, "America's Top Soldier."

(20) **Colleagues warned that** . . . Alsop and Kinter, "America's Top Soldier."

(20) **This military and legal infrastructure** . . . See Brooke L. Blower, "A Nation of Outposts: Forts, Factories, Bases, and the Making of American Power," *Diplomatic History* 41, no. 3 (June 2017): 439–59.

(21) Yet this meant, as Marshall said, . . . Alsop and Kinter, "America's Top Soldier."

(21) Many members of Congress . . . Kennett, *G.I.*, 42–45.

(21) At their height . . . Lenore Fine and Jesse A. Remington, *United States Army in World War II: The Technical Services, the Corps of Engineers; Construction in the United States* (Washington, DC: Center of Military History, US Army, 1989), 42–56.

(22) Most of the new camps . . . Kennett, *G.I.*, 44–45; Fine and Remington, *Construction in the United States*, 131.

(23) While the land was mostly cheap . . . Kennett, *G.I.*, 43, 46.

(24) In 1940, the lumber market . . . Fine and Remington, *Construction in the United States*, 131, 213–16.

(24) Part of the problem came from . . . Capt. M. M. Corpening, "Lack Veterans to Rush Training of Draft Army: Recruits Arriving Too Fast to Be Absorbed," *CDT*, June 16, 1941, 4.

(24) Green troops found little help . . . Kennett, *G.I.*, 80–81.

(25) In some ways, the Old Army . . . For the monastic culture of the corps, see O'Connell, *Underdogs*, 24–60.

(25) Although the War Department . . . Carlyle Holt, "Quality First, Army's Plan to Build Fighting Force," *DBG*, October 27, 1940, B31.

(25) With a chronic shortage . . . "This Is What the Soldiers Complain About," *Life*, August 18, 1941, 17.

(25) One army colonel . . . "Col. M'Cormick Says U.S. Army Unfit for War: Contrasts Training with Germans," *CDT*, August 17, 1941, 1.

(25) Privates largely agreed . . . "This Is What the Soldiers Complain About," 18.

(26) *Life* published damaging remarks . . . "This Is What the Soldiers Complain About," 18.

(26) An army-commissioned study . . . The Sulzberg/Railey report and *Yank* letter quoted in Kennett, *G.I.*, 68–70, 85. Kennett also quotes the *Life* report.

(26) Only officers were officially . . . Terkel, *"The Good War,"* 132.

(26) Draftees' distrust of their superiors . . . Fussell, *Wartime*, 37.

(27) Draftees moved into near-open rebellion . . . Arthur Krock, "'Flank Attack' Is Used in Draft-Army Change," *NYT*, July 20, 1941, E3.

(27) Meyer Berger of the *New York Times* . . . Meyer Berger, "American Soldier—One Year After: A First-Hand Report on the Present State of the Civilian Who Went to Camp Last November to Train for National Defense," *NYT*, November 23, 1941, SM3.

(27) One draftee wrote . . . Arthur Krock, "'Flank Attack' Is Used in Draft-Army Change."

(27) One soldier bluntly told *Life* . . . "This Is What the Soldiers Complain About," 18.

(27) Citing the torrent of letters . . . Willard Edwards, "Public Protests on Longer Draft Term Jar Capital," *CDT*, July 13, 1941, 1.

(28) Privately, Marshall warned . . . Kennett, *G.I.*, 68.

(28) A Fort Meade quartermaster company . . . Arthur Sears Henning, "Court Martial Threat Hurled in Fight to Retain Draftees," *CDT*, July 21, 1941, 1.

(28) Some men responded . . . "This Is What the Soldiers Complain About," 17–18. One plan suggested allowing draftees to defer rent, insurance, and tax debts

made it to the House in an effort to allay some of these concerns. See "Soldiers' Relief from Debt Urged," *LAT*, August 13, 1940, 4.

(29) **Hilton Railey—who described** . . . Kennett, *G.I.*, 70.

(29) **Though weakened by the protests** . . . Richard Turner, "Senate Votes 2½ Year Draft, $10 Pay Boost After One Year," *DBG*, August 8, 1941, 1.

(29) **Low morale continued to plague** . . . "70,000 per Month Will Face Draft, Says Gen. Hershey," *DBG*, August 20, 1941, 13.

(29) **"I was willing to sacrifice** . . . "This Is What the Soldiers Complain About," 18.

(29) **Marshall eased some of the pressure** . . . Kennett, *G.I.*, 70.

(30) **"It's our duty as a nation** . . . Sparrow, *Warfare State*, 56.

(30) **Another asserted that the United States** . . . Sparrow, *Warfare State*, 63.

(30) **Men flocked to recruiting stations** . . . Terkel, *"The Good War,"* 254.

(30) **The navy in Boston** . . . "Recruits: Enlistment Rush Closes Navy Station," *DBG*, December 10, 1941, 11.

(30) **"It was the greatest wave** . . . "Volunteers May Fill Up Draft Quota," *WP*, December 9, 1941, 10.

(30) **The recruit Charles L. Gilley** . . . John G. Norris, "Volunteers Swamp Recruiting Offices," *WP*, December 8, 1941, 10.

(30) **Men fantasized** . . . Sparrow, *Warfare State*, 56.

(30) **The government created six thousand** . . . Elizabeth Mullener, *War Stories: Remembering World War II* (Baton Rouge: Louisiana State University Press, 2002), 35–36. For an in-depth overview of the draft boards, see Kennett, *G.I.*, 6–31.

(30) **Many boys hoped to be selected** . . . Kennett, *G.I.*, 27.

(31) **But men also faced community pressure** . . . Kennett, *G.I.*, 15.

(31) **The administration was pleased** . . . Kennett, *G.I.*, 10.

(31) **Some women's professional groups** . . . "Women Protest Draft Board Ban," *LAT*, October 9, 1940, 5.

(31) **One member explained that** . . . Kennett, *G.I.*, 12.

(31) **Military authorities brought in psychiatric examiners** . . . Bérubé, *Coming Out under Fire*, 22.

(31) **Walter White, the secretary** . . . Quoted in Ulysses Lee, *United States Army in World War II: Special Studies; The Employment of Negro Troops* (Washington, DC: Center of Military History, US Army, 2000), 82.

(32) **Nationwide, draft officials** . . . Kennett, *G.I.*, 11.

(32) **The state selective service director** . . . Lee, *United States Army in World War II*, 411–12.

(32) **Each branch eventually fielded** . . . African Americans made up only 8.5 percent of marine inductees, whereas they constituted 11 percent of registrants. Compare this number to those of the other branches: 10.9 percent of army inductees, 10 percent of navy inductees, and 10.9 percent of coast guard inductees were African American. See Lewis B. Hershey, *Selective Service and Victory: The 4th Report of the Director of Selective Service* (Washington, DC: US Government Printing Office, 1948), 187.

(32) **African American papers** . . . "Now Is the Time Not to Be Silent," *The Crisis* 49 (January 1942): 7 (quoted also in Lee, *United States Army in World War II*, 83).

(32) **The legacy of World War I** . . . Richard S. Faulkner, *Pershing's Crusaders: The American Soldier in World War I* (Lawrence: University Press of Kansas, 2017), 13, 24.

(32) **Devising a unifying narrative** . . . O'Connell, *Underdogs*, 32.

(33) **Few attempted to flee** . . . "His Smashing Draft Protest Is Futile; in the Army Now!," *CDT*, October 15, 1941, 10.

(33) **Men often confessed** . . . Kennett, *G.I.*, 31.

(33) **Awkward young men** . . . Kennett, *G.I.*, 46.

(33) **There recruits lingered** . . . Berger, "American Soldier."

(33) **Most would also receive** . . . Robert W. Coakley and Richard M. Leighton, *United States Army in World War II: The War Department, Global Logistics and Strategy, 1943-1945* (Washington, DC: Center of Military History, US Army, 1968), 13-14.

(34) **Noncoms forced the sleep-deprived men** . . . Berger, "American Soldier"; Sledge, *With the Old Breed*, 8.

(34) **Others jeered that the recruits** . . . Kennett, *G.I.*, 34.

(34) **"The recruits," wrote one observer** . . . Elizabeth R. Valentine, "This Is How We Make a Soldier," *NYT*, August 29, 1943, SM8.

(34) **Draftees soon received** . . . Kennett, *G.I.*, 39.

(34) **At Fort Benning and other posts** . . . Kennett, *G.I.*, 44.

(34) **Superior officers demanded** . . . Ross Parmenter, *School of the Soldier: An Essay in the Form of a Memoir* (New York: Profile, 1980), 27-38.

(34) **Fort Dix featured streets** . . . Marshall Newton, "Sticky Mud Halts Fort Dix Training," *NYT*, December 17, 1940, 21.

(34) **Latrines required** . . . Parmenter, *School of the Soldier*, 28.

(34) **Hastily constructed huts** . . . Berger, "American Soldier."

(34) **Long marches took place** . . . H. I. Brock, "Our Forty-Eight Best States: E Pluribus Unum Has a New Meaning for . . . ," *NYT*, March 14, 1943, SM9.

(35) **Sledge recalled sleeping** . . . Sledge, *With the Old Breed*, 11.

(35) **In Texas, men told of** . . . Kennett, *G.I.*, 44.

(35) **Though conditions improved** . . . Berger, "American Soldier."

(35) **One Indiana recruit lamented** . . . Kennett, *G.I.*, 54.

(35) **Another recalled the** . . . Parmenter, *School of the Soldier*, 38.

(35) **The vast majority of the men** . . . Parmenter, *School of the Soldier*, 22.

(35) **At times, men were quarantined** . . . "Tests Rushed to Determine Cause of Soldier's Death," *LAT*, December 2, 1941, 10.

(35) **Continued equipment shortages** . . . Kennett, *G.I.*, 46.

(35) **Teaching improved** . . . Kennett, *G.I.*, 49.

(35) **Paul Fussell** . . . Fussell, *Wartime*, 76, 80.

(36) **Petty injustices** . . . Fussell, *Wartime*, 80.

(36) **Chickenshit was being forced to dig** . . . Kennett, *G.I.*, 80-81.

(36) **Chickenshit was not being allowed** . . . Kennett, *G.I.*, 54.

(36) **Some of the more intellectual draftees** . . . Parmenter, *School of the Soldier*, 25, 38-39.

(36) **One returning veteran argued** . . . "Voice of the People: Army Training," *CDT*, January 28, 1945, 14.

(36) **Quoting Napoléon, an army colonel** . . . Walter Duranty, "A Challenge to All Americans," *NYT*, May 16, 1943, BR3.

(36) **In 1943, soldiers at Camp Hood** . . . "Private John Rivers to Military Police Division," November 20, 1943, 250.1 General #1, box 65, Administrative Division: Mail and

Records Branch, Classified Decimal File 1941–1945, 250 to 251, RG 389 (Provost Marshal General), NACP.

(37) **The irony, of course,** . . . "Strength of the Army Reports." See also McGrath, *The Other End of the Spear*, 105.

(37) **Their lack of direct experience** . . . Parmenter, *School of the Soldier*, 22.

(37) **In March 1941, the department** . . . "Civilian Workers to Free Soldiers from Camp Jobs," *DBG*, March 20, 1941, 1.

(37) **Even though soldiers also received** . . . Sparrow, *Warfare State*, 212, 224.

(37) **The black press covered** . . . "Summary—Statistical Analysis of Apprehensions," August 14, 1944, 251.2 General #1, box 66, Administrative Division: Mail and Records Branch, Classified Decimal File 1941–1945, 251.2 Gen. to 251.2H, RG 389 (Provost Marshal General), NACP.

(37) **In Bastrop, Louisiana,** . . . "Cavalry Troopers Tell of New Army, Police Brutality," *CD*, September 13, 1941, 1.

(38) **The *Afro-American* reported** . . . *Afro-American* report quoted in Jane Dailey, "The Sexual Politics of Race in World War II America," in *Fog of War: The Second World War and the Civil Rights Movement*, ed. Kevin M. Kruse and Stephen Tuck (Oxford: Oxford University Press, 2012), 151.

(38) **Yet incidents outside the South** . . . For such incidents, see chapter 2.

(38) **Georgia's Camp Stewart** . . . Dailey, "The Sexual Politics of Race in World War II America," 154.

(38) **Europeans consistently noted** . . . Kennett, *G.I.*, 82–83.

(39) **The Office of War Information eventually** . . . "Are you like Benny, without a rating?," created and produced between March 9, 1943, and September 15, 1945, Office for Emergency Management, Office of War Information, Domestic Operations Branch, Bureau of Special Services, Series: World War II Posters, 1942–1945, RG 44 (Records of the Office of Government Reports, 1932–1947), NACP.

(39) **One recruit declared** . . . Kennett, *G.I.*, 82–83.

(39) **Men also shared "rumor-jokes"** . . . Fussell, *Wartime*, 90.

(39) **The Yoo-Hoo Affair started** . . . Louis Lyons, "Tough Gen. Ben Lear Is on a Tough Spot: Nonmilitary Nation Like United States Gets Excited When a Big Mogul of the Army Cracks Down on Selectees Who Yoo-Hoo at Girls," *DBG*, July 13, 1941, C1. For additional coverage of the incident, see Westbrook Pegler, "Fair Enough," *LAT*, July 14, 1941, 1A; "Didn't Know He Was the General," *NYT*, July 15, 1944, 14; and "Yoo-Hooing Soldiers Defended, Gen. Lear Criticized in House," *WP*, July 10, 1941, 1.

(41) **Privately, the brass worried** . . . Kennett, *G.I.*, 67.

(41) **After the story was publicized** . . . Though one congressman asserted that one punished man was "lying prostrate and near death," the camp's commanding officer denied this and said that the injuries were actually a broken rib, one headache, and "three gastronomical disturbances." "Army Orders Lear to Explain Discipline of 'Yoo-Hoo' Troops," *WP*, July 11, 1941, 11.

(41) **To the public, the soldiers** . . . Earl J. Wilson, "Girls OK 'Yoo Hoos'; Say It's Only Natural," *WP*, July 12, 1941, 22.

(41) **One editorial asked** . . . "Brief Note on Shorts," *NYT*, July 17, 1941, 18.

(41) **One woman did maintain** . . . Wilson, "Girls OK 'Yoo Hoos.'"

(41) **The general was unrepentant** . . . "Yoo-Hooing Soldiers Defended."

(41) **Lear believed in the dignity** . . . Lyons, "Tough Gen. Ben Lear Is on a Tough Spot."

(41) **Congress soon put pressure** . . . "Yoo-Hooing Soldiers Defended."

(41) **The War Department eventually** . . . "'Yoo Hoo' Case Delays Action on Lear's Rank," *CDT*, May 13, 1943, 7.

(42) **When Lear returned** . . . "G.I.'s 'Yoo Hoo' Cheer Welcomes Gen. Lear Home," *LAT*, July 21, 1945, 5.

(42) **The incident also inspired** . . . "Yoo-Hoo Incident Ends: War Department Backs Lear in Disciplinary Measures," *NYT*, July 18, 1941, 11; "'Yoo-Hoo' Number Wins Laughter," *LAT*, October 3, 1941, 17; Louella O. Parsons, "Caviar for General!," *WP*, August 11, 1941, 9.

(42) **The Australian war correspondent** . . . Moorehead quoted in Kennett, *G.I.*, 94.

(43) **The men also rejected the patriotic** . . . For the impact of patriotism in driving men to serve in World War I, see Faulkner, *Pershing's Crusaders*, 13, 24.

(43) **Where many doughboys** . . . Faulkner, *Pershing's Crusaders*, 76. Some civil-military conflict did occur, of course. Faulkner, e.g., cites a marine disappointed with the unwelcoming civilians in Galveston. See Faulkner, *Pershing's Crusaders*, 75. For the most part, however, the men of the American Expeditionary Forces did not encounter chronic conflict with locals, nor was the anticivilian ethos baked into their lives in the barracks.

(43) **These experiences outside camp** . . . This view differs from that of Aaron B. O'Connell and others who argue that the army never achieved a truly service-wide identity and emphasized a Taylorist training system focused of shuffling men into their specialized roles. Officially, the army certainly implemented this philosophy. Yet, in the barracks and the camps, most soldiers created a common identity of aggressive hetero-sexuality with a strong anticivilian ethos. Command eventually accepted this mostly organic identity and baked elements of it into training doctrine. See O'Connell, *Underdogs*, 25, 32.

(43) **One GI acknowledged the diversity** . . . Kennett, *G.I.*, 60.

(43) **Whether bullshitting, gambling** . . . For a fascinating breakdown of gambling in the armed forces, see John Desmond, "Help for G.I. Suckers," *NYT*, October 10, 1943, SM14.

(43) **An army study later identified** . . . Army study quoted in Kennett, *G.I.*, 61.

(43) **Men identified different characters** . . . See John Robert Elting, Dan Cragg, and Ernst Deal, *A Dictionary of Soldier Talk* (New York: Scribner, 1984); and Kennett, *G.I.*, 61.

(44) **A flatpeter was more charming** . . . Fussell, *Wartime*, 91.

(44) **Draftees also developed** . . . Elting, Cragg, and Deal, *A Dictionary of Soldier Talk*; Kennett, *G.I.*, 61.

(44) **This "army Creole"** . . . Kennett, *G.I.*, 62.

(44) **Contemporary psychologists identified** . . . Irving L. Janis, "Psychodynamics of Adjustment to Army Life," *Psychiatry*, May 1945, 171; and Kennett, *G.I.*, 62.

(44) **Sociologists agreed** . . . "Sociologists Find Soldier Is No Hero," *NYT*, April 28, 1940, 32.

(44) **Each company produced "weaklings,"** . . . Kennett, *G.I.*, 64.

(44) **These men were bullied** . . . Bérubé, *Coming Out under Fire*, 12–13, 19–20.

(45) **This emphasis was a departure** . . . Bérubé, *Coming Out under Fire*, 12–13, 19–20. For more on wolfish masculinity, see Henry Elkin, "Aggressive and Erotic Tendencies in Army Life," *American Journal of Sociology* 51, no. 5 (March 1946): 408–13; and Talbert Josselyn, "Sailors Ashore," *Collier's*, December 1, 1945, 26–33.

(45) **Some gay draftees found ways** . . . Bérubé, *Coming Out under Fire*, 20, 37–38, 139. For more on the way in which this swaggering masculinity was equated with the full benefits of GI service, see Margot Canaday, "Building a Straight State: Sexuality and Social Citizenship under the 1944 G.I. Bill," *Journal of American History* 90 (December 2003): 935–57, and *The Straight State*.

(45) **General Patton observed** . . . Carlo D'Este, *Patton: A Genius for War* (New York: HarperCollins, 1996), 925–26 n. 42.

(45) **A 1941 navy review of** . . . Navy review quoted in John Costello, *Love, Sex, and War: Changing Values, 1939–1945* (London: Collins, 1985), 115.

(45) **The *US Infantry Journal* concurred** . . . *US Infantry Journal* quoted in Costello, *Love, Sex, and War*, 120.

(45) **"Soldiers," the chief of** . . . Arthur Bartlett, "Best Outfit in the Army: Ask Any Soldier. He'll Tell You What It Is. . . . And Here Is the Man behind the Answer," *LAT*, July 6, 1941, H4.

(46) **Troops obsessed over women's bodies** . . . Elkin, "Aggressive and Erotic Tendencies in Army Life," 411.

(46) **The army's "brass hats"** . . . Meyer Berger, "Morale," *NYT*, May 25, 1941, SM10.

(46) **One soldier wrote** . . . Robert Welker quoted in Kennett, *G.I.*, 80.

(46) **War Department surveys** . . . Forty-six percent responded that were more at ease among soldiers, while 43 percent responded that they felt about the same among both groups. For polling, see "The American Soldier in World War II: Planning Survey 5: Attitudes toward Civilians," Samuel A. Stouffer, USAMS 1942-PS05, War Department, Army Service Forces, Records of the Office of the Secretary of Defense, 1921–2008, RG 330, NACP (retrieved from the Access to Archival Databases at https://catalog.archives.gov/id/620483). See also Samuel A. Stouffer, *The American Soldier: Adjustment during Army Life*, 2 vols. (Princeton, NJ: Princeton University Press, 1949).

(47) **Troops reserved particular antipathy** . . . Kennett, *G.I.*, 78.

(47) **Soldiers regularly complained** . . . "From a Soldier to Civilians," *CDT*, September 21, 1942.

(47) **Men with deferments** . . . Terkel, *"The Good War,"* 121.

(47) **"A Soldier's Guide to the U.S.A." captured** . . . Pfc. Jerome B. Skalka, "A Soldier's Guide to the U.S.A.," *NYT*, August 6, 1944, SM10.

(47) **Yet troops also feared** . . . Bill Downey, *Uncle Sam Must Be Losing the War* (San Francisco: Strawberry Hill, 1982), 25.

(47) **Army psychologists (and enemy psychological warfare divisions)** . . . Clubs similar to those for jilted GIs developed throughout the various theaters of war. Kennett, *G.I.*, 76.

(47) **Several camps spread "Keep 'Em Happy Clubs"** . . . John Cornell, "Southland Soldiers: News and Chatter of Army Camps," *LAT*, July 28, 1941, 7.

(47) **Army researchers became fascinated** . . . Kennett, *G.I.*, 76–77.

(48) **Military life created** . . . Elkin, "Aggressive and Erotic Tendencies in Army Life," 411.

(48) **Many women, too, clearly sensed** . . . Westbrook, "'I Want a Girl, Just Like the Girl That Married Harry James.'"

(48) **Even women's rights advocates** . . . Banning quoted in Judy Barrett Litoff and David C. Smith, eds., *American Women in a World at War: Contemporary Accounts from World War II* (Wilmington, DE: SR, 1997), 10.

(48) **Women's advice authors told** . . . Ethel Gorham, *So Your Husband's Gone to War!* (New York: Doubleday, Doran, 1942), 123.

(48) **One private lamented** . . . Berger, "Morale."

(49) **The men at big training centers** . . . "This Is What the Soldiers Complain About," 18.

(49) **The women who would talk** . . . Berger, "Morale."

(49) **Red-light districts also flourished** . . . Costello, *Love, Sex, and War*, 128–29.

(49) **After Pearl Harbor** . . . Kennett, *G.I.*, 44; Berger, "Morale."

(50) **They would be able to serve** . . . By June 1941, 1,460,998 men were in the army. By 1942, that figure had risen to 3,075,608. See "Strength of the Army Reports"; and Mark Skinner Watson, *United States Army in World War II: The War Department, Chief of Staff; Prewar Plans and Preparations* (Washington, DC: US Army, 1991), 16.

(50) **Carousing with fellow soldiers constituted** . . . Richard Courchene, *"Hell, Love, and Fun"* (West Point, MT: self-published, 1969), 7.

(50) **Before their first time on liberty** . . . Downey, *Uncle Sam Must Be Losing the War*, 23.

(50) **The soldier Walter Bernstein** . . . Walter Bernstein, *Keep Your Head Down* (New York: Viking, 1945), 32. See also Kennett, *G.I.*, 77–78.

(50) **Before shipping out, soldiers** . . . Corporal's story from Cpl. Thomas R. St. George, *C/O Postmaster* (New York: Thomas Y. Crowell, 1943), 1.

(50) **Hilton Railey observed men** . . . Kennett, *G.I.*, 69.

(51) **Only Senator Joshua Lee** . . . Edward Ryan, "Mothers Ask Safeguards for Teen-Age Draft Group: Protests May Bring Provisions for Schooling, Training of 18-19-Year-Olds," *WP*, October 21, 1942, 1.

(51) **One concerned pastor** . . . "M. G. Dickinson to Archie Edwards," February 20, 1941, "C. D. Giauque to Frank Bane," March 3, 1941, "Frank Bane to C. D. Giauque," March 12, 1941, and "Johnathan Daniels to Lewis Polster," March 20, 1942, all in 250, box 86, National Headquarters: General Correspondence, 1940-1942, 250 to 250, RG 171 Records of the Office of Civilian Defense, NACP.

(51) **The Office of Civilian Defense** . . . "A Few of the Many Things All America Does for the Men in Uniform through War Camp Community Service," n.d. (before April 30, 1941), 250 National United through Apr. 30, 1941, box 86, National Headquarters: General Correspondence, 1940-1942, 250 to 250, RG 171 Records of the Office of Civilian Defense, NACP.

(51) **Carousing in "good-time towns"** . . . Kennett, *G.I.*, 77.

(51) **He could be a powerful** . . . Kennett, *G.I.*, 79.

(51) **Far from the control of hard-ass officers** . . . Kennett, *G.I.*, 77. See also Anthony H. Leviero, "The Making of a Soldier," *NYT*, February 9, 1941.

(52) **The army and the navy** . . . Kennett, *G.I.*, 17–22.

(52) **In contrast, the army lacked** . . . It should be noted, however, that the marines were almost certainly viewed as the least prestigious branch at this time. See O'Connell, *Underdogs*.

(52) **The army's own postwar study** . . . Robert R. Palmer, Bell I. Wiley, and William R. Keast, *United States Army in World War II: The Army Ground Forces; The Procurement and Training of Ground Combat Troops* (Washington, DC: Center of Military History, US Army, 1991), 3–5.

(52) **Overall, the military failed to identify** . . . Kennett, *G.I.*, 26.

(52) **The army also received** . . . "American Prison Association Letter," November 26, 1940, 000.5 Criminology-Crimes, Fraud, box 3, National Headquarters: General Correspondence, 1940–1942, 000.5 to 01, RG 171 Records of the Office of Civilian Defense, NACP; "Acts to Permit Probationers to Enlist in Army," *CDT*, January 10, 1942, 10.

(52) **The decision to let in drunks** . . . Kennett, *G.I.*, 79.

(52) **Two months before Pearl Harbor** . . . "Civilians in Uniform," *CDT*, October 7, 1941, 12.

CHAPTER TWO

(54) **Few realize that the vast majority** . . . "Strength of the Army Reports."

(54) **Troops acted poorly long before** . . . As previously stated, estimates vary widely as to how many troops actually saw combat. Less than half were ever in a combat zone, and one military study estimated that less than 10 percent of all troops participated in combat. See Adams, *The Best War Ever*, 70.

(55) **Bases like Fort Hamilton** . . . Wardlow, *The Transportation Corps: Movements, Training, and Supply*, 113.

(55) **Even in smaller locales like Norfolk** . . . J. Blan van Urk, "Norfolk—Our Worst War Town," *American Mercury*, February 1943, 144–51, 145.

(55) **Before heading out, the men** . . . For men taking liberty without permission, see, e.g., Courchene, "Hell, Love, and Fun," 10. Others found ways to sneak women and "other contraband" back in. Bill Mauldin, *Willie and Joe Volumes One and Two* (Seattle: Fantagraphics, 2008), 187.

(55) **While on leave, they were required** . . . For liberty procedures, see "Thirteenth Naval District Order no. 8-41." See also Mark R. Henry, *The U.S. Navy in World War II* (Oxford: Osprey, 2002); and "Liberty Parties—Inspection of," September 6, 1943, P18-1 Leave, Liberty, and Absence 1943, Eleventh Naval District, Commandant's Office, Central Subject Files, RG 181, NARA, Riverside.

(55) **Sailors and soldiers regularly circled** . . . Wardlow, *The Transportation Corps: Movements, Training, and Supply*, 112.

(56) **Although several air and sea routes** . . . This is an amalgamation of several different transportation hubs—such as the Mediterranean/North African route, the Central African route, the Western Pacific route, the Central Asian route, etc.—but it captures the overall movement of troops and materiel while also demonstrating which liberty ports saw the highest levels of human and commercial traffic.

(56) **The main Atlantic route** . . . Wardlow, *The Transportation Corps: Movements, Training, and Supply*, 100, 332. Philadelphia and Baltimore were ports in this network as well, primarily serving New York and Norfolk, respectively. Also note that these

numbers do not include some Allied materiel shipping and that passenger numbers do not include all Allied troops moving through these ports. For more information on transportation networks, see Joseph Rose, *American Wartime Transportation* (Boston: Crowell, 1953).

(57) **New Orleans stitched** . . . Wardlow, *The Transportation Corps: Movements, Training, and Supply*, 100, 332.

(57) **San Francisco and Los Angeles** . . . Wardlow, *The Transportation Corps: Movements, Training, and Supply*, 100, 332.

(57) **"There was nothing but uniforms** . . . Quoted in Nolte, "San Francisco."

(58) **Los Angeles was the other primary port** . . . Wardlow, *The Transportation Corps: Movements, Training, and Supply*, 100, 332.

(58) **These port networks** . . . Wardlow, *The Transportation Corps: Movements, Training, and Supply*, 306–10.

(59) **As their furlough periods approached** . . . Wilbert L. Walker, *We Are Men: Memoirs of World War II and the Korean War* (Chicago: Adams, 1972), 10–12.

(60) **All thoughts came back** . . . LeRoy Neiman, *All Told*, 28–41; Costello, *Love, Sex, and War*, 115; Milton Bracker, "Beaches in Africa Offer Few Girls," *NYT*, August 22, 1943, 10; Tildon B. Houston, "Sailor Meets City—and Applauds," *NYT*, June 13, 1943, SM6.

(60) **Army officers noted the common** . . . Sgt. Al Hill Jr., "A Soldier's Three Desires," *LAT*, February 21, 1944, A4.

(60) **A sergeant's poem** . . . Costello, *Love, Sex, and War*, 122.

(60) **LeRoy Neiman, later a famous painter** . . . Neiman quoted in *All Told*, 28–41.

(60) **Men often went after girls** . . . Sexual cruelty performed as a kind of male bonding remains quite relevant today. See Jia Tolentino, "Brett Kavanaugh, Donald Trump, and the Things Men Do for Other Men," *New Yorker*, September 26, 2018, https://www.newyorker.com/news/our-columnists/brett-kavanaugh-donald-trump-and-the-things-men-do-for-other-men; and Lili Loofbourow, "Brett Kavanaugh and the Cruelty of Male Bonding," *Slate*, September 25, 2018, https://slate.com/news-and-politics/2018/09/brett-kavanaugh-allegations-yearbook-male-bonding.html.

(60) **Troops flocked to bars** . . . Courchene, "Hell, Love, and Fun," 7.

(61) **Despite the threat** . . . "Disciplinary Proceedings," September 1, 1945, box 178, [Restricted] P13 Misconduct and Discipline Restricted [2 of 2] THRU [Restricted] P14 Appointment #2, Commander in Chief, Atlantic Fleet (CINCLANT)/(RED 7), Entry #P 110 Confidential and Restricted General Administrative Files, 1945–1945, RG 313 Naval Operating Forces, NACP.

(61) **Absenteeism—a catchall term** . . . "Naval Offenders Including Deserters and Stragglers—Procedure for Handling," March 31, 1945, box 178, [Restricted] P13 Misconduct and Discipline Restricted [2 of 2] THRU [Restricted] P14 Appointment #2, Commander in Chief, Atlantic Fleet (CINCLANT)/(RED 7), Entry #P 110 Confidential and Restricted General Administrative Files, 1945–1945, RG 313 Naval Operating Forces, NACP.

(61) **Army and navy archives** . . . For examples of military archival AWOL/deserter reports, see box 66, Administrative Division: Mail and Records Branch, Classified Decimal File 1941–1945, 251.2 General #1, RG 389, NACP.

(61) **Mess Sergeant Thomas Flynn** . . . "Army Deserter Seized," *NYT*, July 24, 1942, 22. For similar examples, see "Police Seeks [*sic*] AWOL Soldier in Slaying of

Serviceman," *WP*, February 3, 1944, 1; and "'3-State Crime Wave' Captured; Open Phone at Hold-Up Trips Him," *NYT*, October 20, 1942, 1.

(61) **Other deserters left the military** . . . "2 AWOL Soldiers Called 'Fagins' in Gang Roundup," *CDT*, January 10, 1943, 13.

(61) **One absentee serviceman** . . . "Bazooka Soldier, AWOL, Found," *NYT*, September 15, 1944, 21; "AWOL Soldier Gets Year for Cheese Theft," *CDT*, February 20, 1946, 9.

(62) **Some, like Richard Lee Bailey,** . . . "Statement of Richard Lee Bailey," August 22, 1944, box 66, Administrative Division: Mail and Records Branch, Classified Decimal File 1941–1945, 251.2 B, RG 389 (Provost Marshal General), NACP.

(62) **Initially, military commanders** . . . "Leave and Liberty," December 20, 1941, "Boston. Memo on Navy Employees," July 16, 1941, and "Thirteenth Naval District Order no. 8-41, July 14, 1941," all in P18-1 Leave, Liberty and Absence folder, box 347, 1rst Naval District, Commandant's Office, General Correspondence "District Files," 1941, RG 181, NARA, Waltham. See also "Stragglers from Ships of the Support Force," October 17, 1941, P-13 Discipline folder, box 340, 1rst Naval District, Commandant's Office, General Correspondence "District Files," 1941, RG 181, NARA, Waltham.

(62) **In November 1942, the War Department** . . . "Measures to Forestall Desertions and to Rehabilitate Deserters," March 29, 1943, 250.4 General, box 65, Administrative Division: Mail and Records Branch, Classified Decimal File 1941–1945, 250 to 251, RG 389 (Provost Marshal General), NACP.

(62) **By demonstrating that a serviceman** . . . Surveys confirmed that many men wished to avoid combat. See Kennett, *G.I.*, 113, 133.

(63) **Trials by court-martial** . . . For concern among military authorities over perverse incentives, see "Measures to Forestall Desertions and to Rehabilitate Deserters."

(63) **Confronted with a strained manpower pool** . . . "Eleventh Naval District Circular Letter no. 104-42," October 5, 1942, P 13 Misconduct 1942, RG 181, NARA, Riverside.

(63) **While the navy set up** . . . "Eleventh Naval District Circular Letter no. 104-42."

(63) **Chief of Staff George C. Marshall** . . . For Marshall, see "Discipline and Courts-Martial," November 10, 1942, 250.4 General, box 65, Administrative Division: Mail and Records Branch, Classified Decimal File 1941–1945, RG 389 (Provost Marshal General), NACP.

(64) **The welfare of civilians proved** . . . "Statement of Principles of Discipline for Women's Reserve," December 14, 1942, P-13 Discipline folder, 1 of 2, box 422, 1rst Naval District, Commandant's Office, General Correspondence "District Files," 1942, RG 181, NARA, Waltham. Despite its title, this document contains important regulations on male behavior and crime. See also "Bureau of Naval Personnel Circular Letter no. 165-42," November 27, 1942, P-13 Discipline folder, 1 of 2, box 422, 1rst Naval District, Commandant's Office, General Correspondence "District Files," 1942, RG 181, NARA, Waltham. The key memorandums on crime and shore leave include the measures first conceived in "Secretary of the Navy Restricted Letter," File P3-1 (400226) B, July 19, 1940, RG 181, NARA, Waltham. These measures were expanded on and reinforced in the "Principles of Discipline" memos.

(64) **For example, while troops** . . . "Disciplinary Proceedings." See also "Eleventh Naval District Circular Letter no. 104-22, Subject: Discipline, and Violations of

Traffic Laws by Naval Personnel," October 5, 1942, P 13 Misconduct 1942, RG 181, NARA, Riverside.

(64) **In early 1943, Stimson** . . . "Measures to Forestall Desertions and to Rehabilitate Deserters."

(64) **Officers took this to mean** . . . "Naval Personnel—Absent over and without Leave—Lack of Information concerning Seriousness of Offenses," January 19, 1944, P 13 Misconduct, RG 181, NARA, Riverside.

(64) **Despite these complaints, district officials** . . . "Speedy Trial of Summary Court Martial Cases," September 12, 1944, A17 Law and Justice, RG 181, NARA, Riverside.

(64-65) **At the end of 1943** . . . "Rear Admiral Wilder D. Baker to Vice Admiral J. K. Taussig," December 7, 1943, box 272, [1944-45] P12 to P13 Religion and Misconduct and Discipline THRU P16-1 Strength and Distribution Personnel, Commander-in-Chief Pacific Fleet (CINPAC)/(RED 107), Entry #P 89 Confidential and Secret Administrative Files, 1943-1945, RG 313 Naval Operating Forces, NACP.

(65) **The fleet finally saw an improvement** . . . "Officers and Men Absent without Leave and Absent over Leave on Returning Landing Craft," February 16, 1945, box 178, [Restricted] P13 Misconduct and Discipline Restricted [2 of 2] THRU [Restricted] P14 Appointment #2, Commander in Chief, Atlantic Fleet (CINCLANT)/(RED 7), Entry #P 110 Confidential and Restricted General Administrative Files, 1945-1945, RG 313 Naval Operating Forces, NACP.

(65) **Infantrymen even began to redesignate** . . . This lack of concern about behavior in ports and cities and a general apathy about enforcing moral and religious codes mark another divergence from World War I, during which the May Act was strictly enforced. For appropriating the term *AWOL*, see Blower, "V-J Day, 1945, Times Square," 78.

(65) **Military authorities relied** . . . See, e.g., Dailey, "The Sexual Politics of Race in World War II America," 154.

(66) **But other orders, like when the army** . . . "Jurisdiction of Court-Martial," October 9, 1943, and "Prior Authorization of General Court-Martial Trail [sic] of Civilians," February 15, 1944, both in 250.401 General, Administrative Division: Mail and Records Branch, Classified Decimal File 1941-1945, box 65, RG 389 (Provost Marshal General), NACP.

(66) **Some military decrees, like one preventing** . . . "Army, Navy Issue 'Toughest' Curbs to Miami Night Clubs; New Curfews," *Variety*, July 8, 1942, 45.

(66) **The War Department relied heavily** . . . "Coordination between Civil and Military Law Enforcement Agencies," August 28, 1943, 250.4 Court Martials, Office Management Division: Decimal File 1920-1945, 250.1 Morals & Conduct—Misc. to 291.1 Baptisms Vol. 1, box 195, RG 247 (Chief of Chaplains), NACP.

(66) **Article 74 established** . . . *A Manual for Courts-Martial* (Washington, DC: US Government Printing Office, 1943), app. 1, 220-21.

(66) **One official regulation stipulated that** . . . For the written and unwritten legal measures used by the military, see "Army Service Forces Domestic Situation Report," November 1945, 319.1 Weekly Intell. Summary, Administrative Division: Mail and Records Branch, Classified Decimal File 1941-1945, box 78, 319.1 Weekly Intell. Summary to 320.2 Bolera Mission, RG 389 (Provost Marshal General), NACP; "Arrest Procedure for Military Personnel," March 17, 1941, 370.093, Administrative Division: Mail and Records

Branch, Classified Decimal File 1941–1945, 370.093, box 111, RG 389 (Provost Marshal General), NACP; and "Clashes between Civil and Military Police in Tuskegee, Alabama," June 24, 1942, 250.1 General #1, Administrative Division: Mail and Records Branch, Classified Decimal File 1941–1945, box 65, RG 389 (Provost Marshal General), NACP.

(67) **Army leaders also relied** . . . Eugene O. Porter, "The Articles of War," *Historian* 8, no. 2 (March 1946): 77–102, 77, 79.

(67) **The navy also took advantage of the vagueness** . . . Capt. Donald I. Thomas (Ret.), "Rocks and Shoals," *Shipmate* 54, no. 7 (September 1991): 31, https://www.history.navy.mil/research/library/online-reading-room/title-list-alphabetically/r/rocks-and-shoals-articles-for-the-government-of-the-us-navy.html.

(67) **Legal scholars noted** . . . *Articles for the Government of the United States Navy* (Washington, DC: US Government Printing Office, 1932).

(67) **Navy personnel picked up on this** . . . Robert S. Palsey Jr. and Felix E. Larkin, "Navy Court Martial Proposals for Its Reform," *Cornell Law Review* 33, no. 2 (November 1947): 199–201.

(67) **The articles sometimes referred** . . . *Articles for the Government of the United States Navy.*

(67) **In 1942, a sailor** . . . *Rosborough v. Rossell*, 150 F.2d 809 (1st Cir. 1945).

(68) **The resulting case** . . . Palsey and Larkin, "Navy Court Martial Proposals for Its Reform," 199–200.

(68) **Using a legal justification** . . . For the military's legal justification for putting civilians under military justice, see "Jurisdiction of Court-Martial"; and "Prior Authorization of General Court-Martial Trail [sic] of Civilians."

(68) **Chief of Staff Marshall reiterated** . . . A federal judge previously rejected the army's argument that civilians might be tried outside areas under martial law, but the army circumvented the ruling by defining bases, ports, and transports as "in the field."

(68) **Here, *the field* referred to** . . . For Marshall's justification, see "Authority of Commanders and Jurisdiction of the Military Tribunals of the United States with Respect to the Crews of Merchant Vessels," October 9, 1942, 250 General, Administrative Division: Mail and Records Branch, Classified Decimal File 1941–1945, box 65, RG 389 (Provost Marshal General), NACP.

(68) **Much of Marshall's legal reasoning** . . . *A Manual for Courts-Martial*, app. 1, 203.

(69) **Even outside US ports and bases** . . . For the claim to confine civilians, see "Confining Civilians in Post Guard House," September 18, 1941, 370.093, Administrative Division: Mail and Records Branch, Classified Decimal File 1941–1945, 370.093, box 111, RG 389 (Provost Marshal General), NACP.

(69) **In one publicized case, a Shore Patrol officer** . . . See "Judge Censures Shore Patrol for Arrest, Beating of Civilian," *DBG*, September 25, 1943, 3.

(69) **The municipal court judge overseeing the case** . . . For Judge James Fee's rejection of military legal authority, see "DeWitt Denied Powers over Citizens on Coast," *LAT*, November 17, 1942, 15.

(69) **A merchant seaman** . . . "Upholds Military on Convoy Seaman," *NYT*, February 10, 1944, 12.

(69) **In Shanghai, for instance, the army** . . . For the Shanghai case, see "U.S. Army Holds 3 Americans for 133 Days," *CDT*, April 14, 1946, 2.

(69) **Hawaiian civilians described** . . . "Charge Abuse of Civilians in Army Courts: Tell of Judges in Hawaii with Guns at Side," *CDT*, July 2, 1944, 1.

(70) **Territorial officials argued that** . . . "Army, Court Controversy in Hawaii at White Heat," *WP*, August 27, 1943, 1.

(70) **After a civilian naval employee** . . . Dillard Stokes, "Ruling Bars Army Trials for Civilians," *WP*, February 26, 1946, 1.

(70) **The civilians' attorney charged** . . . "Charge Abuse of Civilians in Army Courts"; "Tyranny in Hawaii Rebuked," *CDT*, February 27, 1946, 12. For more on the wartime situation in Hawaii, see Bailey and Farber, *The First Strange Place*. See also Harry N. Scheiber and Jane L. Scheiber, *Bayonets in Paradise: Martial Law in Hawai'i during World War II* (Honolulu: University of Hawaii Press, 2016).

(70) **These cases were more likely to garner** . . . For the order preventing MPs from testifying in court, see "W. W. Smith Memo," August 2, 1941, 370.093, Administrative Division: Mail and Records Branch, Classified Decimal File 1941–1945, 370.093, box 111, RG 389 (Provost Marshal General), NACP.

(70) **At a meeting of the International Association of Chiefs of Police** . . . Quotes from International Association of Chiefs of Police from "Planning for Police Emergency and Disaster Mobilization and a General Discussion of National Defense Problems Affecting Police," December 9, 1940, no folder, National Headquarters General Correspondence, 1940–1942, 501 to 502, box 110, RG 171 Records of the Office of Civilian Defense, NACP.

(71) **Civil police were also supposed** . . . "Eleventh Naval District Circular Letter no. 97-42, Subject: Infringement on Jurisdiction of Civilian Law Enforcement Officers," September 16, 1942, P 13 Misconduct 1942, RG 181, NARA, Riverside.

(71) **In a memo to district police officers** . . . "Procedure regarding Arrest and Release of United States Army, Navy, Marine, Coast Guard, and State Guard Personnel," *Daily Police Bulletin*, August 17, 1943, A17-6 Agents, Legal Matters, Eleventh Naval District, Commandant's Office, Central Subject Files, RG 181, NARA, Riverside; "Walter H. Lentz to All Officers," October 1, 1943, A17-6 Agents, Legal Matters, Eleventh Naval District, Commandant's Office, Central Subject Files, RG 181, NARA, Riverside.

(72) **The army's head of policing occasionally** . . . "Misconduct of Military Personnel Resulting from Drinking."

(72) **Even civilians recognized** . . . For civilian criticism of cops, see "Frank Merwin to Mr. James M. Landis," May 8, 1942, Public Relations—4 Criticism-Complaints, Office of Civilian Defense, National Headquarters, Washington, DC: General Correspondence, 1941–May 1945, box 88, RG 171, NACP.

(72) **Some cities felt compelled** . . . For civilians giving the military city hall space, see "Colonel Charles B. Elliott Memo," September 10, 1941, 370.093, Administrative Division: Mail and Records Branch, Classified Decimal File 1941–1945, 370.093, box 111, RG 389 (Provost Marshal General), NACP.

(72) **Men often hit the bars** . . . Alexander Feinberg, "Curfew Viewed as Breeder of Unbridled Drinking, Vice: Consensus of Service Men and Women, Café and Bar Owners Is Curfew Viewed as Breeder of Unbridled Drinking Fear of Speakeasy Evils," *NYT*, March 14, 1945, 1.

(73) **Whether with beer, whiskey, moonshine** . . . Courchene, *"Hell, Love, and Fun,"* 4.

(73) **The navy actually began adding croton oil** . . . Mike Ostlund, *Find 'Em, Chase 'Em, Sink 'Em: The Mysterious Loss of the WWII Submarine USS Gudgeon* (Guilford, CT: Globe Pequot, 2006), 88-89.

(73) **Other soldiers began looting** . . . "Pilfering of Whiskey Cargo," September 20, 1943, Administrative Division: Mail and Records Branch, Classified Decimal File 1941-1945, 250 to 251, General #1, box 65, RG 389 (Provost Marshal General), NACP.

(74) **Others snuck booze onto trains** . . . For train drinking, see "St. Paul Train Report," February 3, 1945, and "San Francisco Train Report," April 3, 1945, both in Administrative Division: Mail and Records Branch, Classified Decimal File 1941-1945, 250 to 251, General #2, box 65, RG 389 (Provost Marshal General), NACP.

(74) **British officers remarked that American soldiers** . . . Fussell, *Wartime*, 102.

(74) **Subsequent medical studies** . . . C. Dennis Robinette, Zdenek Hrubec, and Joseph F. Fraumeni Jr., "Chronic Alcoholism and Subsequent Mortality in World War II Veterans," *American Journal of Epidemiology* 109, no. 6 (1979): 687-700.

(74) **In November 1942, Chief of Staff Marshall** . . . "G. C. Marshall to General Gullion."

(74) **Months later, however,** . . . "Misconduct of Military Personnel," February 19, 1943, Administrative Division: Mail and Records Branch, Classified Decimal File 1941-1945, 250 to 251, box 65, RG 389 (Provost Marshal General), NACP.

(74) **Once again, however, naval protocol warned** . . . "Disciplinary Proceedings."

(75) **Civilian police did little better** . . . Feinberg, "Curfew Viewed as Breeder of Unbridled Drinking, Vice."

(75) **In July 1942, Miami's Rear Admiral James L. Kauffman** . . . A similar ban was implemented in San Francisco, to little effect. For the Miami midnight liquor ban, see "Army, Navy Issue 'Toughest' Curbs to Miami Night Clubs."

(75) **In March 1943, the *Daily Boston Globe*** . . . William H. Clark, "Servicemen Have Given Miami a Strong Home Town Atmosphere," *DBG*, March 14, 1943, C37.

(75) **Similar attempts in New York** . . . Feinberg, "Curfew Viewed as Breeder of Unbridled Drinking, Vice."

(76) **In Colón and Panama City** . . . Robert Edson Lee, *To the War* (New York: Knopf, 1968), 54-57.

(76) **Privately, the army conceded that MPs** . . . "Report from Theaters of Operation on Military Police Subjects," September 24, 1942, Administrative Division: Mail and Records Branch, Classified Decimal File 1941-1945, 319.1 General, 319.1 (Caribbean Defense Command) Gen, box 72, RG 389 (Provost Marshal General), NACP.

(77) **Some Panamanians—including the local police** . . . Lee, *To the War*, 54-57.

(77) **Troops and MPs in Colón** . . . "U.S. Soldiers Hurt in Panama Riot," *NYT*, May 5, 1941, 2.

(77) **Later, in Natal, Brazil,** . . . "U.S. Sailors in Brazil Riot," *NYT*, December 20, 1945, 5.

(77) **These brawls and riots** . . . "Panama Says No," *NYT*, December 28, 1947, E2; "Troops Pulled Out," *NYT*, December 24, 1947, 1.

(77) **For many men it was "Last Stop** . . . Richard Goldstein, *Helluva Town: The Story of New York City during World War II* (New York: Free Press, 2013), 55-56.

(77) **Entering New York Harbor** . . . Lee, *To the War*, 47-48.

(77) And, in "the Crossroad of the World," . . . Alistair Cooke, *The American Home Front, 1941–1942* (New York: Grove, 2006), 281.

(78) Seeing the hordes of bluejackets . . . Lee, *To the War*, 47–48.

(78) On Broadway, women filling . . . "Times Sq. Is Enjoying Its 'Greatest Boom' as Civilian and Military Visitors Fill Area," *NYT*, October 28, 1943, 25.

(78) But this was not a peaceful . . . See Blower, "V-J Day, 1945, Times Square," 75–79.

(78) "Canteens, above-the-street dance halls . . . Berger, "Times Square Diary."

(78) In this aggressive mix of violent masculinity . . . "Times Sq. Is Enjoying Its 'Greatest Boom.'"

(78) In Times Square, women . . . Berger, "Times Square Diary."

(78) The film critic Pauline Kael . . . Terkel, *"The Good War,"* 124.

(79) Secretary of the Navy Frank Knox . . . Knox Memos and SP Reports.

(79) In the early hours of the morning . . . Berger, "Times Square Diary."

(79) After beginning the night by pouring . . . Lee, *To the War*, 49.

(79) Reporters ominously wrote . . . Feinberg, "Curfew Viewed as Breeder of Unbridled Drinking, Vice."

(79) From the beginning of the war . . . "Instructions for Reporting Detention of Canadian Absentees," May 22, 1944, and "Apprehension of French Absentees," May 4, 1944, 251.2 General #1, box 66, Administrative Division: Mail and Records Branch, Classified Decimal File 1941–1945, 251.2 Gen. to 251.2 H, RG 389 (Provost Marshal General), NACP; "37 Chinese Sailors Held," *NYT*, April 13, 1942, 4.

(79) Many hotels refused to give rooms . . . Gorham, *So Your Husband's Gone to War!*, 114.

(79) The *New York Times* noted . . . Feinberg, "Soldiers Tour City in Vain for Rooms." La Guardia occasionally opened up the park for sleeping in the summer, though troop behavior did not seem to be affected by his decrees.

(80) Like other servicemen, gay troops . . . Bérubé, *Coming Out under Fire*, 123.

(80) In Los Angeles, sailors found vice . . . "Taverns and Bars—Out of Bounds," (August?) 1942, P8-5 1940 11 ND, RG 181, NARA, Riverside; "Special Investigation Report of T/4 Hugh Nelson and Pvt. Lcl. John Hollinger," July 17, 1942, P8-5 1940, Eleventh Naval District, Commandant's Office, Central Subject Files, RG 181, NARA, Riverside; "Statement of T/4 Pvt. Lcl. Robert Upton and Pvt. Lcl. Charles Rolfe," July 10, 1942, P8-5 1940, Eleventh Naval District, Commandant's Office, Central Subject Files, RG 181, NARA, Riverside.

(81) Locals suggested that visiting servicemen . . . Lee Shippey, "Lee Side o' LA," *LAT*, November 26, 1943, A4.

(81) Mexico and the United States . . . "Apprehension of Deserters by Mexican Authorities," July 21, 1944, "Return of Absentees to Military Control from Mexico," October 10, 1944, and "U.S.W.D. Policy to Deserters and Soldiers AWOL in Mexico," May 25, 1944, all in 251.2 General #1, box 66, Administrative Division: Mail and Records Branch, Classified Decimal File 1941–1945, 251.2 Gen. to 251.2 H, RG 389 (Provost Marshal General), NACP.

(81) After a night of drinking . . . "Illinois Soldier Is Killed by Mexico Police," *CDT*, May 12, 1941, 24; "Camp Callan Soldier Slain; Policeman Held at Tijuana," *LAT*, May 12, 1941, 9.

(81) **In Reynosa** . . . "Weekly Intelligence Summary, 1 September 1945 to 10 September 1945," September 10, 1945, Administrative Division: Mail and Records Branch, Classified Decimal File 1941-1945, 319.1 (Weekly Intelligence Summary) 8th SC., box 78, RG 389 (Provost Marshal General), NACP; "Conduct of Military Personnel in Vicinity of El Paso, Texas, and Juarez, Mexico," April 15, 1944, 250.1 General, box 65, Administrative Division: Mail and Records Branch, Classified Decimal File 1941-1945, 250 to 251, RG 389 (Provost Marshal General), NACP.

(82) **Across American liberty ports** . . . "Protest Letter to Admiral in Command 11th Naval District," March 8, 1944, Eleventh Naval District, Commandant's Office, Central Subject Files, RG 181, NARA, Riverside.

(82) **Other servicemen would "hide** . . . "Protest Letter to the Commandant."

(82) **At the Pike in the Long Beach Amusement Zone** . . . "John L. MacNamara to Admiral L. J. Hiltse."

(82) **On trains and railways, women often** . . . "Statement of Jillson, Edward T. regarding Conditions aboard Southern Pacific Train," December 8, 1944, P18-1 Leave, Liberty, and Absence 1944, Eleventh Naval District, Commandant's Office, Central Subject Files, RG 181, NARA, Riverside.

(82) **Soldiers and sailors regularly engaged** . . . Schiff, *Scollay Square*, 25, 48.

(83) **After witnessing the violent carousing** . . . "Misconduct of Service Personnel."

(83) **Lieutenant General Brehon Somervell** . . . "Brehon Somervell on Discipline," July 14, 1942, 250 Discipline, box 193, Office Management Division: Decimal File 1920-1945, 246.8 Enlisted Personnel—Allowances of to 250.1 Morals and Conduct Vol. 1 (Entertainment), RG 247 (Chief of Chaplains), NACP.

(83) **This ideology informed** . . . "Misconduct of Service Personnel."

(83) **While the admiral chose** . . . Kennett, *G.I.*, 17-22.

(84) **Hampton Roads's struggles** . . . "Misconduct of Service Personnel."

(84) **Male civilians—thought of as 4-Fs** . . . Emily Post, "If He's in Civvies . . . ," *LAT*, April 2, 1944, F21; "Soldiers Find 4-F Civilian Is A-1 Fighter," *WP*, February 10, 1944, 2.

(84) **On many nights, reporters watched** . . . "Rowdies in Times Square," *NYT*, June 11, 1943, 21.

(84) **On other nights, service personnel** . . . Feinberg, "Curfew Viewed as Breeder of Unbridled Drinking, Vice."

(84) **Store owners expected riots and vandalism** . . . Meyer Berger, "Roosevelt Crowd in Times Square Quiet, Very Young, Middle-Aged," *NYT*, November 8, 1944, 7.

(84) **In New York and elsewhere, soldiers drinking** . . . Cases of joyriding, drunk driving, and grand theft auto appear throughout Military Police and Shore Patrol reports. They also made regular appearances in the papers. See, e.g., "Held in Auto Thefts: Sailors Accused of Taking Car from Russian Embassy," *NYT*, April 7, 1944, 21; "Held in Police Car Theft: Sailors Accused of Taking Auto from in Front of Station House," *NYT*, February 23, 1944, 21; "Sailor, Marine Killed in Traffic," *LAT*, February 22, 1945, A12; and "Sailor Escapes Death When Car Skids Off Road," *LAT*, May 1, 1944, A1.

(84) **Stories of sailors even murdering civilians** . . . "Dies After Row with Sailor," *NYT*, August 13, 1944, 19; "Tavern Wrecked as 3 Policemen Battle Civilians, Sailors in Astoria," *NYT*, April 9, 1945, 1.

(84) **Servicemen's targeting of civilian men** . . . "Sailors Barred at Sacramento After Rioting," *CDT*, July 28, 1944, 9.

(85) **Men sought out establishments** . . . "Special Investigation Report of T/4 Hugh Nelson and Pvt. Lcl. John Hollinger"; "Statement of T/4 Pvt. Lcl. Robert Upton and Pvt. Lcl. Charles Rolfe."

(85) **On San Diego's Mission Beach** . . . "Complaint of Rex A. Smith," July 9, 1942, P8-5 1940, Eleventh Naval District, Commandant's Office, Central Subject Files, RG 181, NARA, Riverside.

(85) **In August 1942, over twelve hundred people** . . . "Fight over Girl Starts Dance Hall Riot: 15 Jailed, Scores Hurt in Cambridge," *CD*, August 15, 1942, 2. For other examples, see "Riot Is Started as Soldier and Civilian Fight," *CDT*, August 6, 1943, 19; "Servicemen, Civilians Clash in Lynn, One Hurt and Soldier Held," *DBG*, July 21, 1943, 3; Enoc P. Waters Jr., "Inside Story of Arizona: Blame Girls for Fatal Battle," *CD*, December 5, 1942, 1: and "Soldier Is Shot, 2 Policemen Hurt in So. End Fracas," *DBG*, May 10, 1944, 1.

(85) **The "Battle of Astoria" in New York** . . . "Tavern Wrecked as 3 Policemen Battle Civilians, Sailors in Astoria."

(86) **These interservice brawls could be massive** . . . "Weekly Intelligence Summary," September 29, 1945, Administrative Division: Mail and Records Branch, Classified Decimal File 1941–1945, 319.1 (Weekly Intelligence Summary) 9th SC., box 78, RG 389 (Provost Marshal General), NACP.

(86) **In Bermuda** . . . William Fulton, "Troop Rivalries Keep Bermuda Police on Alert: British and U.S. Sailors Engage in Brawls," *CDT*, September 2, 1941, 7.

(86) **Relations between them eventually** . . . The joint American-British training program was called the "Inter-Attachment Scheme." Here, British and American army forces trained together in Northern Ireland and other home command zones in an attempt to avoid the conflicts that had developed over the course of the war. See "The Army Council: Inter-Attachment of British and American Army Personnel in the United Kingdom: 1944," NA: WO 32/10268.

(86) **Many British soldiers and sailors** . . . For British jealousy over American access to women, see "Minutes of a Conference Held at the Home Office on the 16th April, 1943," NA: WO 32/10267.

(86) **Prominent Bostonians responded** . . . Nat Burrows, "Union Jack Club for Naval Men of Britain Opens Here Tomorrow," *DBG*, November 7, 1941, 9.

(87) **British sailors seen with American** . . . Fussell, *Wartime*, 39.

(87) **Some British servicemen deserted** . . . For British deserters marrying American women, see "Amnesty-Ruling for Deserters Now Residing in (U.S.A.)," NA: WO 32/15261. For the Australian-American war bride example, see "Aussie Sailor Wins Bride in Beach City," *LAT*, October 20, 1945, A3. For Australian women who became American war brides, see Overseas War Brides Association Staff, *Overseas War Brides: Stories from the Women Who Followed Their Hearts to Australia* (East Roseville, NSW: Simon & Schuster, 2001).

(87) **While the British assented** . . . For unequal treaties, see "Offences by Merchant Seamen in Foreign Countries," NA: WO 32/10645. For an example of a British sailor tried in an American civil court, see "Head of the British Advisory Repair Mission to the Secretary of the Admiralty on Alfred Thompson," May 26, 1942, ADM1/12036.

(87) **The Americans additionally demanded . . .** For the United States rejecting UK attempts to try American sailors, see "Disciplinary Status of U.S. Troops in South Africa," June 29, 1942, 250.1 General #1, box 65, RG 389 (Provost Marshal General), NACP.

(87) **Military officials readily understood . . .** "Naval Offenders and Their Treatments by Lt. Comdr. Richard A. Chappell," April-June 1945 Issue of "Federal Probation," A17 Law and Justice, RG 181, NARA, Riverside.

(87) **Following General Marshall's complaints . . .** "Conduct of Military Personnel on All Public Carriers"; "Misconduct of Military Personnel Resulting from Drinking"; "Allen W. Gullion to International Association of Chiefs of Police."

(88) **After Gullion demanded more . . .** "War Department to General Gullion, Military Police Assigned to Public Carriers," September 24, 1942, 250.1 General, Administrative Division: Mail and Records Branch, Classified Decimal File 1941-1945, box 65, RG 389 (Provost Marshal General), NACP.

(88) **A report in August 1942 . . .** For August 1942 report, see "Determination of the Requirements of Military Police Units Necessary for the Internal Security of the United States," August 7, 1942, 320.2 General #1, Administrative Division: Mail and Records Branch, Classified Decimal File 1941-1945, box 79, RG 389, NACP.

(88) **By January 1945, Military Police . . .** "Strength of the Army Report," January 31, 1945, 320.2 Strength of the Army, Administrative Division: Mail and Records Branch, Classified Decimal File 1941-1945, box 80, RG 389, NACP.

(89) **Rather than addressing servicemen's alcohol abuse . . .** For more on vice boards, see the P Vice files and P Misconduct files in RG 181.

(89) **When the Los Angeles Shore Patrol . . .** "Vice Admiral J. K. Taussig to Commodore S. F. Heim," November 25, 1944, P18-1 Leave, Liberty, and Absence 1944 Eleventh Naval District, Commandant's Office, Central Subject Files, RG 181, NARA, Riverside.

(89) **A 1942 army study . . .** "Study of Personnel Problems in the Corps of Military Police," April 30, 1942, box 1185, Military Police Division, Military Police Board Reports, 1942-1947, MP Bd Rpt's # 1 to 17, RG 389 (Provost Marshal General), NACP.

(89) **By the war's end . . .** "Major General James L. Collins to Brigadier General Joseph F Battley," June 23, 1945, 370.093 General, box 111, Administrative Division, Mail and Records Branch, Classified Decimal File 1941-1945, 370.093, RG 389, NACP.

(89) **Other commanders pleaded that . . .** "Lt. Colonel Charles Meyers to Major General Archer L. Lerch," September 1, 1944, 370.093 General, box 111, Administrative Division, Mail and Records Branch, Classified Decimal File 1941-1945, 370.093, RG 389 (Provost Marshal General), NACP.

(90) **Jokes abounded . . .** For MP jokes and "flatfoot," see Sgt. Lloyd Shearer, "A Night with an M.P.," *NYT*, December 6, 1942, SM23.

(90) **GIs like Bill Mauldin . . .** Mauldin, *Willie and Joe Volumes One and Two*, 25.

(90) **Other troops hypothesized that . . .** Kennett, *G.I.*, 85.

(90) **A 1943 War Department report . . .** "What Soldiers Think about Army Branches," April 30, 1943, 461 General #2, box 125, Administrative Division, Mail and Records Branch, Classified Decimal File 1941-1945, 461 to 463.7, RG 389 (Provost Marshal General), NACP.

(90) **One brigadier general . . .** "Disrespect toward and Acts of Violence against Military Police; Misconduct Outside Military Reservations," June 21, 1945, 370.093

General, box 111, Administrative Division, Mail and Records Branch, Classified Decimal File 1941–1945, 370.093, RG 389 (Provost Marshal General), NACP.

(90) **Naval files swell** . . . "Sailors Barred at Sacramento After Rioting."

(90) **Army reports include grisly accounts** . . . "MP Assault Report," June 8 1945, Administrative Division: Mail and Records Branch, Classified Decimal File 1941–1945, 250.1 General #1, box 65, RG 389 (Provost Marshal General), NACP.

(91) **A naval district patrol officer** . . . "Memorandum of T. M. Leovy," March 8, 1944, P8-5, box 297, Eleventh Naval District, Commandant's Office, Central Subject Files, RG 181, NARA, Riverside.

(91) **But how could undermanned patrols** . . . "Bureau of Naval Personnel Circular Letter no. 165-42."

(91) **One woman complained** . . . "Anonymous to Admiral in Command 11th Naval District."

(91) **Instead, "patrols," one civilian seethed** . . . "John L. MacNamara to Admiral L. J. Hiltse."

(91) **When women complained** . . . "Anonymous to Admiral in Command 11th Naval District."

(91) **Several women told the** *Chicago Defender* . . . Waters, "Inside Story of Arizona."

(92) **The army's weekly intelligence summaries** . . . Numerous weekly intelligence summaries can be found in RG 389, Administrative Division, Mail and Records Branch, Classified Decimal File 1941–1945, 319.1 Weekly Intell. Summary, boxes 76–78, NACP. The individual incident reports are found in RG 389, Administrative Division, Mail and Records Branch, Classified Decimal File 1941–1945, 322 General #1, box 81, NACP.

(92) **Black marines lusted** . . . Downey, *Uncle Sam Must Be Losing the War*, 23, 25, 137, 153.

(93) **First, their exhibition of military identity** . . . Sparrow, *Warfare State*, 186.

(94) **In early 1942, Houston city cops** . . . For the Houston case, see John H. Thompson, "Texas Police Insult, Arrest Race Soldiers," *CD*, February 14, 1942, 1; and "Investigation of Negro Situation in Houston Area," March 14, 1942, 291.2 General, Administrative Division: Mail and Records Branch, Classified Decimal File 1941–1945, 251.26 to 300.6, box 68, RG 389 (Provost Marshal General), NACP.

(95) **The War Department investigated** . . . For an example of riots occurring because of a lack of black MPs, see "2 Soldier Riots in Tallahassee," *CD*, October 14, 1944, 11.

(95) **The specter of riots** . . . "Investigation of Negro Situation in Houston Area."

(95) **A different solution presented itself** . . . "Weekly Intelligence Summary, 5th SvC," July 28, 1945, 319.1 (Weekly Intelligence Summary) 5th SC, Administrative Division: Mail and Records Branch, Classified Decimal File 1941–1945, box 77, RG 389 (Provost Marshal General), NACP.

(96) **While police commanders in Houston** . . . For an overview of hypersegregation, see Douglas S. Massey and Nancy A. Denton, "Hypersegregation in U.S. Metropolitan Areas: Black and Hispanic Segregation along Five Dimensions," *Demography* 26, no. 3 (August 1989): 373–91.

(96) **In July 1942, a navy lieutenant commander** . . . "Navy Sets Up 'Jim Crow' Area in Chicago," *CD*, July 25, 1942, 1.

(96) **For example, in New York, . . .** "Weekly Intelligence Summary, 5th SvC."

(96) **Naval authorities in Chicago . . .** "Navy Sets Up 'Jim Crow' Area in Chicago."

(97) **In the army's weekly intelligence summaries . . .** "Weekly Intelligence Summary, 4th SvC," August 11, 1945, 319.1 (Weekly Intelligence Summary) 4th SC. Administrative Division: Mail and Records Branch, Classified Decimal File 1941–1945, 319.1 (Weekly Intelligence Summary) 4th SC., box 77, RG 389 (Provost Marshal General), NACP.

(97) **Detroit witnessed the power of race . . .** For an analysis of how rumor affected the riots, see Marilynn S. Johnson, "Gender, Race, and Rumors: Re-Examining the 1943 Race Riots," *Gender and History* 10, no. 2 (August 1998): 252–77.

(97) **While the Detroit Riot had many . . .** For a short overview, see Sparrow, *Warfare State*, 228.

(97) **In the summer's heat . . .** For Detroit's rumors, see Patricia A. Turner, *I Heard It through the Grapevine: Rumor in African-American Culture* (Berkeley and Los Angeles: University of California Press, 1994), 51.

(97) **Brawling, looting, and firefights . . .** "Detroit Calmer; Troops on Guard," *WP*, June 23, 1943, 1; "23 Killed; U.S. Army Rules Detroit," *DBG*, June 22, 1943, 1; Alfred E. Smith, "Wartime Rioting History Repeats: Will the President Speak Out?," *CD*, August 28, 1943, 8.

(97) **Only a day before the riot . . .** "Army Race Riots Grow! 4 Killed, 16 Wounded in Dixie Clashes," *CD*, June 19, 1943, 1.

(97) **For five days in June 1943 . . .** For the Zoot Suit Riots, see "Riot Alarm Sent Out in Zoot War," *LAT*, June 8, 1943, 1; "Zoot Suit War Grows; Army and Navy Act," *CDT*, June 9, 1943, 1; "Zoot Suit War Runs Course as Riots Subside," *LAT*, June 12, 1943, A; "Zoot Suiters Learn Lesson with Servicemen," *LAT*, June 7, 1943, A1; and "Los Angeles Barred to Sailors by Navy to Stem Zoot-Suit Riots," *NYT*, June 9, 1943, 23. See also Pagan, *Murder at the Sleepy Lagoon*; and Sparrow, *Warfare State*, 228–37.

(97) **The *Chicago Daily Tribune* claimed . . .** "Zoot Suit War Grows."

(98) **The military men stationed in Los Angeles . . .** "Zoot Suit War Grows."

(98) **Eventually, the navy temporarily banned . . .** "Zoot Suiters Learn Lesson with Servicemen."

(98) **Weeks later in Harlem . . .** Turner, *I Heard It through the Grapevine*, 52.

(98) **Crowds formed . . .** "6 Dead in Harlem Riot," *CD*, August 7, 1943, 1; "Harlem Normal Again After Wild Rioting," *CD*, August 14, 1943, 8.

(98) **Riots, fights, and protests . . .** For examples of the continuing conflicts, see "Police Kill Negro Soldier in Arizona," *WP*, July 12, 1942; Charley Cherokee, "National Grapevine," *CD*, October 14, 1944, 13; and "Three Jailed After Soldier, Civilian Fight," *CD*, July 17, 1943, 1.

(99) **The War Department anticipated . . .** "A Plan to Aid in Maintaining a High Standard of Discipline in the Armed Forces After the Defeat of Germany," n.d., Administrative Division: Mail and Records Branch, Classified Decimal File 1941–1945, 370.01 Demobilization to General #2, box 109, RG 389 (Provost Marshal General), NACP.

(99) **In Boston, army officials wisely . . .** "Army to Confine N.E. Soldiers to Bases V-J Day," *DBG*, August 14, 1945, 1.

(99) **Store owners . . .** Seymour R. Linscott, "Boston Becomes Bedlam of Jubilant Demonstrators," *DBG*, August 15, 1945, 1; George McKinnon, "Touring in Police Car: Delirious North End, Lights Bonfires in Streets, Yards," *DBG*, August 15, 1945, 3.

(100) **"When the excitement really** . . . Linscott, "Boston Becomes Bedlam of Jubilant Demonstrators."

(100) **Compelled mass kissing** . . . Leonora Ross, "Joyous, Friendly Crowd Surges through Streets," *DBG*, August 15, 1945, 18.

(100) **Well into the second day** . . . "Boston Keeps Up Victory Whoopee," *DBG*, August 16, 1945, 1.

(100) **Alison Arnold** . . . Arnold quoted in Roy Hoopes, *Americans Remember the Homefront* (New York: Berkley, 2002), 134.

(100) **In New Bedford** . . . "Riot in New Bedford Halted by State Guard and Shore Patrols," *DBG*, August 17, 1945, 1.

(100) **Throughout the Boston area** . . . "Boston Keeps Up Victory Whoopee."

(101) **In Los Angeles, thousands of** . . . "Street Kisses and Embraces to Servicemen Order of Day," *LAT*, August 15, 1945, 7; Art Ryon, "Word of Peace Brings Bedlam in Los Angeles," *LAT*, August 15, 1945, 1.

(101) **"Masses of humanity"** . . . Ryon, "Word of Peace Brings Bedlam in Los Angeles."

(101) **Marines, GIs, and bluejackets** . . . "Los Angeles Rests After Victory Celebrations Night," *LAT*, August 16, 1945, A1.

(101) **An alternate angle likewise focuses** . . . Victor Jorgensen, "New York Celebrating the Surrender of Japan: They Threw Anything and Kissed Anybody in Times Square," August 1945, General Photographic File of the Department of the Navy, 1943–1958, RG 80, NACP.

(101) **The woman, Greta Friedman,** . . . Friedman quoted in Blower, "V-J Day, 1945, Times Square," 80. For interpretations of the photo, see Lawrence Verria and George Galdorisi, *The Kissing Sailor: The Mystery behind the Photo That Ended World War II* (Annapolis, MD: Naval Institute Press, 2012), 3–4; and Blower, "V-J Day, 1945, Times Square," 72–73. The photo is continuously re-created. See Sewell Chan, "62 Years Later, a Kiss That Can't Be Forgotten," *NYT*, August 14, 2007, http://cityroom.blogs.nytimes.com/2007/08/14/62-years-later-a-kiss-that-cant-be-forgotten/?_r=0.

(102) **Over two million crowded** . . . "N.Y.'s Celebration Is Gayest of All Time," *PM*, August 15, 1945, 14–15.

(103) **Police stood by as** . . . "V-J Day Revelry Erupts Again with Times Sq. Its Focus," *NYT*, August 16, 1945, 1.

(103) **Indeed, "kissing became** . . . Feinberg, "All City 'Let's Go'"; "City Takes a Holiday," *New York Post*, August 15, 1945, 5.

(103) **One woman, seized** . . . "N.Y.'s Celebration Is Gayest of All Time"; Verria and Galdorisi, *The Kissing Sailor*, 87–90.

(103) **Reporters later witnessed GIs** . . . "Festal Mode."

(103) **Alexander Feinberg** . . . Feinberg, "All City 'Let's Go.'"

(103) **Over the next two days** . . . "V-J Day Revelry Erupts Again with Times Sq. Its Focus."

CHAPTER THREE

(105) **The history of American women** . . . Some of the key works on women and sex on the American home front are Karen Anderson, *Wartime Women: Sex Roles, Family Relations, and the Status of Women during World War II* (Westport, CT: Greenwood, 1981);

Campbell, *Women at War with America*; Costello, *Love, Sex, and War*; Maureen Honey, *Creating Rosie the Riveter: Class, Gender and Propaganda during World War II* (Amherst: University of Massachusetts Press, 1984); Margaret Randolph Higonnet, Jane Jenson, Sonya Michel, Margaret Collins Weitz, eds., *Behind the Lines: Gender and the Two World Wars* (New Haven, CT: Yale University Press, 1987); Penny Summerfield, *Women Workers in the Second World War: Production and Patriarchy in Conflict* (New York: Routledge, 1984); Hegarty, *Victory Girls, Khaki-Wackies, and Patriotutes*; and Meghan K. Winchell, *Good Girls, Good Food, Good Fun: The Story of USO Hostesses during World War II* (Chapel Hill: University of North Carolina Press, 2008). Marilynn Johnson's portrait of wartime Oakland also offers a look into how defense work transformed a city's economy, space, and amusements for laborers, including the new female war workers. See Johnson, *The Second Gold Rush*.

(105) **When Beth first meets Jerry** . . . For the shoulders quote, see Schiff, *Scollay Square*, 8. For the naval lieutenant quote, see ibid., 102.

(106) **Other women hoped** . . . Bosley Crowther, "The Screen in Review," *NYT*, June 15, 1944, 16.

(106) **In Schiff's *Scollay Square*** . . . Schiff, *Scollay Square*, 9.

(106) **Schiff repeatedly describes** . . . Schiff, *Scollay Square*, 20.

(106) **Jerry's forearm tattoo** . . . Schiff, *Scollay Square*, 17-18.

(106) **When Jerry softly brushes her hair** . . . Schiff, *Scollay Square*, 13.

(107) **After she tells him of her** . . . Schiff, *Scollay Square*, 15.

(107) **For the first two months** . . . Schiff, *Scollay Square*, 85.

(107) **At other times Jerry kisses** . . . Schiff, *Scollay Square*, 131.

(107) **When they have sex for the first time** . . . Schiff, *Scollay Square*, 155-56.

(107) **Another character, Emily,** . . . Schiff, *Scollay Square*, 48.

(107) **Popular works from the era** . . . Margaret Mitchell, *Gone with the Wind* (New York: Macmillan, 1936); *Gone with the Wind*, dir. Victor Fleming (1939; Culver City, CA: Selznick International Pictures, 2000), DVD; Zelda Popkin, *The Journey Home* (Philadelphia: Lippincott, 1945), 5, 41, 95. By contrast, Ann Petry's *The Street* featured a sexually aggressive and obsessed navy vet assaulting and attempting to rape a woman. See Ann Petry, *The Street* (New York: Houghton Mifflin, 1946).

(107) **These desires fall into** . . . For an overview of the literature on rape fantasies and forced seduction, see Joseph W. Critelli and Jenny M. Bivona, "Women's Erotic Rape Fantasies: An Evaluation of Theory and Research," *Journal of Sex Research* 45, no. 1 (January–March 2008): 57–70.

(108) **One of Schiff's female characters** . . . For the "dark sailor" quote and the description of wholesome and shy boys, see Schiff, *Scollay Square*, 48.

(108) **Many women echoed the themes** . . . For "uniform-crazy," see Jean Bartlett in Terkel, *"The Good War,"* 246. For "handsomest thing," see Malvina Lindsay, "The Gentler Sex: Man on Furlough," *WP*, November 20, 1943, B2.

(108) **Married women worried** . . . Gorham, *So Your Husband's Gone to War!*, 78–79.

(108) **Print columnists readily dispensed** . . . Mary Day Winn, "Will War Weddings Last?," *LAT*, September 12, 1943, G4.

(108) **Civilian groups** . . . For the WCCS, see "A Few of the Many Things All America Does for the Men in Uniform through War Camp Community Service."

(108) **Appearing before a Senate subcommittee** . . . For Healey's comments, see "Parental Neglect Blamed for Rise in Delinquency," *WP*, December 1, 1943, 1.

(109) **One seventeen-year-old girl** . . . For the quotes from teenage boys and girls, see Dorothy Gordon, "As the Youngsters See Juvenile Delinquency," *NYT*, August 6, 1944, SM16.

(109) **Spending time with a uniformed man** . . . Gorham, *So Your Husband's Gone to War!*, 76–77.

(109) **Women sometimes banded together** . . . "Twelve Chicago Girls Adopt a Lonely Sailor!," *CDT*, February 1, 1944, 5.

(109) **The navy even went so far** . . . "Most Sailors Not Lonely, Navy Warns All 'Juliets,'" *NYT*, August 16, 1942, 9.

(110) **These proclamations could not** . . . Dellie Hahne in Terkel, *"The Good War,"* 117.

(110) **In 1944, twenty-five hundred** . . . "Service Men Dance in Park Moonlight," *NYT*, June 29, 1944.

(110) **Papers featured front-page stories** . . . ". . . Happily Ever After: Bill the Sailor and Josephine Who Slept in Subways Will Wed: 'Cinderella' Finds Her Bill the Sailor," *WP*, November 13, 1941, 1.

(110) **At Fort Jackson's hospital** . . . "Anonymous Communication to War Dept of the Army," January 26, 1943, 319.1 (M.I.D.) General (Military Investigation Division), Administrative Division: Mail and Records Branch, Classified Decimal File 1941–1945, 319.1 (M.I.D.) General (Military Investigation Division), box 73, RG 389 (Provost Marshal General), NACP.

(110) **Even after being warned** . . . Gorham, *So Your Husband's Gone to War!*, 78.

(110) **Dellie Hahne, a substitute teacher** . . . Dellie Hahne in Terkel, *"The Good War,"* 117.

(110) **Going out during wartime** . . . Juanita Loveless in Sherna Berger Gluck, *Rosie the Riveter Revisited* (Boston: Twayne, 1987), 139.

(110) **Some women remembered** . . . Betty Jeanne Boggs and Juanita Loveless in Gluck, *Rosie the Riveter Revisited*, 113, 143.

(110) **Workers said that** . . . Juanita Loveless in Gluck, *Rosie the Riveter Revisited*, 143.

(110) **Some spent too much time** . . . Peggy Terry in Terkel, *"The Good War,"* 114.

(110) **At Lockheed, young female** . . . Gluck, *Rosie the Riveter Revisited*, 15.

(110) **The GI or sailor** . . . Gorham, *So Your Husband's Gone to War!*, 76.

(111) **One riveter remembered** . . . Betty Jeanne Boggs in Gluck, *Rosie the Riveter Revisited*, 113–14.

(111) **Another young woman, Margarita Salazar McSweyn,** . . . Margaret Salazar McSweyn in Gluck, *Rosie the Riveter Revisited*, 87–89.

(111) **One worker said: "Most of the fellows** . . . Juanita Loveless in *Rosie the Riveter Revisited*, 140.

(111) **Other women, like Marilyn Renner of Iowa,** . . . "Soldier Weddings in Australia Hit," *LAT*, August 23, 1942, 5.

(111) **Jean Bartlett** . . . Terkel, *"The Good War,"* 242–47. Gorham also acknowledges the war's boredom and the potential fun that can be had with men. See Gorham, *So Your Husband's Gone to War!*, 71.

(112) **Women quickly found sport** . . . Gorham, *So Your Husband's Gone to War!*, 173–74.

(112) **Women shared sodas** . . . "Aussie Sailor Wins Bride in Beach City."

(112) **Some women expressed a particular preference** . . . Gorham, *So Your Husband's Gone to War!*, 174.

(112) **Observers in marriage license bureaus** . . . "War Is Powerless to Halt Romance as Business at Marriage Bureau Booms—Husbands in Uniforms," *NYT*, June 19, 1943, 10.

(112) **Most USO hostesses** . . . Eleanor Stierhem, "They Want to Dance . . . ," *LAT*, May 9, 1943, G10.

(112) **"Center girls"** . . . "Job in Service Center? It's Fun for Girls," *CDT*, March 7, 1943, NW1.

(113) **Here, a girl or young woman** . . . For treating idea, see Kathy Peiss, *Cheap Amusements: Working Women and Leisure in Turn-of-the-Century New York* (Philadelphia: Temple University Press, 1986).

(113) **Rather than rotting away** . . . Schiff, *Scollay Square*, 65.

(113) **They remembered being** . . . Gorham, *So Your Husband's Gone to War!*, 70.

(113) **War wives argued** . . . "Why Army Wives Crack Up," *CDT*, August 27, 1944, 16.

(113) **"Don't decide against going out** . . . Gorham, *So Your Husband's Gone to War!*, 78.

(113) **Full control of the pocketbook** . . . Nancy MacLennan, "Wives—but without Husbands," *NYT*, April 26, 1942, SM14.

(114) **Guides advised wives** . . . Gorham, *So Your Husband's Gone to War!*, 43, 70–72, 78. Gorham offers similar advice in ibid., 79.

(114) **Boston's hostesses found that** . . . Robert Allen, "500 Servicemen, 600 Girls Dance at Block Party," *DBG*, September 4, 1942, 1.

(114) **Although only 8 percent** . . . The 8 percent figure is taken from Adams, *The Best War Ever*, 70. See also Gluck, *Rosie the Riveter Revisited*, 13.

(115) **Her guidebook—full of interviews** . . . Major papers recommended Gorham's guide to war wives. See, e.g., Hope Ridings Miller, "If Your Husband Has Gone to War, or May Go Soon, You'll Need Some of Ethel Gorham's Advice," *WP*, September 24, 1942, B7; and Peggy Capron, "For Wives of Service Men: *So Your Husband's Gone to War!* by Ethel Gorham," *NYT*, October 4, 1942, BR20.

(115) **Wives tried to use liberty** . . . Gorham, *So Your Husband's Gone to War!*, 102–3.

(115) **After weeks obsessing** . . . Gorham, *So Your Husband's Gone to War!*, 146.

(116) **Guides advised that a poor appearance** . . . Gorham, *So Your Husband's Gone to War!*, 146.

(116) **The women's columnist Antoinette Donnelly** . . . Antoinette Donnelly, "Wives of Men in the Service: Keep Beauty," *CDT*, October 22, 1942, 26.

(116) **Gorham advised that** . . . Gorham, *So Your Husband's Gone to War!*, 146.

(116) **Women ought to wear** . . . Gorham, *So Your Husband's Gone to War!*, 108, 115, 156.

(116) **Thinking about the inevitable departure** . . . Gorham, *So Your Husband's Gone to War!*, 2.

(116) **The *New York Times* called them** . . . MacLennan, "Wives—but without Husbands."

(116) **They feared a daunting** . . . Gorham, *So Your Husband's Gone to War!*, 123.

(117) **The *Chicago Daily Tribune* reported** . . . Doris Blake, "Lonely Wife Should Find Work to Do," *CDT*, January 31, 1944, 15. Doris Blake was the pseudonym of the women's advice columnist Antoinette Donnelly.

(117) **Besides, some wives argued,** . . . Gorham, *So Your Husband's Gone to War!*, 123 (see also 53).

(117) **An army chaplain declared** . . . Blake, "Lonely Wife Should Find Work to Do."

(117) **In Brooklyn, a sailor** . . . "Two Women Slain, Police Hunt Sailor," *NYT*, July 10, 1944, 17.

(117) **One husband viciously stabbed** . . . "Woman Slashed, May Die, Soldier Cut, Husband Held," *DBG*, November 29, 1943, 12.

(117) **The opera singer Grace Moore** . . . "Unfaithful Wives of Soldiers Stirs [*sic*] Grace Moore's Ire," *WP*, July 29, 1945, 2.

(118) **Presiding over a petty officer's divorce case** . . . "Judge Assails Philandering by Sailor's Wife," *CDT*, December 15, 1943, 13.

(118) **Beyond granting more divorces** . . . "Faithless Wives," *WP*, August 12, 1945, B4.

(118) **Representative Dewey Short** . . . "Army Opposes Move to Check Wives' Morals," *CDT*, October 2, 1943, 13.

(118) **Here, World War I** . . . For women worrying about the effect of World War II, see Winn, "Will War Weddings Last?," G4; and Gorham, *So Your Husband's Gone to War!*, 80. For divorce statistics and wartime bumps in the divorce rate, see Randal S. Olson, "144 Years of Marriage and Divorce in 1 Chart," Randal S. Olson, June 15, 2015, http://www.randalolson.com/2015/06/15/144-years-of-marriage-and-divorce-in-1-chart. Olson pulls data from CDC reports.

(119) **During World War II** . . . For divorce and marriage rates, see Olson, "144 Years of Marriage and Divorce in 1 Chart."

(119) **They were told: "You'd be a foolish wife** . . . Gorham, *So Your Husband's Gone to War!*, 74.

(119) **One wife recalled that** . . . Winn, "Will War Weddings Last?," G4.

(119) **A twenty-one-year-old bride** . . . MacLennan, "Wives—but without Husbands."

(119) **Another young furlough bride mused** . . . Gorham, *So Your Husband's Gone to War!*, 74–75.

(119) **Wives also despaired** . . . Dorothy Dix, "No One Can Help Woman When Prosperity Changes Husband," *DBG*, August 27, 1943, 9.

(119) **Beyond the difficulties of maintaining** . . . Gorham, *So Your Husband's Gone to War!*, 10.

(119) **This mandate provided wives** . . . "Soldiers' Wives' Hobby Club Is Just the Thing," *CD*, March 13, 1943, 16.

(119) **"Don't think there won't be any men,"** . . . Gorham, *So Your Husband's Gone to War!*, 70–71.

(120) **There were men seeking to use women** . . . Gorham, *So Your Husband's Gone to War!*, 72.

(120) **Gorham cautioned fellow wives** . . . Gorham, *So Your Husband's Gone to War!*, 76–80.

(121) **If wives were not faithful** . . . Gorham, *So Your Husband's Gone to War!*, 80.

(121) **Other wives ruefully noted** . . . "Why Army Wives Crack Up."

(121) **Gorham offered these wives** . . . Gorham, *So Your Husband's Gone to War!*, 80.

(121) **Women's columnists also advised** . . . Doris Blake, "Girl Workers: Learn Escort's Marital Status," *CDT*, February 28, 1943, F6.

(121) **Books like *Sailor's Star*** . . . Fanny Heaslip Lea, *Sailor's Star* (New York: Dodd, Mead, 1944).

(121) **"Let your blood run cold,"** . . . Gorham, *So Your Husband's Gone to War!*, 74–75.

(122) **Housing thus became scarce** . . . See Barbara Klaw, "Camp Follower," in Litoff and Smith, eds., *American Women in a World at War*, 128–37, 132; "Soldier's Wife Works," *DBG*, November 26, 1943, 12; and "Service Men's Wives Praised," *NYT*, February 14, 1944, 16.

(122) **Workers sometimes resorted to** . . . Juanita Loveless in Gluck, *Rosie the Riveter Revisited*, 134.

(122) **Marie Baker, a worker** . . . Marie Baker in Gluck, *Rosie the Riveter Revisited*, 231.

(122) **Early in 1942, the Women's Bureau** . . . Adelaide Handy, "Housing Sought for the Women in Defense Jobs," *NYT*, January 11, 1942, D4. See also Johnson, *The Second Gold Rush*.

(122) **According to the *Women's Bureau Special Bulletin*** . . . Dorothy Kraft Newman, *The Woman Counselor in War Industries: An Effective System*, Women's Bureau Special Bulletin no. 16 (Washington, DC: US Government Printing Office, 1944), quoted in Gluck, *Rosie the Riveter Revisited*, 240.

(122) **Even though women were** . . . "Women Face Bias as Room Tenants," *NYT*, April 22, 1944, 10.

(122) **Even military wives struggled** . . . Klaw, "Camp Follower," 132.

(122) **Upscale hotels** . . . Gorham, *So Your Husband's Gone to War!*, 113–14.

(123) **Many decent and even shabby hotels** . . . Chapin Hall, "What Goes On?," *LAT*, April 27, 1942, 7.

(123) **In New York, hotel associations** . . . "Hotels Ask Help of Soldier's Wives," *NYT*, March 5, 1943, 12.

(123) **Work could also be difficult** . . . Peggy Terry and Sarah Killingsworth in Terkel, *"The Good War,"* 109, 114.

(123) **Female war workers** . . . Elizabeth Hawes, "Woman War Worker," *NYT*, December 26, 1943, SM9.

(123) **Other women struggled against stereotypes** . . . Juanita Loveless in Gluck, *Rosie the Riveter Revisited*, 141.

(123) **Beauty columns pressuring** . . . Dorothy Dix, "Women's Beauty Burden Grows Heavier with War Activities," *DBG*, March 16, 1943, 17.

(124) **Gorham described trains as** . . . Gorham, *So Your Husband's Gone to War!*, 112–14.

(124) **Sailors and soldiers took up** . . . Hall, "What Goes On?," 7.

(124) **Given the difficulties of travel** . . . Winn, "Will War Weddings Last?," G4.

(124) **One report acknowledged** . . . "Instructions for Military Police on Railroad Trains (Not Troop Trains) and in Railroad and Bus Terminals and Stations," 1943, Administration Division: Mail and Records Branch, Classified Decimal File 1941–1945, 250.1 General, box 65, RG 389, NACP.

(124) **Nevertheless, women still faced** . . . Mauldin, *Willie and Joe Volumes One and Two*, 33 (*Star Spangled Banter*, March 14, 1941).

(124) **Chief of Staff George C. Marshall** . . . "Memorandum for General Gullion, from Marshall."

(124) **Chicago's Phyllis Blair** . . . "Hunt Assailant of War Worker on North Side," *CDT*, August 1, 1943, 21; "Robbery Motives Seen in Murder of Girl Worker," *CDT*, August 3, 1943, 12.

(126) **Private Edward Green** . . . "Soldier Is Seized in Park Rape Case," *NYT*, June 12, 1943, 28.

(126) **Many women experienced** . . . "Cambridge Soldier Is Charged with Chorus Girl Attack," *DBG*, April 20, 1944, 20.

(126) **In Los Angeles, women described** . . . "Two Women Report Attacks," *LAT*, August 14, 1945, A2.

(126) **Some women, like Fanny Christina Hill** . . . Hill in Gluck, *Rosie the Riveter Revisited*, 35.

(126) **Another woman testified that** . . . "Woman War Welder Fights Off Attacker," *NYT*, January 20, 1945, 24.

(126) **After the rape and strangling of Jessie Strieff** . . . "First Lady Warns Defense-Job Girls," *NYT*, June 18, 1941, 23.

(126) **The House District Committee** . . . "Randolph Asks Military Police Help for DC," *WP*, June 21, 1941, 14.

(127) **Similarly, by 1945** . . . "War on Rapists Mapped as Sex Crimes Mount," *CDT*, August 17, 1945, 5.

(127) **Attacks like these** . . . Elizabeth Gurley Flynn, "Women in the War," in Litoff and Smith, eds., *American Women in a World at War*, 11–23, 18.

(127) **Early on, the National Council for Women** . . . "Women Lay Plans for Post-War Era," *NYT*, October 25, 1941, 20.

(127) **Even worse was** . . . In fact, if servicemen were put on trial, they almost always wore their uniforms and as many medals as they could. Prosecuting attorneys even argued that a uniform could unfairly sway female jurors. See "Women Convict Soldier Who Led $16,150 Robbery," *CDT*, March 4, 1943, 18.

(127) **The papers became especially infatuated** . . . For examples of more concern for white, middle-class women, see "2 Women, Girl Attacked by Sex Criminals," *CDT*, September 6, 1943, 19.

(127) **In Detroit, the furloughed coast guardsman Mike Stephanchenko** . . . "White Sailor Cleared of Rape Charge," *CD*, November 21, 1942, 4. This pattern of exoneration for servicemen followed a fairly standard pattern, especially when the victim was poor or nonwhite. For one notable exception in Bermuda, see "Life for White Soldier in Rape of Negro Woman," *CD*, January 9, 1943, 4.

(127) **Jerry—Beth's sailor love interest** . . . Schiff, *Scollay Square*, 256, 258–59.

(128) **One riveter, Helen Studer,** . . . Studer, Juanita Loveless, Boggs, and Margarita Salazar McSweyn in Gluck, *Rosie the Riveter Revisited*, 189, 138, 113, 85.

(129) **Gorham told working wives** . . . Gorham, *So Your Husband's Gone to War!*, 119–20.

(129) **The *Chicago Defender*, however,** . . . "Warns Workers Not to Spend All They Make," *CD*, May 22, 1943, 8.

(129) **Confronted with the question of** . . . A young man's propensity to be violent or sexually aggressive toward women seems more predicated on factors like antisocial behavior and hostility toward women than, e.g., alcohol consumption. See Maria Testa and Michael J. Cleveland, "Does Alcohol Contribute to College Men's Sexual Assault Perpetration? Between- and within-Person Effects over Five Semesters," *Journal of Studies on Alcohol and Drugs* 78, no. 1 (January 2018): 5-13.

(129) **Psychologists, doctors, and military officials** . . . "Be Tolerant, Understanding to Avoid Beating, Wives Told," *WP*, December 28, 1945, 1.

(129) **"Suddenly, single women** . . . Dellie Hahne in Terkel, *"The Good War,"* 117-18.

(130) **"Listen little lady** . . . Joan Merrill singing "You Can't Say No to a Soldier," by Mack Gordon and Harry Warren, in *Iceland*, dir. H. Bruce Humberstone (1942; Century City, CA: 20th Century-Fox, 2013), DVD.

(130) **On the radio, in magazine shorts** . . . Dellie Hahne in Terkel, *"The Good War,"* 117-18.

(130) **Women who did not fulfill** . . . Westbrook, "'I Want a Girl, Just Like the Girl That Married Harry James.'"

(130) **For government officials** . . . For an overview, see Hegarty, *Victory Girls, Khaki-Wackies, and Patriotutes*, 1-10.

(131) **A typical instance of harassment** . . . "Weekly Intelligence and Security Summary," August 22, 1945, 319.1 General #3, Administrative Division: Mail and Records Branch, Classified Decimal File 1941-1945, 319.1 General, box 72, RG 389 (Provost Marshal General), NACP.

(131) **Gorham warned women** . . . Gorham, *So Your Husband's Gone to War!*, 146.

(131) ***Good Housekeeping* published guides** . . . Florence Howitt, "How to Behave in Public without an Escort," *Good Housekeeping*, September 1943, 40, 160.

(132) **A Doris Blake column** . . . Doris Blake, "Problem of Beauless Girl Needing Escort," *CDT*, January 10, 1941, 16. For similar advice, see Gorham, *So Your Husband's Gone to War!*, 77.

(132) **The Catholic priest and writer Daniel A. Lord** . . . Lord quoted in Doris Blake, "Escort Role Is That of a Protector," *CDT*, January 22, 1942, 17.

(132) **Imogene Stevens** . . . "Woman Held in Sailor's Death," *LAT*, June 30, 1945, 2; "Piano Playing Sailor Slain; Woman Is Held," *CDT*, June 25, 1945, 7.

(133) **Although Stevens was initially** . . . "Mrs. Stevens Free in Slaying Sailor," *NYT*, October 18, 1945, 23.

(133) **At Terminal Island in Los Angeles** . . . "Woman Foils Sailor's Try at Robbery," *LAT*, December 29, 1945, A1.

(133) **In San Diego, a navy wife** . . . "Woman Held in Shooting of Sailor at San Diego," *LAT*, August 7, 1942, 12; "Woman Jailed as Sailor Dies of Gun Wounds at San Diego," *LAT*, August 10, 1942, A13.

(133) **Sarah Killingsworth** . . . Terkel, *"The Good War,"* 115.

(134) **One young woman accused** . . . "Woman Tells Attempt to Make Her Call Girl," *LAT*, August 9, 1941, 16.

(134) **The FBI became so concerned** . . . Susan Laughlin in Gluck, *Rosie the Riveter Revisited*, 250.

(134) **Most workers, however,** . . . Sarah Killingsworth in Terkel, *"The Good War,"* 115.

(134) **Men flocked to the bars** . . . Courchene, *"Hell, Love, and Fun,"* 14.

(134) **Most of these establishments** . . . "Elimination of B-Girls Sought by Government Authorities," *LAT*, August 22, 1942, A14.

(134) **Enterprising operators developed** . . . "Crime against Military Personnel Becomes Flourishing Business: Shore Patrol's Records Show Rise of Menace," *LAT*, January 19, 1945, A1.

(135) **In saloons and soda shops** . . . "Taverns and Bars—Out of Bounds."

(135) **Men would buy the girls liquor** . . . "Elimination of B-Girls Sought by Government Authorities"; "Crime against Military Personnel Becomes Flourishing Business."

(135) **These fears and suspicions** . . . See Hegarty, *Victory Girls, Khaki-Wackies, and Patriotutes*.

(135) **Los Angeles became a port plagued** . . . "Crime against Military Personnel Becomes Flourishing Business."

(136) **"When is a bottle of pop dangerous** . . . "Elimination of B-Girls Sought by Government Authorities."

(136) **Employing crackdowns, raids** . . . "New B-Girl Ban Approved," *LAT*, September 11, 1940, A2.

(136) **As the men poured out of their ships** . . . "City, Army and Navy Patrols Battle Racketeers Who Prey on Servicemen," *LAT*, January 27, 1946, A1; "Griffith Charges Soldiers Rooked," *LAT*, April 12, 1944, 1.

(136) **One pair of young women** . . . "City, Army and Navy Patrols Battle Racketeers Who Prey on Servicemen."

(136) **Girls in the West End of Boston** . . . "British Sailor, Lured by Women, Attacked by Man; Loses $1500," *DBG*, October 3, 1943, B19.

(137) **Sailors could be stabbed to death** . . . "Crime against Military Personnel Becomes Flourishing Business."

(137) **Teenage girls, including a thirteen-year-old** . . . "Police Arrest 5 Boys, Girls; Smash West End Crime Club," *DBG*, December 23, 1945, D2.

(137) **In Staten Island** . . . "Two 'Glamour Girl' Burglars Get $1,000 Loot in Staten Island Home," *NYT*, October 10, 1942, 17.

(137) **In Washington, DC, women** . . . "Police Helped Woman Take Sailor's Wallet," *WP*, June 3, 1945, R5.

(137) **Back in Los Angeles** . . . "Two Women Accused of Dating for Holdups," *LAT*, October 17, 1943, A3.

(137) **Los Angeles authorities estimated** . . . "City, Army and Navy Patrols Battle Racketeers Who Prey on Servicemen."

(137) **Yet officers also admitted** . . . "Crime against Military Personnel Becomes Flourishing Business."

(137) **Nationwide, officials worried** . . . "Spawning Ground of Evil," *WP*, July 24, 1943, 1.

(137) **FBI director J. Edgar Hoover** . . . "Sharp Crime Rise Shown for Girls," *NYT*, March 21, 1943, 16. See also "Women 11% Less Honest," *NYT*, March 14, 1942, 17.

(137) **Subsequent years saw similar increases** . . . "FBI Crime Report Reveals 49.9% Jump in Girl Arrests."

(137) **Women's police bureau officials** . . . "Spawning Ground of Evil."

(138) **The sociologist Elizabeth K. Norton** . . . "Sociologists Find Soldier Is No Hero," *NYT*, April 28, 1940, 32.

(138) **Female troops even got military tattoos** . . . Barbara Brooks, "WAVES and WACS Are Being Tattooed," *DBG*, April 25, 1943, C1.

(138) **Like male soldiers, female troops** . . . Several cases involving WACs and WAVES appear in Military Police misconduct reports.

(138) **In one example, a female first lieutenant** . . . "Misconduct Report for 1st Lt. Mary Hodges Parsons," October 12, 1945, 319.1 Weekly Intell. Summary, Administrative Division: Mail and Records Branch, Classified Decimal File 1941-1945, 319.1 Weekly Intell. Summary to 320.2 Bolera Mission, RG 389 (Provost Marshal General), box 78, NACP.

(140) **On Union Street in Memphis** . . . "Statement of 1st Lt. Wayne H. Allen and Other MPs," August 27, 1945, 250.1 General #3, Administrative Division: Mail and Records Branch, Classified Decimal File 1941-1945, 250 to 251, box 65, RG 389 (Provost Marshal General), NACP.

(140) **Getting drunk and disorderly** . . . For the severe challenges and hostility that some female troops faced as well as the efforts to control female sexuality (and screen out lesbians and working-class women), see Leisa D. Meyer, *G.I. Jane: Sexuality and Power in the Women's Army Corps during World War II* (New York: Columbia University Press, 1998).

(140) **A contingent of African American WACs** . . . "Weekly Intelligence Summary 5th SvC," August 11, 1945, 319.1 (Weekly Intelligence Summary) 5th SC, Administrative Division: Mail and Records Branch, Classified Decimal File 1941-1945, 319.1 Weekly Intell. Summary, RG 389 (Provost Marshal General), box 77, NACP.

(141) **For example, profiles of Coney Island** . . . Murray Schumach, "It's the Old Coney—with War Overtones," *NYT*, July 4, 1943, SM8; John Martin, "Shangri-La of Joe Doakes," *NYT*, August 13, 1944, SM16.

(141) **A San Francisco naval lieutenant** . . . "Brief of Report of Investigation," July 17, 1945, 333.4 (710th M.P. Btn.) Gen, Administrative Division: Mail and Records Branch, Classified Decimal File 1941-1945, 333.5 to 333.9, RG 389 (Provost Marshal General), box 85, NACP; "Captain Taylor Report of Criminal Investigation," n.d., 333.5 (710th M.P. Btn.) Gen, Administrative Division: Mail and Records Branch, Classified Decimal File 1941-1945, box 85, RG 389 (Provost Marshal General), NACP.

CHAPTER FOUR

(142) **Writing in 1990, Mike Davis** . . . Mike Davis, "Fortress Los Angeles: The Militarization of Urban Space," in *Variations on a Theme Park: The New American City and the End of Public Space*, ed. Michael Sorkin (New York: Hill & Wang, 1992), 154-80, 154-56.

(142) **Cities had previously been militarized** . . . For an example of the study of urban militarization focused on the growth of defense industries and military dollars, see Roger W. Lotchin, ed., *The Martial Metropolis: U.S. Cities in War and Peace* (New York: Praeger, 1984).

(143) **Each city frequented by troops** . . . "Well-stacked" from Courchene, *"Hell, Love, and Fun,"* 14.

(144) **Boston's history of catering** . . . Anne Street is also sometimes termed Ann Street. Today it is North Street. For an overview of Anne Street and Richmond Street (Black Sea), see George Weston, *Boston Ways: High, By, and Folk* (Boston: Beacon, 1974), 182-84.

(144) **Originally a cow pasture** . . . For background on Scollay Square, see Weston, *Boston Ways*, 184–86.

(145) **In one tale, marines** . . . Schiff, *Scollay Square*, 1.

(145) **Civilians recalled GIs wandering** . . . *Boston: The Way It Was* (Boston: WGBH/PBS, 2000), VHS.

(145) **Boston mothers employed it** . . . Schiff, *Scollay Square*, 1.

(145) **High school boys and undergraduates** . . . *Boston: The Way It Was*.

(146) **The actual square featured** . . . For description of Scollay Square and its surrounding area, see Weston, *Boston Ways*, 187; and Schiff, *Scollay Square*, 2–3.

(146) **Boston's Pearl Schiff** . . . Schiff, *Scollay Square*, 3, 86.

(146) **"Scollay Square was the** . . . *Boston: The Way It Was*.

(146) **The district offered** . . . "Make believe," "drink and make love," and "infinite choice of pleasures" from Schiff, *Scollay Square*, 62, 24, 73.

(146) **Spots like the Tasty** . . . *Boston: The Way It Was*.

(148) **Originally famous as the site** . . . Stewart H. Holbrook, "Boston's Temple of Burlesque," *American Mercury*, April 1944, 411–16.

(148) **By World War II, Corio** . . . For more on Corio, see "Lives Lived Well and the Lesson That They Teach," *NYT*, January 2, 2000; and *Boston: The Way It Was*.

(148) **Other theaters featured** . . . For fan dances and tassel dancers, see WGBH's *Boston: The Way It Was*.

(148) **Shore Patrol officers** . . . Schiff, *Scollay Square*, 8.

(148) **Civilian men who had not joined** . . . Hoopes, *Americans Remember the Homefront*, 134.

(148) **"Jack Ashore" understood** . . . Weston, *Boston Ways*, 187.

(148) **Furloughed sailors were greeted** . . . Schiff, *Scollay Square*, 5.

(148) **The air was heavy** . . . Jonathan Kaufman, "From Scollay Sq. Tattoo Parlors to Combat Zone Porno Films," *DBG*, December 27, 1984, 25; Schiff, *Scollay Square*, 3.

(149) **At the beginning of the night** . . . Schiff, *Scollay Square*, 3–4, 28.

(149) **Street hawkers and shops** . . . Weston, *Boston Ways*, 187.

(149) **The Rialto Theatre** . . . George McKinnon, "Edict Ends Hub's All-Night Movie: Little Scollay-Sq. House Was Refuge of Night Owls," *DBG*, February 22, 1945, 17.

(150) **Scollay's tattoo parlors** . . . For quotes and information on tattoo parlors, see Brooks, "WAVES and WACS Are Being Tattooed."

(150) **In Schiff's *Scollay Square*** . . . "The tradition of its narrow streets" and "the beer joints" both from Schiff, *Scollay Square*, 28, 200.

(150) **Other troops sentimentally remembered** . . . Weston, *Boston Ways*, 189.

(150) **As the end of the war approached** . . . "Scollay Square Reserved for V-E Day Celebrations," *DBG*, March 30, 1945, 17.

(151) **Many denounced this shift** . . . Schiff, *Scollay Square*, 28.

(151) **In 1942, Boston police** . . . For the Boston Common/Scollay curfew and the step-up in police presence, see "Boston Common Deserted Before 10 p.m. Curfew," *DBG*, July 10, 1942, 1; and "Scollay Square, Common Get More Policemen," *DBG*, July 2, 1942, 9.

(151) **Timilty, for instance,** . . . For Timilty's planned recreation center and its failure, see "Servicemen's Center in Dutton Building Urged," *DBG*, August 6, 1942, 22; and "Charge U.S.O. Fails in Recreation Denied," *DBG*, August 11, 1942, 6.

(151) **Undeterred, the Boston Licensing Board** . . . "Scollay Square Grill Closed on Complaint of Health Officials," *DBG*, April 12, 1943, 9.

(151) **Occasional citywide blackouts** . . . For dimouts and blackouts, see Louis Lyons, "Big Blackout Success," *DBG*, April 1, 1942; and Janet Jones, "Boston Hasn't Grasped Meaning of Dimout, Col. Sullivan Finds," *DBG*, June 19, 1942, 2.

(151) **Even one soldier from Massachusetts** . . . "Stories of Scollay Sq. Disturb Boston Boys," letter to the editor, *DBG*, March 19, 1944, 16.

(152) **Boston's Watch and Ward Society** . . . Salvatore M. Giorlandio, "The Origin, Development, and Decline of Boston's Adult Entertainment District: The Combat Zone" (MA thesis, Massachusetts Institute of Technology, 1986), 11–12; New England Watch and Ward Society Records, 1918–1957, Bound Volumes, 1927–1957, boxes 14 and 16, Harvard Law School Library, Harvard Library, Harvard University.

(152) **A Boston judge said Scollay** . . . Quotes from Kaufman, "From Scollay Sq. Tattoo Parlors to Combat Zone Porno Films."

(152) **Under the onslaught of wartime mobilization** . . . Salvatore M. Giorlandio, "The Origin, Development, and Decline of Boston's Adult Entertainment District: The Combat Zone" (MA thesis, Massachusetts Institute of Technology, 1986), 11–12; New England Watch and Ward Society Records, 1918–1957, Bound Volumes, 1927–1957, boxes 14 and 16, Harvard Law School Library, Harvard Library, Harvard University.

(153) **By the 1920s, both Central Park** . . . Robert Caro, *The Power Broker: Robert Moses and the Fall of New York* (New York: Vintage, 1975), 334–35, 374.

(153) **But the war brought unexpected challenges** . . . "Central Park Beachhead," *NYT*, July 16, 1944, SM16.

(154) **One woman was found** . . . For the murder and the "day or night" quote, see "Dog Finds a Body in Central Park," *NYT*, November 3, 1942, 25. For the attempted rape, see "Policemen Rescue Girl," *NYT*, August 15, 1943, 41.

(154) **One sailor abducted** . . . "Girl, 13, Vanishes: Met Sailor in Park," *NYT*, November 2, 1943, 46.

(154) **One eleven-year-old boy** . . . "Sailor Held in Assault: Tossed Boy, 11, into Lake because He Was Annoyed, He Says," *NYT*, May 25, 1945, 9.

(154) **In a highly publicized case** . . . "3 Veterans Seized as Park Slayers," *NYT*, June 21, 1946, 1.

(154) **At times, he took alternate** . . . "Moses Bars Free Golf to Soldiers on Ground They Don't Like Game," *NYT*, April 22, 1944, 1.

(154) **A longtime refuge** . . . See Louis J. Parascandola and John Parascandola, eds., *A Coney Island Reader: Through Dizzy Gates of Illusion* (New York: Columbia University Press, 2014), 1–27 (introduction).

(155) **Moses despised the beaches** . . . Moses quoted in Parascandola and Parascandola, eds., *A Coney Island Reader*, 26.

(155) **Rather than "bemoaning the end** . . . Parascandola and Parascandola, eds., *A Coney Island Reader*, 26; Caro, *The Power Broker*, 335; Schumach, "It's the Old Coney—with War Overtones."

(155) **Taking control of zoning** . . . Parascandola and Parascandola, eds., *A Coney Island Reader*, 26; Robert Moses, "Attachment to Letter to Mayor Fiorello La Guardia" (1937), in ibid., 224–25.

(155) **Even New York's most powerful** . . . Parascandola and Parascandola, eds., *A Coney Island Reader*, 27; Frank Elkins, "Boom for the Beaches," *NYT*, June 13, 1943, SR32.

(155) **Servicemen and gas-rationed New Yorkers** . . . Schumach, "It's the Old Coney—with War Overtones."

(155) **It was "sordid, shoddy** . . . Henry Miller, *Black Spring* (Paris: Obelisk, 1936), 159.

(155) **Elderly middle-class patrons** . . . Schumach, "It's the Old Coney—with War Overtones."

(156) **Passersby would hear** . . . Schumach, "It's the Old Coney—with War Overtones"; Martin, "Shangri-La of Joe Doakes."

(156) **In the "old carnival spirit"** . . . Schumach, "It's the Old Coney—with War Overtones."

(156) **Coney was reborn** . . . Martin, "Shangri-La of Joe Doakes."

(156) **In Miami, military officials** . . . Clark, "Servicemen Have Given Miami a Strong Home Town Atmosphere."

(156) **In Atlantic City** . . . For the first report on the Atlantic City takeover, see "3 More Hotels Taken Over by Army in A.C.," *Variety*, July 8, 1942, 45.

(156) **By midway through the tourist season** . . . For subsequent Atlantic City reports, see Bérubé, *Coming Out under Fire*, 123.

(156) **In Chicago, the military moved** . . . William Strand, "Senate Kills Dry Rider to 18 Year Draft: Ghost of Gang Era Haunts Chamber," *CDT*, October 23, 1942, 1.

(157) **By September 1942** . . . "Federal Government Now Largest Operator of Hotels," *LAT*, September 25, 1942, 26.

(157) **This loss of property** . . . For the loss of tax revenue, see "Urge Vigilance in Collection of Local Taxes," *CDT*, December 12, 1942, 26.

(157) **Beyond the vast numbers** . . . This section makes use of the excellent scholarship done by Phyllis A. Hall and Pippa Holloway.

(157) **The civilian population grew** . . . A February 1943 article in the *American Mercury* reports slightly different population figures, suggesting that the area's total population more than doubled, from 366,817 to 778,000. It is unclear whether this number is correct or whether the author was including a larger area. Either way, these figures are similar to the population change recorded above. Numbers taken from Phyllis A. Hall, "Crisis at Hampton Roads: The Problems of Wartime Congestion, 1942–1944," *Virginia Magazine of History and Biography* 101, no. 3 (July 1993): 405–32, 406. Hall cites R. Wayne Kernodle, "Population Changes," in *The Hampton Roads Communities in World War II*, ed. Charles F. Marsh (Chapel Hill, NC: Hampton Roads–Peninsula War Studies Committee, 1951), 76–79.

(157) **The whole area—and Norfolk in particular** . . . Van Urk, "Norfolk—Our Worst War Town," 149–51.

(158) **Terrible working and living conditions** . . . Hall, "Crisis at Hampton Roads," 412–13.

(158) **The region's labor, housing** . . . Walter Davenport, "Norfolk Night," *Collier's*, March 28, 1942, 17, 35; W. Cornell Dechert, "Wartime Dislocations in Norfolk and Baltimore Areas," *Domestic Commerce*, June 4, 1942, 3–6; "What's a War Boom Like?," *Business Week*, June 6, 1942, 22–32; "Norfolk, VA: . . . 'Confusion, Chicanery, Ineptitude,'"

Architectural Forum 76 (June 1942): 366–67. Local papers like the *Norfolk Virginian-Pilot* reprinted the *Architectural Forum* piece, to the consternation of its readers. See Hall, "Crisis at Hampton Roads," 410. The list of publications given above is taken from ibid., 407–10.

(158) **Magazine reporters blasted Norfolk's** . . . "Norfolk, VA: . . . 'Confusion, Chicanery, Ineptitude'"; "Navy and Police Raid Tourist Cabins; 115 Held Near Norfolk," *NYT*, October 19, 1942, 6.

(158) **The *American Mercury*** . . . Van Urk, "Norfolk—Our Worst War Town," 144–45.

(159) **Early war anti-venereal disease** . . . Holloway, *Sexuality, Politics, and Social Control in Virginia*, 169–71.

(159) **After World War I** . . . Holloway, *Sexuality, Politics, and Social Control in Virginia*, 168–69; van Urk, "Norfolk—Our Worst War Town," 144.

(159) **A cop approvingly recalled** . . . Van Urk, "Norfolk—Our Worst War Town," 144.

(159) **The prostitutes working** . . . Holloway, *Sexuality, Politics, and Social Control in Virginia*, 169.

(159) **Early in the war, however,** . . . Van Urk, "Norfolk—Our Worst War Town," 144–45.

(159) **The government and the navy** . . . Holloway, *Sexuality, Politics, and Social Control in Virginia*, 170.

(159) **Each night, a "sea of white caps"** . . . Van Urk, "Norfolk—Our Worst War Town," 145–47.

(160) **Longtime Norfolk residents** . . . For a discussion of these rumors, see Hall, "Crisis at Hampton Roads," 408–9.

(160) **After touring these areas** . . . Van Urk, "Norfolk—Our Worst War Town," 147.

(160) **The federal government proved reluctant** . . . Holloway, *Sexuality, Politics, and Social Control in Virginia*, 173, 175.

(160) **Reporters contended** . . . Van Urk, "Norfolk—Our Worst War Town," 151.

(161) **Outside observers and municipal officials** . . . Van Urk, "Norfolk—Our Worst War Town," 150–51.

(161) **On October 20, 1942, the board listed Hampton Roads** . . . The board also sought to investigate liberty ports like San Diego, the San Francisco Bay area, Portland, Maine, and Newport, Rhode Island. These areas similarly faced an overtaxed public infrastructure and a lack of housing that drove civil-military conflict. See Hall, "Crisis at Hampton Roads," 410–11.

(161) **The board explained that** . . . Hall, "Crisis at Hampton Roads," 411.

(161) **Moses somewhat cryptically explained** . . . Robert Moses, *Public Works: A Dangerous Trade* (New York: McGraw-Hill, 1970), 754. Hall also quotes Moses. See Hall, "Crisis at Hampton Roads," 410.

(161) **He and his group of engineers** . . . Hall, "Crisis at Hampton Roads," 412; "Precepts for Survey of Congested Areas of War Production," November 6, 1942, in *Survey of Congested War Production Areas for the Army and Navy Munitions Board*, Army and Navy Munitions Board Secret and Confidential Correspondence, 1922–1945, entry 5, box 47, RG 225, NAB.

(162) **Even worse, Moses argued,** . . . The section makes use of Hall's excellent research. See Hall, "Crisis at Hampton Roads," 413. See also "Precepts for Survey of Congested Areas of War Production."

(162) **Moses reserved his greatest ire** . . . Hall, "Crisis at Hampton Roads," 413; "Precepts for Survey of Congested Areas of War Production."

(162) **Moses called on officials** . . . Hall, "Crisis at Hampton Roads," 414.

(162) **He explained that "the navy people** . . . Moses, *Public Works*, 754. Hall also quotes Moses. See Hall, "Crisis at Hampton Roads," 414-15.

(162) **The Army and Navy Munitions Board** . . . Hall, "Crisis at Hampton Roads," 415.

(163) **One journalist revealed** . . . "Federal Officials Here Rapped in Moses Report on Wartime Conditions," *Norfolk Ledger Dispatch*, March 23, 1943, 1. See also Hall, "Crisis at Hampton Roads," 419.

(163) **Responding to the outrage** . . . Hall, "Crisis at Hampton Roads," 421.

(163) **The congressmen on the subcommittee** . . . Charles Hoofnagle, "Moses Criticism Refuted as to Simons and Gygax, Congressmen Declare Here," *Norfolk Ledger Dispatch*, March 25, 1943, 1; Hall, "Crisis at Hampton Roads," 423.

(163) **Congressman Winder Harris** . . . Harris quoted in Hall, "Crisis at Hampton Roads," 423.

(163) **The committee's follow-up report** . . . Hall, "Crisis at Hampton Roads," 424; US House of Representatives Naval Affairs Investigating Committee, *Investigation of Congested Areas, I: Report on Hampton Roads Area*, 78th Cong., 1st sess., 1943, 643, 650-51.

(163) **A subsequent president's committee** . . . Hall, "Crisis at Hampton Roads," 431-32.

(164) **As seen in Norfolk** . . . Incoming war workers also created disruptions and challenges. For an examination of how the war industry and the movement of new populations into urban areas changed wartime cities like Oakland, see Johnson, *The Second Gold Rush*. See also Marilynn S. Johnson, "Urban Arsenals: War Housing and Social Change in Oakland and Richmond, California, 1941-1945," *Pacific History Review* 60, no. 3 (August 1991): 283-308, and "War as Watershed: The East Bay and World War II," *Pacific History Review* 63, no. 3 (August 1994): 315-31.

(164) **In the face of government propaganda** . . . For "war-minded" and reverence toward troops, see Sparrow, *Warfare State*, 12-13.

(164) **They mocked the soldier's nemesis** . . . Schiff, *Scollay Square*, 66.

(164) **In multiple incidents** . . . For incidents in which civilians defended troops, see "Fight over Girl Starts Dance Hall Riot"; "Tavern Wrecked as 3 Policemen Battle Civilians, Sailors in Astoria."

(165) **Police brutality may have** . . . For a comprehensive overview of police tactics and police brutality using New York City as a case study, see Marilynn S. Johnson, *Street Justice: A History of Police Violence in New York* (Boston: Beacon, 2004), esp. chap. 6.

(165) **In Vancouver, Washington** . . . "Riot Is Started as Soldier and Civilian Fight."

(165) **In one letter, a "lawabiding citizen"** . . . For the informer letter, see "Informer Letter: Frank Riley," n.d., 251.2 General #1, Administrative Division: Mail and Records Branch, Classified Decimal File 1941-1945, 251.2 Gen. to 251.2 H, box 66, RG 389 (Provost Marshal General), NACP.

(165) **Other civilians wrote** . . . For "loyal to this country" and the son-in-law complaint, see "Informant Letter: Mr. Parks," n.d., 251.2 General #1, Administrative Division: Mail and Records Branch, Classified Decimal File 1941-1945, 251.2 Gen. to 251.2 H, box 66, RG 389 (Provost Marshal General), NACP.

(165) **Citizens sometimes demanded** . . . For the furlough paper inquiry and "continually drunk," see "Thomas A. Conroy Statement on James Philip Nary," n.d., 251.2 General #1, Administrative Division: Mail and Records Branch, Classified Decimal File 1941–1945, 251.2 Gen. to 251.2 H, box 66, RG 389 (Provost Marshal General), NACP. For "boisterous type" and the radio complaint, see "Anonymous Communication," May 27, 1944, 251.2 General #1, Administrative Division: Mail and Records Branch, Classified Decimal File 1941–1945, 251.2 Gen. to 251.2 H, box 66, RG 389 (Provost Marshal General), NACP.

(166) **To incentivize informers** . . . For the army's films, posters, and newspaper postings, see "Brigadier General Archer L. Lerch Memo on AWOL Campaign," May 1944, and "Suggestion concerning Training Film 19-2034, 'AWOL and Desertion,'" October 25, 1944, both in 251.2 General #1, Administrative Division: Mail and Records Branch, Classified Decimal File 1941–1945, 251.2 Gen. to 251.2 H, box 66, RG 389 (Provost Marshal General), NACP. For an examination of the 50,000 Americans and 100,000 British soldiers who deserted, see Charles Glass, *The Deserters: A Hidden History of World War II* (New York: Penguin, 2014). Glass focuses mostly on combat deserters.

(166) **In his April 1942 fireside chat** . . . For this idea of a moral compact between soldier and civilian and the Roosevelt quote, see Sparrow, *Warfare State*, 168 (Roosevelt quote). For additional work on the idea of civilians sacrificing for the military, state, and troops, see Westbrook, *Why We Fought*, and "'I Want a Girl, Just Like the Girl That Married Harry James'"; and Mark H. Leff, "The Politics of Sacrifice on the American Home Front in World War II," *Journal of American History* 77, no. 3 (March 1991): 1296–1318. For an examination of how advertising and music were used as propaganda, see John Bush Jones, *All-Out for Victory! Magazine Advertising and the World War II Home Front* (Waltham, MA: Brandeis University Press, 2009), and *The Songs That Fought the War: Popular Music and the Homefront, 1939–1945* (Waltham, MA: Brandeis University Press, 2006). See also Holly Cowan Schulman, *The Voice of America: Propaganda and Democracy, 1941–1945* (Madison: University of Wisconsin Press, 1990).

(166) **By 1943, unemployment had plummeted** . . . For the economic numbers, see Sparrow, *Warfare State*, 114–15.

(166) **Republicans and Democrats both** . . . For discussions of the soldier vote and Roosevelt's charge, see Ernest Lindley and George Gallup, "Vote of Soldiers Could Decide '44 Election, Gallup Poll Finds," *NYT*, December 5, 1943, 48; "Soldier Vote: Has Become Party Issue," *WP*, March 17, 1944, 9; and "Charges Assault on Morale of Soldiers and Families," *WP*, October 6, 1944, 1.

(166) **Members of Congress, responding** . . . For congressional criticism of military justice, see "Minutes, Meeting of the General Council," July 1945, 337 General Council Meeting June 1945–, Administrative Division: Mail and Records Branch, Classified Decimal File 1941–1945, 337 General Council Nov 1944 to Feb 1945, box 95, RG 389 (Provost Marshal General), NACP. Some of this criticism, however, likely originated from the case of Private Joe McGee, who was convicted by a military court of striking German prisoners. For the McGee case and the military response, see Cabell Phillips, "Army Explains Its System of Administering Justice," *NYT*, July 8, 1945, 35.

(167) **Washington, DC, officials** . . . For the request of Military Police aid, see "Randolph Asks Military Police Help for DC."

(167) **Mayor La Guardia never explicitly** . . . When the military expanded the draft to include older men with families—known popularly as the *father draft*—La Guardia

made his criticism more explicit, declaring that this expansion would exert "a crippling effect" on New York's police. "We just couldn't cover the city. We can't get men," he explained. His commissioner concurred by citing the fact that the draft gutted their recruiting classes. See "Father Draft Held 'Crippling' Police," *NYT*, September 22, 1943, 9.

(167) **In early 1942, La Guardia . . .** For mention of the volunteer city patrol, see "Woman War Welder Fights Off Attacker."

(167) **Not content with this meager augmentation . . .** "Mayor Asking Legion to Form 'Patrol Corps': To Supplant 'City Guard' Brown Banned; Fill Posts Army Will Vacate Soon," *New York Herald Tribune*, February 27, 1942, 8; "Mayor's Patrol to Take Over," *New York Amsterdam Star-News*, March 7, 1942, 4.

(167) **When La Guardia first met . . .** "City Moves Today on Defense Corps: Application for Patrol Unit Will Be Issued at Legion Offices in Brooklyn," *NYT*, March 7, 1942, 18; "Patrol Corps Formed: First Company of Auxiliary Police Organized in Brooklyn," *NYT*, March 8, 1942, 28.

(167) **Veterans crowded the Brooklyn headquarters . . .** "Veterans Flock to Join City's Patrol Corps," *New York Herald Tribune*, March 8, 1942, 19; "Mayor's Patrol to Take Over."

(167) **The legionnaires were armed . . .** "La Guardia, Legion Confer on Patrol," *NYT*, February 27, 1942, 19; "Mayor Reports Set Up Complete for Patrol Corps," *New York Herald Tribune*, March 9, 1942, 12; "Mayor's Patrol to Take Over."

(167) **Ads called on volunteers to join . . .** "Join City Patrol Corps," *NYT*, September 23, 1943, 23.

(167) **One pamphlet warned potential volunteers . . .** "Front Line of City Defense," pamphlet, n.d., Museum of the City of New York's Collection on World War I and World War II, https://blog.mcny.org/2015/02/03/the-civilian-war-effort-in-new-york-city-during-world-war-i-and-world-war-ii.

(167–68) **By October 1942, the force . . .** "Mayor Praises City's Control of War-Time Vice: No Other Large U.S. Center Equals Record, He Tells Patrol Corps Leaders," *New York Herald Tribune*, October 6, 1942, 9. The *New York Times* recorded nearly seven thousand members in December 1942. See "6992 New in City Patrol Corps," *NYT*, December 4, 1942, 7.

(168) **Speaking at a patrol corps ceremony . . .** "Mayor Praises City's Control of War-Time Vice."

(168) **The patrol corps continued to police . . .** "Mayor Praises City Patrol Unit at Last Review: Corps to Be Demobilized Sept. 30 After Working Over 4 Million Hours," *New York Herald Tribune*, August 20, 1945, 24.

(168) **Chicago began by planning for . . .** "Legion to Train Boy Patrols in Defense Work," *CDT*, January 11, 1942, 17; "Sons of Legion Expand County Defense Patrol: 2,700 Youths to Study Emergency Work," *CDT*, January 8, 1942, S3.

(168) **Later that month, Mayor Edward J. Kelley . . .** For the Chicago conflict over the legion police, see "Chicago Civil Liberties Committee Chairman John A. Lapp to Assistant Director Howard Evans," January 29, 1942, 501.1 Auxiliary Police, National Headquarters General Correspondence, 1940–1942, 501 to 502, box 110, RG 171 Records of the Office of Civilian Defense, NACP.

(169) **Soldier establishments also attracted prostitutes . . .** For an overview of the duties of the army-navy vice boards, see "Joint Army-Navy Release: Army-Navy

Disciplinary Control Boards Established," December 4, 1944, 000.7, Office Management Division: Decimal File 1920–1945, box 8, RG 247 (Chief of Chaplains), NACP.

(169) **Thus, the proprietors of bars** . . . For an overview of the anti-venereal disease task force, see Hegarty, *Victory Girls, Khaki-Wackies, and Patriotutes*, 75–84.

(169) **In November 1941, after a bit of prodding** . . . "Frank J. Wetzel, Illinois Association of Breweries Letter," November 25, 1941, 250.1 General #1, Administrative Division: Mail and Records Branch, Classified Decimal File 1941–1945, box 65, RG 389 (Provost Marshal General), NACP.

(170) **Proprietors, however,** . . . For the May Act and the La Guardia quote, see "Mayor Bars Heavy Drinking as a Peril to Nation at War," *NYT*, September 22, 1942, 1.

(170) **After the Hollywood Tropics** . . . Many protest letters and vice reports can be found in the Naval P8-5 files in Record Group 181. For the Hollywood Tropics case, see "Harry Arnheim Telegram," August 10, 1942, P8-5 1940 [1/10], Eleventh Naval District, Office of the Commandant, Central Subject Files: 1924–1958, box 296, RG 181 Records of Naval Districts and Shore Establishments, NARA, Riverside.

(170) **In rejecting this appeal, the Eleventh Naval District** . . . For the district commandant's rejection of the appeal, see "'The Tropics,' Hollywood, Calif.—Complaint of Mr. Harry Arnheim, Pres.; re: placing 'out of bounds,'" September 7, 1942, P8-5 1940 [1/10], Eleventh Naval District, Office of the Commandant, Central Subject Files: 1924–1958, box 296, RG 181, NARA, Riverside.

(170) **It even recruited sailors and soldiers** . . . For sailors' and soldiers' special investigation of businesses, see "Special Investigation Report of T/4 Hugh Nelson and Pvt. Lcl. John Hollinger."

(171) **Shore Patrol commander Fogg** . . . "Crime against Military Personnel Becomes Flourishing Business."

(171) **In one instance, a floor manager** . . . For the Midtown brawl, see "Roosevelt Son Linked to G.I. Street Brawl," November 22, 1944, *CDT*, 1.

(171) **In Chicago, a tavern owner's wife** . . . For the tavern owner's wife breaking up a brawl, see "Former Sailor Stabbed in Tavern Fight; One Held," *CDT*, March 25, 1945, 8.

(171) **In one Louisiana boomtown** . . . For the Louisiana brawl, see "A Disturbing Picture," *CDT*, September 15, 1941, 14.

(171) **In another tavern, this one in Chicago,** . . . For the North Kenwood (Chicago) conflict, see "Purdue Sailor, Shot in Tavern Quarrel, Dies," *CDT*, August 4, 1944, 11.

(172) **In Washington, DC, an army lieutenant** . . . For the Ambassador Hotel incident, see "Delinquency Report and Witness Statements," May 3, 1945, 250.1 General #2, Administrative Division: Mail and Records Branch, Classified Decimal File 1941–1945, box 65, RG 389 (Provost Marshal General), NACP.

(172) **In New York, the district commandant** . . . For the Hotel Astor incident, see "Monroe Kelly to Commanding Officer, USS Augusta," December 13, 1945, "Robert D. Howard to Monroe Kelly, Rear Admiral USN," December 7, 1945, and "Monroe Kelly to Robert D. Howard," n.d., all in P 13 #2 Misconduct and Discipline Restricted, Commander in Chief, Atlantic Fleet (CINCLANT)/(RED 7), Entry #P 110: Confidential and Restricted General Administrative Files, 1945–1945, container 178, RG 313 Naval Operating Forces, NACP.

(172) **The luxury to refuse business** . . . In Bermuda, e.g., the naval authorities implemented a 6:00 p.m. curfew aimed at quelling the "alleged misbehavior" and

"criminal misconduct" of American sailors after a slew of complaints from the island's House Assembly. The legislators and naval authorities soon faced a minor rebellion launched on behalf of merchants "who missed the Americans' free spending." See "Bermuda Changes Mind: Protests Curfew on U.S. Sailors as Business Declines," December 6, 1944, *NYT*, 6.

(172) **Military investigators regularly** . . . For investigation of price gouging, see, e.g., "Minutes of the Meeting of Joint Army-Navy Disciplinary Control Board for Baltimore Area," April 3, 1945, P 13 Misconduct and Discipline Restricted, Commander in Chief, Atlantic Fleet (CINCLANT)/(RED 7), Entry #P 110: Confidential and Restricted General Administrative Files, 1945-1945, container 178, RG 313 Naval Operating Forces, NACP.

(172) **Taverns and cafés pulled a number of tricks** . . . For the running-out-of-draft-beer trick, see "Leopold Gruener Memo," September 21, 1945, 250.1 General #1, Administrative Division: Mail and Records Branch, Classified Decimal File 1941-1945, box 65, RG 389 (Provost Marshal General), NACP.

(173) **In one notable case** . . . For the soldiers' suit against the overcharging bar, see "Soldier Suit Fine Is Paid," *World Herald*, August 27, 1945.

(173) **The military in Hawaii** . . . For military price gouging in Hawaii, see "Fort Shafter to Chief of Staff US Army," March 15, 1942, 370.8 General, Administrative Division: Mail and Records Branch, Classified Decimal File 1941-1945, box 117, RG 389 (Provost Marshal General), NACP.

(173) **Taxi drivers** . . . For taxi price gouging, see "Alan J. Kennedy Memo on 'The Barn,'" March 16, 1944, 250.1 General #1, Administrative Division: Mail and Records Branch, Classified Decimal File 1941-1945, box 65, RG 389 (Provost Marshal General), NACP.

(173) **Other cabbies cut out** . . . For cabbies selling whiskey, see "H. E. Erickson to Provost Marshal General," October 5, 1945, 250.1 General #1, Administrative Division: Mail and Records Branch, Classified Decimal File 1941-1945, box 65, RG 389 (Provost Marshal General), NACP.

(173) **Barbers attempted their own rackets** . . . For the barber racket, see "Statement of Charles C. Crooks," n.d., 250.1 General #1, Administrative Division: Mail and Records Branch, Classified Decimal File 1941-1945, box 65, RG 389 (Provost Marshal General), NACP.

(173) **Young boys would wait** . . . For the Omaha boys' scam, see "B. R. Buening Memo," September 21, 1945, 250.1 General #1, Administrative Division: Mail and Records Branch, Classified Decimal File 1941-1945, box 65, RG 389 (Provost Marshal General), NACP.

(173) **Bases and camps attracted carnivals** . . . For gambling joints, see "Frank W. Choate Memo," September 22, 1945, 250.1 General #1, Administrative Division: Mail and Records Branch, Classified Decimal File 1941-1945, box 65, RG 389 (Provost Marshal General), NACP.

(173) **Troops frequenting downtown Washington, DC,** . . . "John H. Rogaleskie Report," September 25, 1945, 250.1 General #1, Administrative Division: Mail and Records Branch, Classified Decimal File 1941-1945, box 65, RG 389 (Provost Marshal General), NACP.

(173) **Horace Lancaster** . . . "John H. Rogaleskie Report."

(174) **Nightclub operators and bootleggers** . . . For nightclub operators and boot-leggers, see Berger, "Morale."

(174) **Civilian police occasionally worked** . . . For the civilian-police shakedown, see "Aircraft—Delay of and Seizure of Confidential Orders Pertaining to by Civilian Authorities, Jackson, Mississippi," February 5, 1945, 250.1 General #2, Administrative Division: Mail and Records Branch, Classified Decimal File 1941–1945, box 65, RG 389 (Provost Marshal General), NACP.

(174) **At worker recreation halls** . . . For Pearl Harbor gambling, see "Navy Officers Face Gambling Courts Martial," *WP*, August 27, 1946, 2.

(174) **Few, however, surpassed the brazen corruption** . . . For the Captain Taylor case, see "Captain Taylor Report of Criminal Investigation."

(175) **Shortly after Pearl Harbor** . . . For the New York district attorney, see "War Crime Wave Feared by Hogan," *NYT*, January 23, 1942, 21.

(175) **J. Edgar Hoover publicly expressed** . . . For Hoover's concerns, see "FBI Reports 3% Rise in Crime."

(175) **Early on, urban officials** . . . For Dockweiler to La Guardia, see "John F. Dockweiler to Mayor Fiorello La Guardia," December 29, 1941, 000.5 Criminology-Crimes-Fraud, National Headquarters: General Correspondence, 1940–1942, RG 171 Records of the Office of Civilian Defense, box 3, NACP.

(175) **Dockweiler established an anticrime committee** . . . For the Dockweiler anticrime committee and the apple quote, see "Anti-Crime Leader Named," *LAT*, June 10, 1941, A20.

(175) **In tackling the challenges** . . . This concern over an epidemic of youthful criminals wreaking havoc in American cities was partially a racial panic, but many reports focused solely on white children, suggesting that race was a more minor factor. See, e.g., Gordon, "As the Youngsters See Juvenile Delinquency."

(175) **In his letter to La Guardia** . . . For Dockweiler to La Guardia, see "John F. Dockweiler to Mayor Fiorello La Guardia."

(175–76) **Other civil authorities acknowledged** . . . "Urge Crime Fight by Defense Units: Jersey Officials Would Keep Present Organization After War for New Duties," *NYT*, September 25, 1942, 42.

(176) **When New York proposed eliminating** . . . For the Women's City Club, see "Letter to *The Times*: Preventing Juvenile Crime: Proposed Elimination of Aid Bureau Here Is Viewed as Backward Step," *NYT*, April 23, 1942, 22.

(176) **The Department of Labor's Children's Bureau** . . . For Department of Labor statistics, see Robert Guy Spinney, *World War II in Nashville: Transformation of the Home-front* (Knoxville: University of Tennessee Press, 1998), 82.

(176) **Urban officials and groups** . . . Dorothy Johnson, "Warns Nation Is Losing War on Delinquency," *CDT*, February 28, 1945, 17.

(176) **Scholars remain more circumspect** . . . For a summary of scholarly attitudes toward the reality of juvenile delinquency, see David B. Wolcott, *Cops and Kids: Policing Juvenile Delinquency in Urban America, 1890–1940* (Columbus: Ohio State University Press, 2005), 194. A Senate subcommittee found little evidence to corroborate the hysteria over delinquency. See "Senate Group to Sift Facts on Juvenile Delinquency," *WP*, November 29, 1943, 11; and "For Agency to Cut Youth Delinquency: Pepper Committee Supports Proposal for a Federal Commission," *NYT*, September 24, 1944, 48.

(176) **Both experts and young people** . . . For reporters blaming boomtowns and vice, see Sanford Bates, "Johnny—14 Years Old, and a Challenge: 'Juvenile Delinquency,'" *NYT*, November 8, 1942, SM10.

(176) **A Department of Labor report** . . . For the Department of Labor report, see "National Go-to-School Drive" Handbook, U.S. Department of Labor, Federal Security Agency, 1944. Page 17, folder 5, box 31, Defense Council Records, OSA; and "A Community Program for Prevention and Control of Juvenile Delinquency in Wartime," Report, US Department of Labor, September 1943. Page 5, folder 1, box 28, Defense Council Records, OSA. (citations taken from http://sos.oregon.gov/archives/exhibits/ww2/Pages/life -juveniles.aspx). Troops certainly contributed to the possible growth in delinquency and changes in how it was policed. Early in the war, officials and reformers mostly called for delinquents to be educated and uplifted by superior schooling, recreation, and religious instruction. By war's end, a harsher form of policing and punishment took hold as the dominant regimen. Reflecting on the emerging postwar society, Hoover put out sensational warnings that the country faced "a potential army of six million criminals," while Newark's police chief denounced the "mollycoddling" that allowed this threat to grow. For the Hoover and Newark chief quotes, see William Glover, "Some Cities Visit Sin of Child on Parents," *WP*, September 1, 1946, B1. For an overview of the gradual shift to the harsher policing of delinquency, see Wolcott, *Cops and Kids*, 193–97.

(177) **After the millionth serviceman** . . . "The Millionth Serviceman Welcomed at Canteen," *NYT*, October 2, 1944, 32.

(177) **As the draft expanded** . . . For an overview of the Fort Sill–Governor Phillips conflict, see "Oklahoma Dry since 1907: But Liquor Can Be Had at Two or Three Times the Price," *NYT*, October 23, 1942, 11.

(178) **Senator Joshua Lee** . . . "Lee Proposal Would Ban Liquor in Army Areas," *WP*, October 6, 1942, 6.

(178) **Prohibition groups had long campaigned** . . . For Congress receiving support for the Lee amendment, see Arthur Hatchen, "Dry Zone Issue May Hold Up 18–19 Draft: Senator Lee Would Bar Sale of Drinks Near Military Centers," *WP*, October 19, 1942, 1.

(178) **Civilian organizations like** . . . For the WCTU's support, see "W.C.T.U. of State Would Bar Liquor Near Army Camps," *DBG*, October 22, 1942, 9; and Elizabeth La Hines, "Seek Liquor Ban at Army Camps," *NYT*, November 3, 1940. The sale of alcohol to men in uniform was illegal under World War I's Selective Service Act. See Faulkner, *Pershing's Crusaders*, 52.

(178) **Groups opposed to prohibition** . . . For the Goebbels claim, see "Lawless-ness Depicted in Dry Oklahoma; Prohibition Disunity Held to Be Axis Aim," *NYT*, October 23, 1942, 11.

(178) **Secretary of War Henry Stimson** . . . "Stimson Opposes Camp Prohibition as Bad for Morale," *NYT*, October 22, 1942, 1.

(178) **Senator Scott W. Lucas** . . . For Lucas's pragmatic concerns, see Strand, "Senate Kills Dry Rider to 18 Year Draft."

(178) **When Chief of Staff Marshall learned** . . . "G. C. Marshall to General Gullion."

(179) **Judges and prisoner advocacy groups** . . . For linking alcoholism to criminality, see "Links Alcoholism to Major Crimes," *NYT*, October 22, 1942, 44.

(179) **La Guardia toed this line** . . . "Mayor Bars Heavy Drinking as a Peril to Nation at War."

(179) **In Los Angeles, "several hundred civic and religious leaders** . . . For the Los Angeles Police Commission protest, see "Hollywood Vice Charged: Civic Group Tell Police Board How Soldiers 'Clipped,'" *LAT*, January 31, 1945, A1.

(179) **In a letter to the district commandant** . . . "Woman's Christian Temperance Union to Eleventh Naval District."

(180) **As WCTU president Ida B. Wise Smith** . . . "Army Vice-Control Policy Assailed by W.C.T.U. Head," *LAT*, October 31, 1941, 11.

(180) **In Olympia, Washington,** . . . "John S. Lynch Jr. to Captain Charles C. Carroll," November 5, 1941, 370.093 General, Administrative Division: Mail and Records Branch, Classified Decimal File 1941-1945, 370.093, box 111, RG 389 (Provost Marshal General), NACP.

(180) **In North Stelton, New Jersey,** . . . "Telegram from North Stelton Committee, via Senator H. Alexander Smith," n.d., "Disorders Involving Soldiers Near Camp Kilmer, New Jersey, 2S-335605," n.d., "Area Declared Out of Bounds for Soldiers at Camp Kilmer," *Daily Home News*, March 16, 1945, and "Archer L. Lerch to Senator Smith," March 31, 1945, all in 250.1 General #2, Administrative Division: Mail and Records Branch, Classified Decimal File 1941-1945, box 65, RG 389 (Provost Marshal General), NACP.

(181) **When one George A. Turner** . . . For Marshall's response to civilians via Chief of Chaplains, see "George A. Turner to Chief of Staff Marshall," January 7, 1943, and "William R. Arnold to Turner," January 21, 1943, both in 250 Discipline (General) to 250.1 Morals and Conduct, Office Management Division: Decimal File 1920-1945, box 193, RG 247 (Chief of Chaplains), NACP.

(182) **Chief of Chaplains William R. Arnold** . . . "William R. Arnold to Director of Personnel, ASF," March 20, 1945, 250 Discipline (General) to 250.1 Morals and Conduct, Office Management Division: Decimal File 1920-1945, box 193, RG 247 (Chief of Chaplains), NACP.

(182) **Quoting Marshall, one chaplain protested** . . . For the chaplain quoting Marshall, the "gambling" quote, and the "world is imperiled" quote, see "Paul McCullers to Office of the Chief of Chaplains," March 5, 1945, 250 Discipline (General) to 250.1 Morals and Conduct, Office Management Division: Decimal File 1920-1945, box 193, RG 247 (Chief of Chaplains), NACP.

(182) **Another chaplain with experience** . . . "Chaplain C. F. Frith to Chaplain William R. Arnold," June 9, 1944, 250.1 Morals and Conduct, Office Management Division: Decimal File 1920-1945, box 194, RG 247 (Chief of Chaplains), NACP.

(182) **City councilmen in Los Angeles** . . . For other cities' proposals to bolster police numbers, see Meyer Berger, "La Guardia Calls on Armed Forces to Free Policemen," *NYT*, November 24, 1945, 1.

(182) **Council members complained** . . . "Crime Worries City Councilmen," *LAT*, August 25, 1945, A3.

(183) **The most explosive and visible** . . . "Kane Asks Army Aid in Soldier Crime Rise," *NYT*, February 25, 1945, 13.

(183) **Kane's proclamation was a remarkable challenge** . . . "Jurors Again Sift Staten Island Crime," *NYT*, March 24, 1945, 32.

(183) **Tensions deepened after a civilian** . . . "6 Soldiers Assault Civilian, Policeman," *NYT*, March 4, 1945, 29.

(183) **Kane demanded** . . . "Soldiers Beat, Rob Staten Island Man," *NYT*, March 13, 1945, 15.

(183) **Robberies and assaults persisted** . . . For women refusing to walk the streets and the La Guardia quote, see "Staten Island Acts to End Crime Wave," *NYT*, March 15, 1945, 1.

(183) **A grand jury investigated** . . . "Crime in Richmond Put on Army Laxity," *NYT*, April 4, 1945, 23.

(183) **Indeed, the local GIs on Staten Island** . . . For additional background on the case, see "Staten Island Acts to End Crime Wave."

(184) **The *Chicago Defender* considered** . . . For the *Defender's* criticism of the coverage and the transfer of the black troops, see Earl Conrad, "Army Moves Negro GIs in N.Y. Rape Hysteria," *CD*, March 24, 1945, 10.

(184) **The military rarely assented** . . . For Byrnes's ostensible reasons for issuing the order and exemptions to it, see Ben W. Gilbert, "Midnight Closing Edict Effective February 26," *WP*, February 20, 1945, 1.

(184) **Congress launched an inquiry** . . . "What's behind Curfew Edict? House Asked," *CDT*, March 6, 1945, 1.

(185) **Though La Guardia attempted** . . . For enforcement in New York City and La Guardia's competing ordinance, see "La Guardia's Impeachment Talked in N.Y.," *CDT*, March 21, 1945, 13.

(185) **Alexander Feinberg** . . . Feinberg, "Curfew Viewed as Breeder of Unbridled Drinking, Vice."

(185) **Commanders cleared Scollay Square** . . . McKinnon, "Edict Ends Hub's All-Night Movie."

(185) **Earlier in the war, the army imposed an ordinance** . . . For the earlier San Francisco order and the New York City order, see Alexander Feinberg, "La Guardia Eases Curfew to 1 a.m.; Byrnes Is Silent," *NYT*, March 19, 1945, 1.

(185) **In one example, an MP** . . . "Statement of Fred L. Witt," November 3, 1944, and "McDonald Rigdon to the Provost Marshal General's Office," January 24, 1945, both in 250.1 General #2, Administrative Division: Mail and Records Branch, Classified Decimal File 1941–1945, box 65, RG 389 (Provost Marshal General), NACP.

(186) **Train bathrooms** . . . For the report on train bathrooms and the civilian complaints, see "Inspection Report," August 10, 1945, 333 General #2, Administrative Division: Mail and Records Branch, Classified Decimal File 1941–1945, box 254, RG 389 (Provost Marshal General), NACP.

(186) **Riots occurred when the army** . . . "Routine Trip Report of Military Police Inspector," August 3, 1943, and "Inspection Report on Phoenix, Arizona," July 30, 1943, both in 250.1 General #1, Administrative Division: Mail and Records Branch, Classified Decimal File 1941–1945, box 65, RG 389 (Provost Marshal General), NACP.

(186) **Civilians resented the preferential** . . . "Memorandum for the Chief of Transportation," July 30, 1945, 510 General, Administrative Division: Mail and Records Branch, Classified Decimal File 1941–1945, box 128, RG 389 (Provost Marshal General), NACP.

(186) **These men generally suffered** . . . "Willing 4-F," letter to the editor, *DBG*, February 14, 1944, 8.

(186) Regularly seen as cowardly . . . "Plea for the 4-F," *CDT*, October 12, 1943, 16.

(186) *Four-effer* became its own epithet . . . "Work or Fight," letter to the editor, *WP*, January 9, 1945, 6.

(186) In Schiff's *Scollay Square* . . . Schiff, *Scollay Square*, 44.

(186) Radio programs piled it on . . . "The 4-F Club," *CDT*, October 28, 1943, 12.

(187) Emily Post offered a similar . . . Post, "If He's in Civvies . . ."

(187) Occasionally, civilian men confronted . . . "Soldiers Find 4-F Civilian Is A-1 Fighter."

(187) 4-Fs were also seen as . . . For 4-Fs hating uniforms and picking fights, see Schiff, *Scollay Square*, 70.

(187) One 4-F in Los Angeles . . . "4-F Nabbed for Posing as Captain," *CD*, October 2, 1943, 2.

(187) In a nightclub, MPs confronted . . . "Disturbance at Black Eagle, Montana, December 26, 1942," January 28, 1943, 319.1 (M.I.D.) General, Administrative Division: Mail and Records Branch, Classified Decimal File 1941–1945, box 73, RG 389 (Provost Marshal General), NACP.

(187) During the war, fears proliferated . . . Lewis E. Lawes, "Will There Be a Crime Wave?," *NYT*, November 5, 1944, SM16.

(187) The prominent businessman Harvey S. Firestone Jr. . . . . "Pictures Post-War Crime Wave," *NYT*, April 11, 1943, 40.

(187) Criminologists at the Harvard Law School . . . "Increased Delinquency and Crime After War Predicted by Gluecks," *DBG*, June 14, 1945, 20.

(187) Hoover admitted similar concerns . . . "F.B.I. Chief Admits Crime Wave Fears," *LAT*, August 12, 1945, 16.

(188) Some of these fears derived . . . Lawes, "Will There Be a Crime Wave?"

(188) Reports of American troops looting . . . For the comments of the general and the European incidents, see Drew Middleton, "Veterans Called Law-Abiding Men," *NYT*, October 14, 1945, 19.

(188) In one report, the separated wife . . . For the knife quote, see J. Edgar Hoover, "Is the Army Breeding Criminals?," *LAT*, March 11, 1945, F4.

(188) As boredom and waiting time increased . . . "Luther D. Miller to Commanding General," September 6, 1945, and "Unsatisfactory State of Morale," August 10, 1945, both in 330.11 Morale and Welfare of Army Personnel, Office Management Division: Decimal File 1920–1945, box 245, RG 247 (Chief of Chaplains), NACP.

(188) Even before the end of the war . . . For the provost marshal general's 1944 memo on postwar crime, see "Archer L. Lerch on Proposals to Improve the Conduct and Appearance, While in Uniform, of Personnel Being Discharged or Released from Active Service," July 19, 1944, 332.31 General, Administrative Division: Mail and Records Branch, Classified Decimal File 1941–1945, box 84, RG 389 (Provost Marshal General), NACP.

(189) Writing in January 1946 . . . Charles A. Merrill, "Why Hysteria Sweeps Nation: Servicemen, Management, Labor—All of Us—Are Reluctant to Continue in Wartime Roles as Puppets of the State," *DBG*, January 20, 1946, C2.

(189) Civilians had been made part of . . . For the warfare state concept, see Sparrow, *Warfare State*.

EPILOGUE

(190) **After the chronic misbehavior, absenteeism, . . .** For army efforts to recruit a more technical, skilled force, see Brian McAllister Linn, *Elvis's Army: Cold War GIs and the Atomic Battlefield* (Cambridge, MA: Harvard University Press, 2016), 32–33. For some of the effects of demobilization on the military and veterans, see Laura McEnaney, "Veterans' Welfare, the GI Bill and American Demobilization," *Journal of Law, Medicine and Ethics* 39, no. 1 (Spring 2011): 41–47. For the later transition to an all-volunteer force, see Beth Bailey, *America's Army: Making the All-Volunteer Force* (Cambridge, MA: Belknap Press of Harvard University Press, 2009). For an examination of how mobilization and demobilization affected labor in cities, see Marilynn S. Johnson, "Mobilizing the Homefront: Labor and Politics in Oakland, California, 1943–1951," in *Working People of California: Towards a New Social History of the Golden State*, ed. Daniel Cornford (Berkeley and Los Angeles: University of California Press, 1995), 344–68. For another view of the "harsh trade-offs and taxing adaptations for city dwellers," see Laura McEnaney, "Nightmares on Elm Street: Demobilizing in Chicago, 1945–1953," *Journal of American History* 92, no. 4 (March 2006): 1265–91. For the continued militarization of civilian life, see Laura McEnaney, *Civil Defense Begins at Home: Militarization Meets Everyday Life in the Fifties* (Princeton, NJ: Princeton University Press, 2000). See also Gretchen Heefner, *The Missile Next Door: The Minuteman in the American Heartland* (Cambridge, MA: Harvard University Press, 2012).

(190) **They offered an array of incentives . . .** John Thompson, "When Whole Armies Take to the Air!," *CDT*, November 30, 1947, E7.

(190) **The army expanded its elite ranger program . . .** John G. Norris, "Army Forms 'Ranger' Units to Perform Commando Duties," *WP*, October 11, 1950, 1.

(190) **One lieutenant general argued . . .** "Urges Military Training to End Caste in Army," *CDT*, June 11, 1946, 12.

(190) **The force's poor image . . .** For postwar riots/mutinies, see Linn, *Elvis's Army*, 17–18.

(191) **Major Louis Altshuler . . .** Altshuler quoted in Linn, *Elvis's Army*, 34. See Maj. Louis N. Altshuler, Sub: The War Department Venereal Disease Program, 1947, box 2, E12, RG 334, NACP.

(191) **Command took small steps . . .** Linn, *Elvis's Army*, 33.

(191) **Planners therefore envisioned . . .** Gilbert P. Bailey, "'Umtees'—First Soldiers of the 'New Army,'" *NYT*, February 23, 1947, SM11.

(191) **The "Umtees" . . .** Bailey, "'Umtees.'"

(192) **After several months, the army pronounced . . .** Hanson W. Baldwin, "Army's Youth Unit Called a Success," *NYT*, May 18, 1947, 50.

(192) **They saw the Umtee boys . . .** For the results of the Umtee experiment and the reaction of Old Army regulars, see Baldwin, "Army's Youth Unit Called a Success"; Bailey, "'Umtees.'"

(192) **The young recruits of 1946 and 1947 . . .** For education levels, see Gilbert P. Bailey, "Portrait of GI Joe Jr.," *NYT*, June 2, 1946, SM7. For poor training, see Linn, *Elvis's Army*, 42; and Jacob Devers, Sub: Report of Activities of Army Field Forces, 1945–1949, September 30, 1949, 319.1 File, box 41, E32B, RG 337, NACP.

(193) **The grandiose plans for bright . . .** Linn, *Elvis's Army*, 42–43.

(193) **One veteran officer explained** . . . Hanson W. Baldwin, "'Cream Puff Army' Presents Problem: Korea Shows Need for Tougher Men, High Officers Tell Baldwin," *LAT*, November 17, 1950, 4.

(193) **General Mark Clark, the commander** . . . For Clark and Hershey, see "Rougher Training Planned by Army," *NYT*, August 21, 1950, 11.

(193) **Before making their assault** . . . "Students Don Masks; Raid Co-Eds' Dorm," *CDT*, February 26, 1949, 1.

(194) **Though the men acted** . . . For descriptions of the raid, see "Students Don Masks"; and "Students Dump Coeds Out of Bed at Illinois College," *WP*, February 26, 1949, B2.

(195) **One senior woman claimed** . . . "Coeds Battle Males with Water, Fists in Illinois Raid," *DBG*, February 26, 1949, 2.

(195) **Once the cops had ejected the men** . . . "Men Apologize for Invasion of Co-Eds' Dorm," *CDT*, March 2, 1949, 21.

(195) **In one sense, these volatile campus disturbances** . . . For the connection between panty raids and the later campus/sexual revolution, see Beth Bailey, *Sex in the Heartland* (Cambridge, MA: Harvard University Press, 1999), 45-48.

(195) **For example, when Harvard men** . . . "Playful Tech, Harvard Men Invade Wellesley, Radcliff," *DBG*, May 9, 1947, 1.

(195) **A year later, Colorado's Women's College** . . . "Girls' College Black-Lists Mines Students for Raid," *LAT*, April 14, 1948, 1.

(196) **In 1950, for example,** . . . "Harvard Students Raid Radcliffe during Darkness," *DBG*, November 20, 1950, 1.

(196) **Reports routinely utilized military language** . . . For "surprise sorties," see "Thousands of College Men Invade Coeds' Dormitories: Lingerie Grabbing Spreads," *LAT*, March 20, 1952, 1. For "undie sorties," see "Hurl Rocks, Eggs," *CDT*, May 23, 1952, A13. For "under siege," see "Police Block Raid on Women [sic] Dorm at U. of I.," *CDT*, May 7, 1952, 3.

(196) **Bugle calls** . . . Bailey, *Sex in the Heartland*, 45.

(196) **At the University of California, Berkeley,** . . . "3000 Take Part in California 'Panty Raid' Riot," *WP*, May 18, 1956, 3.

(197) **At the University of Missouri** . . . "Panty Rioters Pillage Dorms at Missouri U.: Damage Near $50,000; 3,000 Join Raids," *CDT*, May 21, 1952, 6.

(197) **Similar assaults occurred** . . . "Six Students Jailed in Kansas Panty Raid," *LAT*, May 23, 1956, 40.

(197) **Women also fought back** . . . "Panty Rioters Pillage Dorms at Missouri U."

(197) **With "sexy souvenirs" in hand** . . . "Sexy souvenirs" from "Panty Raiders Storm Dorms, Find Some Coeds Play Rough," *WP*, May 21, 1952, 1. For street destruction, see "Panty Raiders Invade Dorms at E. Lansing," *CDT*, May 12, 1953, 11.

(197) **Not wishing to harm** . . . "Police Block Raid on Women [sic] Dorm at U. of I."

(197) **The resulting melees lasted hours** . . . "U. of I. Suspends 6 Men in Raid on Girls' Dorm: Police in 3 Hour Melee; 2 Students Fined," *CDT*, May 8, 1952, B2.

(197) **Battling against a hail of rocks** . . . "Hurl Rocks, Eggs."

(198) **One police sergeant explained** . . . "Thousands of College Men Invade Coeds' Dormitories."

(198) **In one instance, an officer** . . . "Cop Unclothed in Madison Raid on Co-Ed Dorms," *CDT*, May 20, 1952, 3.

(198) **At Northwestern University** . . . "1000 Northwestern Students Raid Dorms, Take Police Along," *DBG*, May 20, 1952, 7.

(198) **At other times, however, policemen's** . . . Bailey, *Sex in the Heartland*, 45.

(198) **They also argued that officers** . . . "3 Co-Eds Hurt in Panty Riot at S. Illinois U.," *CDT*, A13, May 23, 1952.

(198) **During almost every raid, women** . . . "Tufts Men Go Bra-Hunting, but Get Wetting Instead," *DBG*, May 20, 1952, 1.

(198) **When men managed to break into** . . . "Panty Raiders Invade Dorms at E. Lansing."

(198) **Others favored baseball bats** . . . "3 Co-Eds Hurt in Panty Riot at S. Illinois U."

(199) **Tulane's raid** . . . "Students Raid Iowa Dorms for Co-Ed Panties," *CDT*, May 15, 1952, 12.

(199) **Whether to entice or to placate** . . . For the Tulane raid and tossing lingerie out preemptively, see "Panty Raid at Tulane Reaches Riot Proportions," *LAT*, October 19, 1954, 17.

(199) **Women also regularly rejected** . . . For "party poopers," see "U. of I. Suspends 6 Men in Raid on Girls' Dorm." For "let 'em in!," see "3 Co-Eds Hurt in Panty Riot at S. Illinois U."

(199) **At Missouri's violent raid** . . . "Panty Raiders Invade Dorms at E. Lansing."

(199) **Co-eds even began undertaking** . . . "100 Coeds Stage 'Shorts' Raid on Men's Dorm," *CD*, May 21, 1958, 4.

(199) **Panty raids appear to have** . . . Soldiers regularly described the later period of the Korean War as a punishing trench war. See "British Veterans of Korean War: 'It Was Like Stepping into Medieval Time,'" *Guardian*, June 24, 2010, https://www.the guardian.com/world/2010/jun/25/british-veterans-korean-war.

(199) **After *Stars and Stripes* published** . . . Disgusted G.I., "Panty Raid Reaction," letter to the editor, *LAT*, June 1, 1952.

(200) **A civilian concurred** . . . John W. Burks, "Panty Raid Reaction," letter to the editor, *LAT*, June 1, 1952.

(200) **Senators demanded the boys be drafted** . . . "Panty Raiders under Fire in Courts, Senate," *DBG*, May 28, 1952, 9.

(200) **The square's now-infamous status** . . . Richard O'Donnell, "Scollays (of Square) Have Left Hub," *DBG*, June 30, 1963, A5.

(201) **In 1951, a judge claimed** . . . "Jurist Describes Essex St. Area as 'Combat Zone,'" *DBG*, April 28, 1951, 18.

(201) **When the Old Howard Theatre** . . . "Three Stripteasers Barely Break the Law, Old Howard Theatre in Boston Is Padlocked," *Wilmington (DE) Sunday Star*, December 6, 1953, 24.

(201) **Boston's upper class increasingly** . . . "Colonel Scollay's Square," *DBG*, October 31, 1961, 22.

(201) **Just as Robert Moses seized his chance** . . . "Improper Bostonians," *CDT*, December 1, 1961, 14.

(201) **In 1962, Old Boston got its wish** . . . "Rowdy Ways of Scollay Sq. Soon Will Go," *CDT*, March 11, 1962, B8.

(201) **With offices soon to populate** . . . "Remember Scollay Square?," *DBG*, November 2, 1963, 4.

(201) **Crews and trucks soon arrived** . . . Robert L. Levey, "Scollay Square—Same Animal in New Lair," *DBG*, November 8, 1966, 23.

(202) **"Scollay Square was called a bad thing** . . . Levey, "Scollay Square."

(202) **For the moment, however, urban renewal evangelists** . . . Paul Kneeland and Gregory Friedberg, "The Combat Zone," *DBG*, July 31, 1966, D6.

(202) **Spread over four blocks** . . . For the description of the Combat Zone, see Paul Kneeland and Gregory Friedberg, "The Combat Zone," *DBG*, July 31, 1966, D6. For a map of the Combat Zone's main area, see John Kifner, "Boston 'Combat Zone' Becomes Target of Police Crackdown," *NYT*, December 4, 1976, 10.

(203) **Like Scollay, the Combat Zone** . . . Kneeland and Friedberg, "The Combat Zone."

(203) **"Yeah, this is the Combat Zone all right,"** . . . Jeremiah V. Murphy, "Boredom Fills the Barrooms in Boston's 'Combat Zone,'" *DBG*, November 11, 1968, 8A.

(204) **Admitting defeat, Boston chose** . . . Kifner, "Boston 'Combat Zone' Becomes Target of Police Crackdown."

(204) **The story reminds readers** . . . I base some of my thoughts on distinguishing between fronts on Brooke L. Blower, "Fronts" (paper presented at the Spatial Histories Roundtable, Society for Historians of American Foreign Relations, Arlington, VA, June 26, 2015).

(205) **The American empire was partially** . . . Blower, "A Nation of Outposts," 453.

(205) **Perhaps the end of the all-volunteer force** . . . Andrew Bacevich, "Why America's All-Volunteer Force Fails to Win Wars," *Dallas Morning News*, April 18, 2016, https://www.dallasnews.com/opinion/commentary/2016/04/18/andrew-bacevich-why -americas-all-volunteer-force-fails-to-win-wars; Mark Thompson, "Here's Why the U.S. Military Is a Family Business," *Time*, March 10, 2016, http://time.com/4254696/military -family-business.

(205) **Civilians, for their part,** . . . "Confidence in Institutions," Gallup, n.d., https:// news.gallup.com/poll/1597/confidence-institutions.aspx.

(206) **Members of the military were recently** . . . "Public Esteem for Military Still High," Pew Research Center, July 11, 2013, http://www.pewforum.org/2013/07/11 /public-esteem-for-military-still-high.

(206) **Empty phrases like** . . . Bacevich, "Why America's All-Volunteer Force Fails to Win Wars." See also Andrew Bacevich, *The Limits of Power: The End of American Exceptionalism* (New York: Holt, 2009).

(207) **More work needs to be done to uncover** . . . Roberts, *What Soldiers Do*, 260.

(207) **Few periods of American history** . . . For the "victory culture" and an examination of its legacy, see Tom Engelhardt, *The End of Victory Culture: Cold War America and the Disillusioning of a Generation* (Amherst: University of Massachusetts Press, 1995).

BIBLIOGRAPHY OF PRIMARY SOURCES

ARCHIVES

National Archives Building, Washington, DC (NAB)
  RG 225, Records of Joint Army and Navy Boards and Committees
National Archives at College Park, Maryland (NACP)
  RG 44, Records of the Office of Government Reports
  RG 171, Records of the Office of Civilian Defense
  RG 247, Records of the Office of the Chief of Chaplains
  RG 313, Records of Naval Operating Forces
  RG 330, Records of the Office of the Secretary of Defense
  RG 334, Records of Interservice Agencies
  RG 337, Records of Headquarters Army Ground Forces (AGF)
  RG 389, Records of the Office of the Provost Marshal General
National Archives and Records Administration (NARA), New York
  RG 181, Records of Naval Districts and Shore Establishments
National Archives and Records Administration (NARA), Riverside, CA
  RG 181, Records of Naval Districts and Shore Establishments
National Archives and Records Administration (NARA), San Bruno, CA
  RG 181, Records of Naval Districts and Shore Establishments
National Archives and Records Administration (NARA), Waltham, MA
  RG 181, Records of Naval Districts and Shore Establishments
The National Archives of the United Kingdom (NA), Kew, Richmond, Surrey
  Admiralty (ADM) Files
  War Office (WO) Files
New England Watch and Ward Society Records, 1918-57, Harvard Law School Library,
  Harvard Library, Harvard University
  Bound Volumes, 1927-57
Oregon State Archives, https://sos.oregon.gov/archives/Pages/records.aspx
  Defense Council Records

DOCUMENTARIES AND FILMS

Anchors Aweigh. Directed by George Sidney. 1945. Beverley Hills, CA: MGM, 2015.

Boston: The Way It Was. 2000. Boston: WGBH/PBS, 2000. VHS.

The Fleet's In. Directed by Victor Schertzinger. 1942. Hollywood, CA: Paramount Pictures, 2014. DVD.

Gone with the Wind. Directed by Victor Fleming. 1939. Culver City, CA: Selznick International Pictures, 2000. DVD.

Iceland. Directed by H. Bruce Humberstone. 1942. Century City, CA: 20th Century–Fox, 2013. DVD.

Left by the Ship. Directed by Emma Rossi Landi and Alberto Vendermmiati. 2010. PBS, 2011.

On the Town. Directed by Stanley Donen and Gene Kelly. 1949. Beverley Hills, CA: MGM, 2015.

Sailor Beware. Directed by Hal Walker. 1952. Hollywood, CA: Paramount Pictures, 2014. DVD.

Sands of Iwo Jima. Directed by Allan Dwan. 1949. Los Angeles, CA: Republic Pictures, 2014. DVD.

Saving Private Ryan. Directed by Steven Spielberg. 1998. Universal City, CA: Amblin Entertainment, 1999. DVD.

NEWSPAPERS AND PERIODICALS

Afro-American
American Mercury
Cairns Post
Chicago Daily Tribune/Chicago Tribune
Chicago Defender
Collier's
The Crisis
Daily Boston Globe/Boston Globe
Daily Californian
Daily Home News
Good Housekeeping
The Guardian
Harper's Magazine
Life
Los Angeles Times
New York Amsterdam Star-News
New York Herald Tribune
New York Post
New York Times
Norfolk Ledger Dispatch
PM
San Francisco Chronicle
SFGate
Shipmate

Stars and Stripes
The Telegraph
Time
Variety
Washington Post
Wilmington Sunday Star
World Herald
Yank

COLLECTIONS, GUIDES, MEMOIRS, NOVELS, AND ORAL HISTORIES

Bernstein, Walter. *Keep Your Head Down*. New York: Viking, 1945.
Cooke, Alistair. *The American Home Front, 1941–1942*. New York: Grove, 2006.
Courchene, Richard. *"Hell, Love, and Fun."* West Point, MT: self-published, 1969.
Downey, Bill. *Uncle Sam Must Be Losing the War*. San Francisco: Strawberry Hill, 1982.
Elting, John Robert, Dan Cragg, and Ernst Deal. *A Dictionary of Soldier Talk*. New York: Scribner, 1984.
Gorham, Ethel. *So Your Husband's Gone to War!* New York: Doubleday, Doran, 1942.
Hoopes, Roy. *Americans Remember the Homefront*. New York: Berkley, 2002.
Klaw, Barbara. *Camp Follower: The Story of a Soldier's Wife*. New York: Random House, 1943.
Lea, Fanny Heaslip. *Sailor's Star*. New York, Dodd, Mead, 1944.
Leckie, Robert. *Helmet for My Pillow: From Parris Island to the Pacific*. New York: Random House, 1957.
Lee, Robert Edson. *To the War*. New York: Knopf, 1968.
Litoff, Judy Barrett, and David C. Smith, eds. *Since You Went Away: World War II Letters from American Women on the Home Front*. Lawrence: University Press of Kansas, 1991.
———. *American Women in a World at War: Contemporary Accounts from World War II*. Wilmington, DE: SR, 1997.
Mauldin, Bill. *Willie and Joe Volumes One and Two*. Seattle: Fantagraphics, 2008.
Miller, Henry. *Black Spring*. Paris: Obelisk, 1936.
Mitchell, Margaret. *Gone with the Wind*. New York: Macmillan, 1936.
Neiman, LeRoy. *All Told: My Art and Life among Athletes, Playboys, Bunnies, and Provocateurs*. Guilford, CT: Lyons, 2012.
Overseas War Brides Association Staff. *Overseas War Brides: Stories from the Women Who Followed Their Hearts to Australia*. East Roseville, NSW: Simon & Schuster, 2001.
Parascandola, Louis J., and John Parascandola, eds. *A Coney Island Reader: Through Dizzy Gates of Illusion*. New York: Columbia University Press, 2014.
Parmenter, Ross. *School of the Soldier: An Essay in the Form of a Memoir*. New York: Profile, 1980.
Peckham, Howard, and Shirley Snyder, eds. *Letters from Fighting Hoosiers*. Bloomington: Indiana War Commission, 1948.
Petry, Ann. *The Street*. New York: Houghton Mifflin, 1946.
Popkin, Zelda. *The Journey Home*. Philadelphia: Lippincott, 1945.
St. George, Corporal Thomas R. *C/O Postmaster*. New York: Thomas Y. Crowell, 1943.
Schiff, Pearl. *Scollay Square*. New York: Rinehart, 1952.

Sledge, Eugene B. *With the Old Breed: At Peleliu and Okinawa*. New York: Presidio, 1981.

Tatum, Chuck. *Red Blood, Black Sand: Fighting alongside John Basilone from Boot Camp to Iwo Jima*. New York: Berkley Caliber, 2012.

Terkel, Studs. *"The Good War": An Oral History of World War II*. New York: New Press, 1984.

Walker, Wilbert L. *We Are Men: Memoirs of World War II and the Korean War*. Chicago: Adams, 1972.

INDEX

The letter *f* following a page number denotes a figure.

mobilization, 12, 131, 152, 267; attack on Pearl Harbor and manly nationalism, 30; construction difficulties, 23; decline of funding and supplies, 10; delays, 16; draft boards, 30–32, 70; equipment shortages, 25, 32, 35; expansion of camps and bases, 21–24, 23f; impact on civilians, 186; lumbar shortage, 21–24; opportunities for women, 104; opposition to, 16; recreation camps, 49–50; recruitment, 13; rejection of physical handicaps, 30–31; rise in crime, 176; supply and training problems, 20

Moses, Robert: attempts to remake Central Park, 153–54; attempts to remake Coney Island, 155–56, 201; conflict with military, 162–64; Hampton Roads inquiry, 161–64; view of Coney Island, 154

My Secret Garden (Friday), 108

NAACP, 31, 38, 94, 96
Natal, Brazil, riots in, 77
National Council for Women, 127
National Education Association, 17
National Guard: morale, 20; prewar strength, 20
nationalism, after Pearl Harbor, 30
National Maritime Union, 15, 69
Neiman, LeRoy, 60
New England Watch and Ward Society, 152
Newfoundland, Canada, ports of embarkation, 57
New Mexico, segregated training camps in, 95
New Orleans, LA: ports of embarkation, 57; recreation camps in, 49
Newport, RI, 161
New York: crime in, 177; housing troops, 79–80; Juvenile Aid Bureau, 176; legal restrictions in, 75–76
New York City, 2–3; leave and liberty in, 77–78; militarization of, 142; ports of embarkation, 56–57; profiteering in, 172; protests in, 15, 19; violence in, 171

New York City Patrol Corps, 167–68
Norfolk, VA, 55; attempts to clean up city, 160; burlesque in, 159; congestion in, 157, 160–64; liberty in, 159–60, 205; militarization of, 142–43, 159; ports of embarkation, 56–57; prewar era, 159; troop behavior in, 131; vice in, 159
Normandy, Battle of, 4, 207
Normandy, France, 6–7
North Carolina: Fort Bragg, 23; recreation camps in, 49
North Stelton, NJ: civilian complaints of troops, 180–81; crime in, 180–81

Office of Civilian Defense, 51, 168
Office of War Information, 39, 124
Office of War Mobilization, 184
Ohio, segregated training camps in, 95
Okinawa, Japan, civil-military conflict in, 5
Oklahoma: drinking prohibition in, 177–78; Fort Sill, 177
Old Howard Athenaeum, 145–46, 148, 152, 201. *See also* Scollay Square, MA
Olympia, WA: attempts to police, 180; Fort Lewis, 23, 180
Omaha, NE, scams in, 173
On the Town (film), 106
Oxnam, G. Bromley, 14–15

Pacific Fleet, destruction of, 29
Panama City, Panama, ports of embarkation, 57, 76–77
panty raids, 193–200; impact on postwar sexuality and masculinity, 195, 197, 199–200
Paris, France: fall of, 18; invasion of, 12; surrender, 18
"patriotute," 130, 134
Patton, George S., 39, 45
Peace Day Riots, 1–2, 11, 99
Peace Mobilization League, 19
Peace Mobilization Society, 15
Pearl Harbor, HI, 27, 29, 33, 175, 207; martial law in, 69–70; psychological impacts of, 10–11, 30